D0897587

A FOOL
and
FORTY ACRES

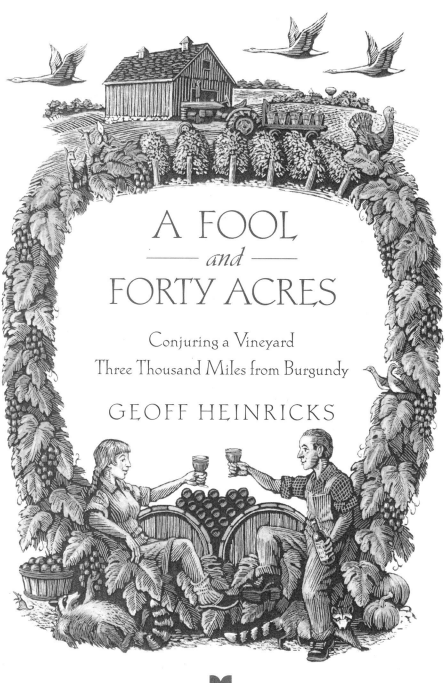

A FOOL
— and —
FORTY ACRES

Conjuring a Vineyard
Three Thousand Miles from Burgundy

GEOFF HEINRICKS

M&S

National Library of Canada Cataloguing in Publication

Heinricks, Geoffrey
    A fool and forty acres : conjuring a vineyard three thousand miles from Burgandy / Geoff Heinricks ; with a foreword by Jamie Kennedy.

Includes bibliographical references.
ISBN 0-7710-4054-7

    1. Heinricks, Geoffrey.   2. Vineyards – Ontario – Prince Edward.
3. Viticulture – Ontario – Prince Edward.   4. Country life – Ontario –
Prince Edward.   5. Prince Edward (Ont.) – History.   I. Title.

TP547.H44A3 2004   634.8'09713'587   C2004-901237-1

Excerpts from Andrew Jefford, *The New France: A Complete Guide to Contemporary French Wine* (London: Mitchell Beazley, 2002) and George Ordish, *The Great Wine Blight* (London: Sedgwick & Jackson, 1972 and 1987) are reproduced here by permission. The poetry of Al Purdy reproduced in this book as chapter epigraphs and in Chapter Thirteen is included here by kind permission of Eurithe Purdy and Harbour Publishing. "You Fit Into Me" from *Power Politics*, copyright © 1971 by Margaret Atwood, is reprinted with the permission of House of Anansi Press, Toronto.

We acknowledge the financial support of the Government of Canada through the Book Publishing Industry Development Program and that of the Government of Ontario through the Ontario Media Development Corporation's Ontario Book Initiative. We further acknowledge the support of the Canada Council for the Arts and the Ontario Arts Council for our publishing program.

Typeset in Bembo by M&S, Toronto
Printed and bound in Canada

This book is printed on acid-free paper that is 100% recycled, ancient-forest friendly (100% post-consumer recycled).

McClelland & Stewart Ltd.
The Canadian Publishers
481 University Avenue
Toronto, Ontario
M5G 2E9
www.mcclelland.com

1 2 3 4 5   08 07 06 05 04

For Noreen, Robert, Betty, and Garn

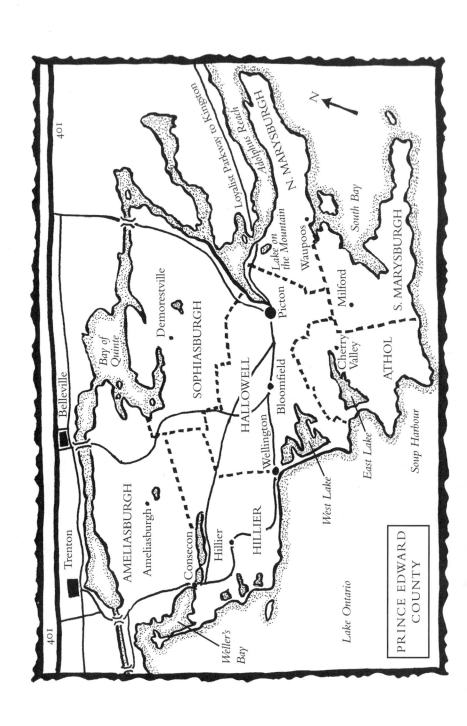

PRINCE EDWARD COUNTY

It's midnight, and I've just arrived in Hillier. I left my restaurant in the city at around ten. Service was beginning to wind down, so I could make my escape. I roll down the windows and turn off the engine. It is the first time I have stopped all day. It is pitch black and the air is sweet. The only sounds I hear are the cicadas and the babbling brook. Tension eases. I contemplate tomorrow.

I have started a new career. Thirty years ago, I took up an apprenticeship in the kitchen. Now I've taken up a new apprenticeship, principally in winegrowing, and this time Geoff Heinricks is my master. Although he is teaching me a lot about cultivating the Pinot Noir vine, I suspect there will be more to this apprenticeship. Geoff and I are kindred spirits. He has a great vision that extends beyond the borders of his vineyard.

I know there must have been a moment when Geoff decided unconsciously to change the road he was travelling. Many of us decide this. Few of us actually make the change and follow our heart's desires. It is Prince Edward County where Geoff decided to settle, but this isn't really a story about the County. This story could take place anywhere. It is more about the philosophy of the man and the dedication to the dream.

In this book, you will learn about viticulture through the entire growing season. There is much information, but it is delivered lyrically, even poetically. You will learn about Geoff's first forays into the world of making wine. You will learn about Canadian history as it pertains to this region; in Geoff's hands it becomes a vital part of this great story.

Geoff's narrative also introduces us to the cast of characters who, in addition to his young family, are part of his daily life, because farming grapes and making exceptional wine sets the stage for the larger drama, being part of a working community. In this sense, Geoff is a Renaissance man. He embraces the ideology of the working rural community as it existed many years ago. To find the right model means looking back to a time when these communities thrived, when everyone in them had a practical role to play in the success of the local economy. Geoff is trying to recapture that harmony which fed people on many levels and encouraged them to care about each other.

Geoff dreams about starting a viable gastro-centric community. One that would favour the artisanal approach. There would be winemakers, cheesemakers, bakers, growers of organic fruits and vegetables. Perhaps a restaurant with a tavern attached. He wants to take the ideology of old and contribute something new, on a human scale, that is absolutely local and of the highest possible quality. As one reads through these pages one starts to imagine the possibilities. There used to be a mill in this little hamlet. It was the lifeblood of the community. Now that we've had our love affair with the internal-combustion engine, perhaps we are ready to look back. We don't need the mill to saw logs any more, nor to card textiles, but we could use it to grind wheat into flour. There could be a wood-fired bake oven perched on the rise above the creek. The limestone smokehouse constructed those many years ago just needs to be fired up again. There could be local sheep's-milk cheese for sale with the bread in the little tavern next to the highway. Inside the restaurant that used to be the blacksmith's shop, one could dine from an absolutely terroir-based menu, with foods and wines striking chords with each other for reasons not to be analyzed too deeply but to be enjoyed and celebrated as something unique to this little place.

In a few years' time, after you have read this book, you might discover the wine that Geoff and others like him have made. As you look into the glass, and then smell, and then taste the wine, you will discover an inner core of vibrancy that resonates with a delicious somewhereness that is truly unique. Geoff wouldn't have it any other way.

Jamie Kennedy

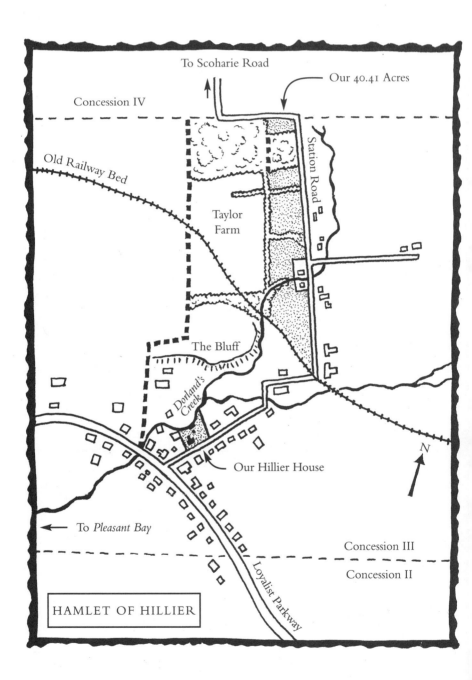

To Scoharie Road

Our 40.41 Acres

Concession IV

Old Railway Bed

Station Road

Taylor Farm

The Bluff

Dorland's Creek

Our Hillier House

To *Pleasant Bay*

N

Concession III

Concession II

Loyalist Parkway

HAMLET OF HILLIER

This is an island and you know
it's like being dressed in lace
as only a woman may be
and not be laughed at
around her neck and throat
the silver dance of coastlines
and bells rung deep in limestone

•   *Al Purdy, "Prince Edward County"*

I still don't know who snapped the photo.

It's of our last few minutes living in Toronto. The usual shutterbugs are all in the picture, standing on the house steps, a few hundred feet from the eastern edge of High Park where the College streetcar loops and rumbles back downtown. My wife, Lauren, holds Jemima, our five-month-old daughter. Joanne, one of Lauren's three older sisters, holds Winona, our two-year-old. Below the four of them I'm cradling a wooden case of very nice Bordeaux on my thigh (1989 Lagrange St-Julien, if you must know), on my way to one of the cars in which we were personally driving valuables and breakables like framed prints and china.

It must have been my dad who captured the moment; he was there to help transport our wine cellar to Prince Edward County.

Lauren and I and our unknowing (and so as yet uncomplaining) daughters were giving up the city to become winegrowers in a forgotten but unforgettable portion of Ontario.

Why? I still can't give any ready answers. I've tried, but there's nothing that truly makes sense. No rumour of viticulture exists in either of our family histories: we're pretty blandly, solidly Canadian. The closest thing to a solution lies in Blaise Pascal's aphorism, "Le coeur a ses raisons que le raison ne connaît point" (The heart has its reasons which reason knows nothing of). The whispers of the heart. They had urged me to prepare for this move for over a decade.

A little over two hours later our convoy of people, wine, and small treasures approached Consecon. We deftly weaved our way to tiny Bay Street, past the warning sign that announced "No Exit." Bay Street did end about seventy-five yards on, in a string of huge, half-submerged granite boulders that stretched out into Weller's Bay.

Until a few months before, I didn't even know how to pronounce the name of the village. Was it Con-*see*-con? No. We learned that in – of all places – Alberta.

A good friend from university had invited me to be a godfather to his son. Peter was now a Mountie, living in Mayerthorpe, well northwest of Edmonton. A Cambridge overeducated Mountie. A poet Mountie. And also the son of a Mountie; Peter's father had grown up in Trenton, just outside Prince Edward County.

"Geoff's buying a farm in Hillier," Peter laconically told his dad while we were all drinking in the kitchen the day before the christening. Our deal was to close a few weeks after we returned to Toronto.

I half-remembered that Peter's dad knew the County. At university in Kingston, Peter would talk of his father as a boy hanging around with his friends on the embankment of the Murray Canal. They'd dive for the silver dollars the American tourists flipped into the water from their pleasure boats. I always thought it was one of those brilliant late-1940s or early-1950s scenes: quintessentially Canadian; perfectly American.

"So I'm hoping we can find a place nearby to rent until we get a house up on the farm," I said. "There's not much in Hillier. Maybe Con-*see*-con."

"*Con*-seh-con."

"Thanks. *Con*-seh-con."

~§

Lauren and I had never even been through Consecon on our frequent trips across Prince Edward County over the years before our move. The village is about five miles south of Carrying Place. That narrow five-mile neck between the Bay of Quinte and Weller's Bay was all that connected Prince Edward County to the north shore of Lake Ontario. A little to the north of the old portage road was the Murray Canal – the canal Peter's dad dove in to grasp the sinking coins. Dug in 1881, it completed the circle of water all around the County. The canal had a short commercial life. It survives as a pleasure-boat artery up the Trent–Severn Waterway.

Technically, the County is still a peninsula, dangling like a cow's udder below the Canadian shore of the east end of Lake Ontario, kept apart from the mainland by the Bay of Quinte as it zigzags its way to the lake. Yet it's an island by natural fiat and a pinch of manmade engineering. The canal is actually located in one of the mainland municipalities; the County line doesn't officially begin for a mile or so south of the Murray.

Unless you fly, waft down by parachute, or have a nautical bent, there are only five routes into Prince Edward County: two small swing bridges across the Murray Canal in the west; a large span over the Bay of Quinte at Belleville; another farther east, arching across from the Mohawk territory near Deseronto; and the ferry from Adolphustown to Glenora.

The bridges are for those in a hurry, or at least the two main bridges are. The pair of tiny spans are not. If the traffic of pleasure craft using the Murray Canal is heavy, and the swing bridge you're gunning for goes out before you can cross, you may be forced to wait five to fifteen minutes until it clicks back into place. Those are joyless minutes. Smouldering lines of cars and trucks idle impatiently; irritable pods of tourists heading for the beach fret that things don't operate on their time, the time of Toronto and its vast suburb. The operation of the swing bridges is as seasonal as the visitors, so for most of the year residents can zip back and forth unimpeded, the operator booths (both on the County side) boarded up and as neglected as an East German border post.

But the ferry . . .

If one has only one chance to come into the County, it should be by the ferry. Ferries across Long Reach have been running in some form for over two centuries. (At one point, just after the War of 1812, it was operated by a relative of U.S. president John Quincy Adams.) Cartographically, the route links the old Loyalist townships of Marysburgh and Fredericksburgh across this last leg of the Bay of Quinte. Emotionally, it crosses time.

After driving along the Loyalist Parkway from Kingston, with the Lake Ontario shore one's constant companion, passing a melange of old and new (or Ye Olde) Upper Canada, interspersed with clumps of industrial Ontario, one is pulled up short after about forty-five minutes by a notice announcing the highway's end.

The ferry usually leaves the mainland at a quarter past and a quarter to the hour; it returns from the Glenora side at the top and bottom of each hour. In summer, when there are two ferries, one is reasonably assured of catching one every fifteen minutes – if it's not a long weekend or the height of summer vacation.

In mid-May or October (two of my favourite times to cross), there's usually only a handful of vehicles waiting. Surrender to the urge to get out of the car, and look out across the Long Reach on your right and the Adolphus Reach on your left while the ferry loops against the current. The County on the far side rises three hundred feet above the water. Nestled against the cliff is a collection of old stone mills, now used by the provincial government as fish hatcheries and labs. Once fall has started, the road that angles up the cliff and a steeple can be spied; at the top of the cliff there is actually a body of water called Lake on the Mountain – a provincial park – which used to supply the water that powered the mills.

The view has remained almost unchanged over the past two centuries. Those willing to ease their neck and shoulders for even a moment can feel something sweep over them, something difficult to describe accurately, but which comes with meeting the past halfway: an Upper Canadian Zen finds you. By waiting for that ferry, one acknowledges an age older than oneself, and in that gentle act of fealty can feel the pleasant suspension of time, or rather a linking of past and present in one moment.

You find you are breathing more deeply, more slowly, more fully. In tarrying, you sense the short crossing is to somewhere special; the sounds, the peace, the view. (I've always found that for me it creates the same sense of childlike wonder I used to have watching the miniature rural scenes at the beginning of *The Friendly Giant* on TV, the camera panning peacefully along until it hit a giant boot. Especially in mid-winter I half expect to hear the familiar "Look up, waaaay up" amid a vista blanketed in newly fallen snow, with the tiny huts of ice fishermen in the distance, the dark gash of the ferry route across the frozen water, and the sound of ice crunching into the dock.)

I've found that everything that presses artificially upon my mind or humour evaporates during that brief pause. Coming home becomes an event, not a commute. There is something comforting about being on an island – the feeling of boundary, of protection, in a world with little of either now. And yet it's not isolation, the kind of safe haven a modern survivalist might seek in a bomb shelter in a compound in Montana. The sense of a history here, older even than this country, that has survived with a living community nullifies the comparison.

Embarking on the Adolphustown side, aboard an unremarkable vessel, with the vaguely familiar faces of the crew, everything important about life comes back into definition. After the midpoint on the water, the buildings of the stone mill – a mill once managed by the father of our first prime minister – assume their fully material form. The cliff shoots up to its proper height; the right-hand bend in the road to Picton becomes visible; a few of the old buildings of Glenora and up above on the strange Lake on the Mountain take their usual place.

No matter how many times I travel this way, I never tire of it. If you undertake it, be warned – it can become an addiction.

Needless to say, relocating to the County in mid-April, we did not take the ferry.

Coming off Highway 401, you head south on the Wooler Road to meet the Loyalist Parkway on the north shore of the Bay of Quinte. Driving past the small cottages and houses fore and aft of Carrying Place, the countryside looks pretty much like any Ontario cottage route. A few minutes clear of Carrying Place the signs warn of the approaching turnoff for Consecon. On the last bend near the railway tracks and an old cheese factory, you catch sight of a forlorn-looking feed store, and the eye notes a colourful flash of a checkered signboard. By the time you look to the right again, you've sped past Consecon. The Loyalist Parkway loops east of the village rather than through it.

Even though Prince Edward County may begin miles to the north at Carrying Place, for many people it doesn't feel like the County until Consecon is in the rearview mirror. The scenery changes. The trees are no longer scrub juniper and cedar; they have become hardwoods. The fencerows seem lusher. The farmland gently rolls. It's not merely a Consecon problem. Consecon is just one of many places that don't get noticed. A lot of those who live in western Ameliasburgh know that people riding along the Parkway pick up that same feeling. It pisses them off.

When Lauren and I finally did roll into Consecon for our first visit, it was under a wet, gunmetal sky at the end of March. We had to move in a few weeks, and had found no place to move to. The only places for rent we'd seen that day were in Picton. The rain had been flowing into the hall and kitchen of

7

an apartment we looked at atop some rundown Main Street stores. At another place in the rougher side of Picton, the landlord didn't even bother to show up for our appointment.

Killing time in Picton, waiting for the landlord who never showed, I noticed an ad in the *Belleville Intelligencer* offering a small house for rent in Consecon. Lauren and I drove into the village without saying anything, our plans to move out here seeming increasingly foolish. At a phone booth outside the variety store on what looked like the main street I dialled the local number. Maybe we could get a look before heading home. After several rings an answering machine clicked on. I left a message. Then I climbed back into the car and we drove back to Toronto, feeling defeated.

It took three or four days of phone tag to sort things out. The landlord, Lawrence, didn't live in the County; the number in the newspaper ad was for his niece. We arranged to have a look at the place.

The house – or, more truthfully, the cottage – was one of eight on Bay Street, and by no means the worst of them. Butter-yellow paint atop the concrete tile cladding on the outside was doing its best to keep the original factory coat of deep green hidden, but was losing the battle here and there. This was pretty much the only house we could find to rent anywhere near our farm – five miles away.

"This place must've been built by the set designer for *Popeye*," Lauren whispered as we were given the tour.

There was barely a right angle in the place, though many attempts: most amusing, a few mischievous, the odd one menacing. The headroom upstairs in this storey-and-a-half cottage was maybe a hair above six feet. The ascent was steep and ship-like. Actually, the whole building seemed to have washed ashore and been carefully retrofitted by amateurs as a land habitation. The departing tenant worked for an electrical company. He had some kind of deal whereby he got a lower rate for electricity, and so heated the house with space heaters. He didn't bother to use the furnace as he was often on the road. It could get cold, he acknowledged, answering my question about winter, but the house was a lot warmer since Lawrence had installed new vinyl window frames . . . much warmer than the old wooden frames and storms.

The cottage was somewhere between tiny and small. But the property was large. The tenant, when asked, said it was about a two-beer lawn, meaning it took approximately that much to get it cut using a small gas mower. From almost anywhere but inside the cottage you could see Weller's Bay – a fairly large body of water cut off from Lake Ontario by a westerly sandbar. It was a stone's throw from the front door. The Consecon River widened into the bay in front of us. The view *was* nice. Lawrence said he and his wife had really bought the place for the lot. They'd knock this house down, rebuild, and retire here when the time came. All that lay between this cottage and the lake was an even smaller cabin and a stucco house. An old cemetery touched the northwest corner of the yard, with the past inhabitants of Consecon taking up valuable lakeshore real estate. Quiet neighbours.

It really wasn't a bad place. Maybe. For a year or two.

Water came from a well out front. I was shown the small pump room off the kitchen, which housed a small rusty blue device and a number of copper and black-plastic tubes. Off in the corner sat an old electric water heater. The pump could have been a sausage-making machine, or a uranium enricher: I wouldn't have known the difference. But I nodded approvingly, because I could see there was room in here for a few wine shelves, with a little extra space to stack cases on the floor.

Leaving the pump room, I finally noticed the stains on some of the ceiling tiles above the kitchen table, and I asked the tenant about them. He said it was okay. I asked Lauren whether she thought the dining-room table would fit in the kitchen here.

"I don't think I'd put it there," the tenant said. "Maybe over there." He was pointing to a carpeted area off the yellow linoleum.

We took the house, and sent Lawrence one month's deposit and a year's worth of postdated cheques. It was, after all, only a layover until we built at the farm.

≈§

It wasn't raining, but the sky was unsure of itself as we waited for the moving boys to show up. Breakables and prints we carted from the cars into the house. I had begun to haul the wine out of trunks and back seats into what I had thought was the coolest part of the garage/workshed. Lauren and Joanne played with Winona and passed Jemima back and forth as needed. After the last of the wine was in the garage, my dad headed back to Toronto. A few minutes after he left, the moving van pulled up, and our worldly goods started the last few yards of their journey.

Boxes of books were diverted to the garage and stacked. The furniture and household items were gradually unloaded and shoehorned into the cottage.

I didn't see him coming, but at my elbow I suddenly found a smaller man, bearded and somewhere between twenty-five and forty-five years old. His hands were those of a mechanic. I could pick up a slight whiff of Canadian cigarette smoke.

"Moving day, eh?" he said, in a manner that both asked and answered his question. "I'm Andy. From there."

Andy pointed to the small frame bungalow closest to us.

"What're you puttin' in here?" he asked as I shifted a few boxes.

"Books," I replied. "Magazines. Things that can wait a few days before being sorted inside. But mostly books." We knew we had maybe a good quarter-mile of shelf material that wasn't going to make it inside.

"You need some pallets."

"Yeah, that would probably make sense. I'll go looking in a few days, I guess. There's that pallet factory in Bloomfield."

"Naw. Forget that. How many do you think you need? There's a pile at my mother-in-law's. She doesn't need 'em for anything. So how many?"

"Uh, maybe three or four. That'd be great." Remembering the pump room, I changed my mind. "Actually, probably five."

"I'll bring you half a dozen."

"That'd be perfect. How much would that cost?"

"Nuthin'." He cocked his head as though I had said something almost foolish. "Like I said, they're just there. May as well be used for something useful."

Someone yelled from nearby. Andy roared back in that direction. I tried not to notice.

"That's dinner. I'll drop 'em by later. Tonight, maybe tomorrow."

"Thanks. That'll really help a lot."

"No problem." Andy headed for his house in a slightly rolling shamble, and added without turning back, "The water backs up in front of the garage there when it rains. You'll need 'em if those are books."

In less than an hour it came time to settle up with the movers. They presented us with a bill a few hundred dollars over the agreed price. They said they had underestimated the drive and the gas. Lauren and I looked at each other. We opened and closed our mouths like fish for a few moments. Lauren took out her envelope of "retirement" money from her colleagues and friends at work and handed over most of it, along with my cheque for the agreed price.

We were free, and though not poor yet, poorer than we had expected to be. Toronto's last hand in the pocket, I guess.

We stowed our effects and organized the house. It didn't really take that long, given the floor space.

The next morning there was a pile of greying pallets in front of the garage. I carried them in and stacked up three pallets of books that we weren't going to see for a while. I brought another pallet into the pump room of the cottage, and trotted back and forth from the garage with cardboard and wooden cases of wine. About three or four thousand dollars' worth of serious, thick Northern Rhône and Australian Syrahs, sweeter and sunnier Grenache blends from the Southern Rhône, three cases of mid-range Bordeaux, and the rest a mix of Pinot Noirs mainly from Oregon and California. It must have been an odd sight for the neighbours – all that fancy wine in a tiny hamlet that preferred shots and pitchers dispensed at the Legion and Cascades. It seems extravagant or foolish now, but it was the cellar of our youthful improvidence. And those stored contents would transform a simple meal on the hardest, loneliest day out here into a banquet.

Our first Thursday as residents of Prince Edward County dawned a few days later, and I got out my heavy black steel-framed bike. It was bought to ride from High Park to downtown Toronto and back, with strength the first consideration so it, and I, might survive the smash and bump of streetcar tracks. I pedalled the three or four hundred yards to the commercial centre of Consecon, a brick store block that housed a bank and a variety store. Thursday's *Globe and Mail* contained a column, written by a friend, that I always found a worthwhile read. As I was still contributing to *Frank* magazine as national-affairs editor every two weeks, keeping up with the *Globe* was pretty important. Inside the Hamlet Variety, owned by a Korean family who lived on the floor over the shop and bank, there were three or four newspapers. The only Toronto title was the *Star*.

"Do you have any more *Globe*s?" I asked the owner, in case there were one or two behind the counter.

"No. No *Globe and Mail*. They don't come here. Sorry. *Toronto Star*," he informed me.

An older man who had just bought a *Star* turned and said he thought Turner's Variety in Carrying Place carried the *Globe*. Otherwise, the County wasn't on the drop-off route.

I thanked him. And I should have known. The *Globe and Mail* had over the last decade winnowed rural areas from its readership, cutting delivery and even store distribution to the "undesirables." Rubes and yokels lurking in unfashionable postal codes contaminated the readership profiles they used to entice the premium advertisers.

It was a mild April day, with sunshine and a cool breeze off the recently thawed bay. I stopped by the house to tell Lauren

I was going to ride to Carrying Place for a paper, about five miles away.

"Well, okay," she said, cautiously. "Be careful of the cars," she added; I'd be going along the main highway. "And try not to be all day."

"I can't imagine I'll be more than two to two and a half hours. It's only Carrying Place."

Twenty miles later, I barely made it back in time for dinner. Turner's Variety was a small store, coffee counter, and gas station that sat on the north side of the Murray Canal. They were sold out of their few daily copies by the time I had finished pedalling up and down the series of ridges that separated Consecon from Carrying Place.

Since I had come this far, I thought, why not go the further five miles into Trenton? The route was flat and skirted around the start of the Bay of Quinte, continuing along the north shore. It'd be a longer way home, but I was a healthy, strong thirty-five-year old, right?

The route along the bay into Trenton on this stretch of the Loyalist Parkway *was* flat, though not terribly inspiring. The water of the Quinte sparkled and danced, and the shoreline of the County opposite swelled gradually higher than the Trenton shore. But the land along here was thinly populated and unremarkable, probably because the old Marmora rail line that reached into the County and ended at Picton Bay ran close to the water's edge and limited the homes here to unadorned bungalows housing souls willing to endure the rumble of trains.

Overhead roared the powerful props of a pair of Hercules transport planes that were almost as much part of the backdrop out here as water and limestone. This close to Trenton they seemed unnervingly loud and close to the ground. Canadian

Forces Base Trenton was one of the largest in the country and the most common departure or arrival point for military personnel and supplies headed somewhere to keep the peace or attend to manmade or natural catastrophes.

The town of Trenton was now charmless and rough, even though it was sited astride the mouth of the Trent River and near the head of the Bay of Quinte. In the days between the world wars it was the Hollywood of Canada, an unlikely place to produce and shoot silent pictures. That was pretty much the town's time in the sun. Like many small industrial centres it was slowly dying. Apart from the air base, only Quaker Oats and a Domtar pulp plant seemed committed to sticking around. Others were closing. The first plant you saw coming in along the parkway was the FBI juice factory. I'd already heard rumours that it had hit hard times too, after switching to apple-juice concentrate bought cheap from China rather than the hundreds of tons of not-quite-as-cheap local apples from the County, Quinte, and Lake Ontario orchards that ran westward to Cobourg.

I stopped at the first variety store past FBI and bought my *Globe and Mail.* I was fortunate the professional and managerial caste of Trenton hadn't scooped them all up. Outside, as I glanced over the headlines above and below the fold to see what was considered important, dust rose from the nearby large industrial site the town was tearing down and attempting to detoxify.

My legs were rebelling against me. They burned and felt thick with the buildup of acids. My folly was clear, but I had found a paper. I had to get back, even if it killed me, just to show Lauren I hadn't been knocked over and slaughtered like a deer by some pickup or transport.

The sunshine on the way home was less bright, and noticing the change was much worse than the actual loss of warmth. There was little comfort. Pain and monotony took the energy out of me, and the day had none of its earlier cheer. Some factory shift in Trenton had clearly ended, and a handful of times I was forced by a small parade of speeding cars onto the unsteady gravel shoulder of the highway. Yet when I finally reached the crest of the last swelling ridge at County Road 19, I smiled. I could see the curve of Weller's Bay into the hamlet of Consecon. The white steeple from the old Methodist church rose highest and lined up with the painted median of the highway.

It's a tiny detail that few if any speeding into the County notice. But to me it began a tradition. Whenever I reach that spot after being away, it's the first moment it hits me: I'm home.

it's as if a man stuck
both thumbs in the stony earth and pulled

it apart
to make room
enough between the trees
for a wife
and maybe some cows and
room for some
of the more easily kept illusions

•   *Al Purdy, "The Country North of Belleville"*

Our first grapevines arrived with Lauren's parents, Betty and Garn Grice, a few weeks later. They drove the trays of tiny shoots and leaves from their basement two hours away in Weston, filling the trunk and back seat. I had started the cuttings about seven or eight weeks before, so they wouldn't get damaged as we packed and prepared to move from downtown Toronto.

They were the first vines I had ever grown. I had purchased a bundle of a few dozen dormant canes of rootstock. They were, like licence plates or prisoners, known merely by numbers and letters: in this case 41 B. It was a hardship, starting them at the Grices. I couldn't check on them every hour, anxious to see if I could get these sticks to grow into plants. I could fuss over them only once a week, during the large gathering Betty and Garn had each Sunday for dinner. I was like a weekend father trying to take in all the growth and change I had been absent for during the previous six days, wondering if I had missed an important stage or mild crisis since the last visit. Garn watched over them during the week; he was a good steward, as it appealed to his sense of curiosity about plants. He was known to try his hand at germinating any pip or seed he scavenged; one of his proud accomplishments was a monstrous banana plant started from seed, now spreading and lording it over all the other greenery he had in the small room dedicated to his triumphs.

I'd check the pots for moisture, then look carefully to identify vine parts and key stages that up until then I'd seen only in textbooks or photos. Upstairs, Lauren's family would tease, argue, and laugh. They were the first native Torontonians I had ever met – for a few generations back too; most people you meet in Toronto arrived from somewhere else. All six of Betty and Garn's kids (and now their kids) would usually come by on Sunday. Even ex-wives. More unusual was that they all lived in Toronto, though Lauren's two brothers and one of her sisters had lived at times in exotic places around the world.

Growing vines known only by a number may seem rather odd. Where's the Pinot Noir . . . the Syrah . . . even the ubiquitous Chardonnay? *Anything* deliciously recognizable from a wine label? What good can come from something called 41 B?

Well, you're right, certainly not wine. At least not directly. These plants were rootstock, upon which is grafted Pinot Noir, or Syrah, or Chardonnay. A sound rootstock allows the vine married to it to flourish and produce grapes and wine, because otherwise a European grapevine's fat, tender roots are just too tempting for a tiny little North American louse known as phylloxera.

The Europeans called it *Phylloxera vastatrix*, or the devastator, and from its appearance in 1886 it laid waste to vineyards across the continent. In France alone, 6.2 million acres of grapevines were destroyed. The physical and social devastation of phylloxera has been compared to Ireland's potato blight, yet few outside the wine industry are aware it happened at all.

Phylloxera will spread across later pages in this book. The reason for mentioning it now lies in the solution that was fixed upon – to graft European fruiting scions onto pieces of native North American vine. The American vines were immune.

Doing my reading in the years before our move, I had waded into the complex world of rootstocks. There's a bewildering range. Some speed maturity; others delay it. Many are robust; a few are weak. They all have their preferred soil types. The two main rootstocks in Ontario are rather vigorous hybrids of European and North American vines called Sélection Oppenheim 4 and 3309 Couderc. Both are really best used on deeper, wetter, more acidic soils, like those in Niagara. The soils in Prince Edward County are quite alkaline, and for the most part shallow and droughty. The rootstocks available from Niagara nurseries wouldn't really do well in our shallow Hillier Clay Loam. Unfortunately the lime-, drought-, and cold-tolerant rootstocks used in Europe were almost impossible to get in Ontario.

I did manage to get some cuttings of what on paper appeared to be the best of these commercially rare rootstocks, with the help of Dr. Helen Fisher of the Horticultural

Research Institute of Ontario. The institute – a sort of vine library – was able to provide cuttings of the rootstocks I believed would do best on our soil. The 41 B vines would grow to be "mother vines," and if needed provide cuttings for my own grafts.

I intended to plant out a few small rows of 41 B in a week or two in my first plot. But the bulk of what I would put into the earth would be 125 vines sourced from a nursery in Niagara and another in California: 100 Pinot Noir and 25 Syrah.

We unloaded the rootstock vines from Betty and Garn's car, and I placed them in the shade to harden off slowly, so they wouldn't get sun-scalded and dry up. As Winona and Jemima played, we all staked out a small garden and built a teepee of poles to support beans. Once the beans grew and twined up the wood, it'd be a little bean playhouse for Winona.

Like any refugee from the city, we couldn't wait to get a small vegetable garden started. Into the newly turned earth went rows of lettuces, beets, peas, shallots, sweet peppers, and ground cherries. And, of course, around the teepee various beans were pressed into the soil.

After supervising the arrangement of seeds in the little plot, Lauren's parents said goodbye and drove off towards the southeast. Lauren's older sister Joanne had decided that moving to Prince Edward County made as much sense as marking time in a banking job she hated. She had just found a place to rent in Wellington, the largest County village near Consecon, and Betty and Garn were off to inspect the new apartment and help with a little cleaning and painting before she settled in.

Joanne would be the first drop in a small rivulet of emigration from the city. Malcolm MacRury, a Toronto friend from the dangerous world of satirical writing, warned people I was starting a cult out in the County.

❦

We closed our purchase of the farm in August 1994. It was just a few days shy of the property's 198th anniversary on August 16, which marked the original Crown Grant given to Joseph Forsyth, a wealthy Kingston merchant. Lot 20, Concession III, Hillier Township. Technically, it was but a portion on Lot 20; the original two hundred acres of the lot (part of a stunning 1,200-acre block grant Forsyth received) had been carved up over the previous two centuries. Much of the hamlet of Hillier was sliced from Lot 20. What we owned – or at least what our credit union let us pretend we owned – was 40.41 acres. Almost a mile from top to bottom, it was the sliver of the lot that ran along Station Road, so named after the old Hillier train depot on the Prince Edward County Railway Company line, first laid in 1879. It was almost a half-sized version of the original narrow and deep Loyalist lot it derived from. Station Road, primarily a gravel township thing, was our eastern boundary, so we had road access all along our farm. The rail line cut an acute angle for our southern limit. Our western boundary – about half the original lot width in from Station Road – was in fenceline cover of hardwoods, chokecherry, and prickly ash, hiding the old snaking cedar-rail and stone fences that originally separated our property from the western half of Lot 20. At the top of our farm Station Road made a hard perpendicular turn to the west, which defined our northern reach.

This was what our $29,000 purchase had given us: four individual fields south to north, each separated by more fence-bottom cover masking the rails and stones; thirteen acres of a mixed hardwood and swampwood forest; then a final five- or six-acre orphan of a field alone at the north.

Lauren and I had subscribed to the local Picton newspaper when we still lived in Toronto, and it was there that I noticed the listing for the farm. It was carried by a real-estate company called Quinte's Isle, playing on one of the nicknames for the County. The company was really just Sharon Armitage, who had her office on Main Street in Wellington. By temperament, I prefer dealing with independent operations.

An energetic blonde with a raspy voice and warm smile, Sharon had faxed us the details of the property, and a few days later I was walking across a small, gentle ridge that ran across the third field, checking it over.

Everywhere I looked, there were finger-, fist-, and foot-size chunks of light-grey rock. Here and there the grey was broken by round cobbles of garnet or pieces of black or white granite from the Canadian Shield, mischievously abandoned by retreating glaciers, indestructible islands amid the softer limestone.

Along the slight slope I walked, the stone was strewn so generously that I could barely glimpse patches of the reddish brown soil. It was exactly what I'd been looking for. The same sight had caused two centuries of farmers to weep and shake their heads; I strode – well, I probably bounded like a puppy – through the fields with a loopy grin and the certainty I'd found the place.

This was to become our terroir-iste training camp.

Not terrorist. *Terroir-iste.*

While the former are all the rage these days, the latter are far less numerous and much easier to identify. True, it's possible to confuse the two, as both share the true believer's intensity, which at times becomes dogmatic and unreasoning.

It is often pointed out that there is no precise English translation for the French terroir. The concept is a grab bag of everything that combines to make one vineyard, appellation, or region unique. Of course with a word like *terroir*, that naturally includes soil, soil drainage, and subsoils or underlying geological formations, but it is also the topography of the site, and the macro- and micro-climates. The larger weather patterns play off against local variations of precipitation, temperature, sunlight, and air movement. All of the above can be measured individually and give a statistical, scientific idea of vineyard differences. The French, being French, added a certain mystical finish to the picture, saying that the sum of all these things creates a sense of uniqueness, a sense of "hereness" or "somewhereness" that cannot be duplicated. Or measured.

It is this mystical touch of "hereness" that lives in an authentic wine, and it causes most winegrowers and vintners in the New World to yank out handfuls of hair in frustration. Often they see terroir as only a clever marketing ploy – a romantic brand positioning that doesn't hold up under scrutiny. This New World skepticism isn't as solid as it used to be; as the vineyards in North and South America, Australia, and New Zealand grow older, there is increasing talk of terroir in those places. It could be a genuine conversion, or it might have more to do with embracing a very successful European marketing strategy and applying it at home. You just have to read a few of the glossy wine magazines to see the increasing talk of New World terroir.

Terroir completely dominates any discussion of Burgundy. The merits of one tiny vineyard plot are compared to another with an intensity that can be unsettling. But few of us will ever get to taste enough of these overpriced and scarce wines to make up our own minds, and that makes it frustrating.

Chardonnay, the famed white grape of Burgundy, has proved willing to bed down anywhere and still produce fine — and in many, many cases stunning — wines. Pinot Noir, the grape of Côte d'Or reds, hasn't done as well around the world, and the frenzied effort to discover why leads vinegrowers and winemakers back to Burgundy, and so to the concept of *terroir*.

It's not surprising that those in the New World most committed to a belief in *terroir* work with Pinot Noir. Former *Toronto Life* editor Marq de Villiers wrote a book about one of them — Josh Jenson of the Calera Wine Company in California — called *The Heartbreak Grape*. A particularly strong characteristic of the Pinot-based terroir-iste is a belief in limestone soils.

Years ago, when I first seriously started poring over Ontario soil maps, I knew just enough about winegrapes to look for rocky, well-draining soil. I also remembered that the European winegrape developed, and is most at home, on limestone soils. During the years I spent in Kingston, limestone was as much part of one's day as the sky. It is the stone of eastern Ontario. I carefully looked at maps of the area, and explored from Gananoque to Hay Bay at the eastern end of Lake Ontario. Vines had the best chance if they were close to the moderating effect of the lake, so I didn't stray too far north. I also looked closely at the wonderful steep lakeshore hills from Brighton to Port Hope, and at the glacial hills and ridges north to Peterborough.

I had collected Ontario's official soil surveys — published as huge county maps and accompanying booklets — for all these areas, and learned names and details of soils the way a boy memorizes a player's hockey-card statistics: Dummer Loam, Farmington Loam, Brighton Gravelly Sand. Some went into the "avoid" list, others were marked down as possibilities. I compared everything to maps of Niagara and the north shore of Lake Erie and Pelee Island, Ontario's established vineyard areas. And I always kept coming back to Prince Edward County.

In most of the soil, geological, and climate surveys, Prince Edward County is considered its own unique region. After a lot of research, I was satisfied that the growing season was long enough to ripen certain winegrapes (about 160 frost-free days), and that there was enough of a moderating lake effect on temperature to keep the absolutes of winter lows and summer highs from hitting us (though it was not as favourable as Niagara's lake effect). The County also had extremely dry summers, which, theoretically, would keep fungal diseases from ravaging grapes, and the dry periods usually occurred at a time in the season when vines could use a little drought stress to create better fruit.

I was hooked.

In the Prince Edward County Soil Survey, dating from 1948, the special qualities of a soil type called Hillier Clay Loam had jumped out at me. Hillier Clay Loam is often called clay gravel by the farmers here. It is shallow – anywhere from six or seven inches to two and a half feet deep – and full of limestone rubble. The stone reflects sunlight, retains heat well after sundown to continue ripening, and it helps warm and drain the clay soil.

Shallowness, combined with the annual droughts, would have been a huge problem except for the special characteristics of the limestone underneath. The old layer of limestone exposed by the glaciers in this part of the County is well fractured with deep fissures. The beds of limestone are fairly thin, separated by layers of shale. Vine roots are powerful things, and they can work their way into the fissures and keep growing for yards. Some of the old reports said that, even with such shallow soil, tree fruits did well on Hillier Clay Loam because of the limestone and shale fissures. I knew that meant grapes would do even better. Once the roots were down in the limestone and shale, drought would become less of a problem, as limestone and the cracks in it act as a sponge, absorbing water and then slowly releasing it. When the soil dried out in late July, roots deep in the limestone would still be able to suck up water.

Our shallow, rubble-strewn soils are much like those in parts of Côte d'Or, though our rock dates from the Ordovician geological period – about 300 million years older than Burgundy's Jurassic limestone. And as our soil was ground up only in the last ice age, it is both a new and ancient creation.

As noted, terroir-istes are frequently those who are irrationally attracted to, out of all the thousands of winegrapes around the world, Pinot Noir, the famous red-wine grape of the Côte d'Or. "Pinot Noir attracts a much wilder bunch," writes British wine journalist Oz Clarke. "A crowd who don't like being told what to do, a crowd who don't like the marketing manager to have more say in a wine than the winemaker. A self-indulgent crew of men and women who love flavour, love perfume, love the silky tactile experiences of a wine like Pinot, seductive, sultry, steamy, sinful if possible, but always solely there, solely made, to give pleasure."

Pinots are actually a whole wild troupe of performers under the canvas of the old French *pynoz* or *pineau*. Because Burgundian patois would render *pineau* as "peen-yo," the spelling was changed to the standard modern form. The name is thought to come from the tight, small, pine-cone structure of the small-berried clusters. There are four main rings in the Pinot circus: Pinot Noir, the black-skinned grape; Pinot Meunier, like Noir a black-skinned grape, but with downy white leaves and growing tips, and now – at least in the world of genetics – reputed to be a parent of Pinot Noir rather than a mutation of it; Pinot Gris, with a stunning red, burgundy, bluish brown range of hues that do look sort of grey compared to Noir; and Pinot Blanc, which is actually green-skinned, as are most white-wine grapes. Except for the hairs on the Meunier, the leaves on all four Pinots look pretty much the same. That means they can be almost circular in shape, without the deep lobes most people associate with grape leaves, or they can have quite deep lobes. They can even have a mix of these different leaves on the same vine. The Pinot family is an unruly lot.

The Pinots are thought to be quite closely related to the wild grapes of Europe, and for that reason are considered genetically unstable. That genetic weirdness and instability is one of the charms of the variety. It mutates so easily that it has become a battalion of clones, all of which are just slightly different from the next; in each of the rings of that Pinot circus, there are many, many acts.

Clones are vegetatively produced by taking a cutting from a mothervine and in effect generating an identical one. The clones themselves happen in the vineyard for reasons that aren't completely understood. Ultraviolet rays, variations in heat or cold or light during bud formation – who knows? – but a vine may grow a slightly bizarre new cane. The leaves may be different, it may have fruit with thicker skins, more sugar, less acid, or maybe the shoot has more resistance than others to disease. Vinegrowers who constantly walk their rows will notice the differences, and mark unusual canes as something special. When dormant, the cane will be cut, planted out the following spring, and new plants with the same unusual characteristics will grow, because they are really just identical little bits of the same plant. Some clones are in effect hundreds of years old, as vinegrowers continue to propagate them.

Pinot Noir, aside from producing the Gris, Meunier, and Blanc versions, has dozens of scientifically recognized clones, and thousands of unrecognized ones in vineyards across Burgundy and around the world. Some are noted for their fertility, some for growth habits (Pinot Fin, which droops to the ground like a willow; Pinot Droit, which grows upright, with canes arrayed like a military guard of honour), some have the usual thin Pinot skins, others have thicker skins, which help ward off rots and increase colour and flavour. There are early-ripening clones, later-ripening clones, Pinot Noir with high acidity levels for Champagne, others with high sugars for alcohol . . . you get the picture. With Pinot Noir, there is little certainty and safety, which are the most valued commodities in modern America. But the result of certainty and safety is cheap sameness. It explains fast food, Wal-Mart, and most of pop culture.

Pinot Noir growers – being individualists – will often try to get as many different clones as they can. The principle is that the different characteristics combine to create something far greater than the sum of its parts. The French call it *sélection massale*, or a large selection of a number of different plants. Commercial interests have been pushing to identify a handful of the "best" clones and have only those ones planted. The fight between them and the more traditional growers is intense.

A few of the top "official" French clones – known as the Dijon clones, as selected by the Comité technique permanent de la sélection (CTPS) in France – have gained a stranglehold on the New World, after long quarantines and bureaucratic quibbles. One of the reasons I had a very small order of Pinot Noir for our first plot was the lack of the very selection needed for a genuinely good Pinot Noir vineyard. (Now, I have started to make arrangements with other Canadian vineyards that have wider selections of Pinot Noir, and I will be buying cuttings from them and a few scientific collections that have an array of clones.)

It's easy to see why there is an underground world of something called suitcase clones; that is, cuttings smuggled in from the best French vineyards. Some of these may enter disguised as Christmas wreaths during the holidays, complete with red ribbons and best wishes. With Pinot Noir, those who are inclined to take on the challenge are rarely happy to accept mediocrity.

It may seem a bit confusing, or too complex to really care about, but it really does matter. With Pinot Noir, the most interesting wines – wines that, once tasted, can strike a mystic chord in an imbiber that creates a lifelong determination to locate another bottle with the same intense pleasure to it – almost always come from vineyards with a huge number of clones.

Pinot Noir has a reputation for being the most difficult, problematic grape in the world. It could be just a myth artfully designed to cloak the grape and its wine in even more exclusivity, and expense, but there is wide agreement that unlike Chardonnay and Cabernet Sauvignon, which can settle in comfort nearly anywhere, Pinot Noir is much fussier about the terroirs it's dropped into and expected to perform in.

While the soils found through much of Prince Edward County appeared to be hiding tremendous viticultural lights under its bushel, the climate is unforgiving compared to almost all other wine regions. Temperatures plummet to -24 or -25 degrees Celsius nearly every year, while -27 has about a 50-per-cent chance of clocking in each winter. (When -27 was last seen in parts of Burgundy, many thousands of vines in Nuits-St-Georges and Chablis were lifeless stumps by spring.) Here, each decade or so promises the terror of -30. But with the razor-thin protection given to the County by Lake Ontario, and the 160 to 165 days each year of frost-free growing, the area could, conceivably, answer the near-impossible demands of Pinot Noir.

It was Phil Mathewson who gave me the courage to try. A pioneering organic farmer from Toronto, with an established reputation for devotion to authenticity in farming yoked to an ornery temperament, he and his wife, Catherine, had moved to the County in 1981 and had thrown themselves into a deliberate, careful, and wide-ranging study of what would grow, thrive, and succeed in the County. I contacted Phil after a profile of the Mathewsons appeared in 1991 in *The County Magazine*. In the article, Phil said he thought, based on his experiments, that Pinot Noir was a good candidate for "higher quality grapes and higher quality products" than Ontario was producing. He also said there were many similarities between the terroir of Burgundy and of the County.

I first spoke to Phil on the phone. He was initially suspicious and hesitant, gradually warmed to laconic, and then after a few minutes settled into a pace, scope, and length of conversation reminiscent of a university seminar. Ninety minutes disappeared. When I met him in person a few weeks later, he had the lean, lanky, and bearded look of a perpetual doctoral candidate still polishing a thesis.

Phil drove in to Toronto each weekend to help organize and vend at a weekly organic market, and from time to time when we still lived in the city, I'd stop by, enrol in another mini-seminar, and purchase a few items for topping homemade pizza. He was always generous with his time and thoughtful with his answers, and it came as a surprise to me when I heard other hopeful winegrowers complain that he was rude, abrupt, and a dreamer. He sorted people rather quickly both by their questions and answers, and I suspected he'd be the poster boy for those who do not suffer fools gladly. I've always appreciated Phil's selflessness and knowledge . . . and the minor vote of approval implied in my receipt of them.

Oregon is probably the best-known New World area that took a hunch about a grape and terroir and worked to fashion a top Pinot Noir region. Before David Lett (who is considered *the* Oregon wine pioneer) arrived in 1966, most wine geeks know there was Charles Coury, who showed up in Oregon the year before and actually got Lett all fired up about Pinot Noir. (And before Coury there was the lone figure of Richard Sommer, who first planted in 1961.) Coury was the original visionary, theoretically figuring things out, matching Pinot Noir with Oregon's climate. Yet, as all too often happens with visionaries, he didn't reap the benefits of his efforts. Coury eventually left Oregon to return to California, and opened a bicycle shop.

The characteristics that serve trailblazers such as Charles Coury, and steel them for their uncharted exploration, rarely equip them for the shift from original proof to mundane practicality. Phil and Catherine Mathewson had hoped to open a commercial winery and cidery a year or two after the magazine profile was published, but it never materialized. Being too far out in front of everybody often means leaving money too far behind. I believe that Phil and his experiments and investigations will prove him right about Pinot Noir and the County. But sometimes I fear that Lauren and I may be too far in front as well.

If I now had the theoretical fix on the terroir we had selected, and had found a variety of grape to try that seemed a perfect fit both with our terroir and my temperament, then the last task was to settle on a density of vines.

I had resolved to try 3,630 vines per acre, with three feet between the vines in each row, and with rows running four feet apart, similar to the higher vine densities found in France. In Burgundy the minimum density is about 4,050 vines per acre. Vines in North America are usually planted at about 1,000 per acre, spaced with rows nine to ten feet apart, mainly to accommodate large North American tractors.

I decided upon the higher vine density, but not just to ape the French. I had done more study and calculation to come up with something to solve three major problems in Hillier and much of the County: the shallowness of the soil, the almost annual occurrence of summer drought, and the harshness of our winters.

When combined with the very dry summers we most often see, there just isn't enough soil depth, fertility, and moisture to support the large vine needed to fill a trellis at 1,000 vines per acre. In the usual North American system, our vines would have to be four times as big as the European ones, and produce four times as much fruit. They would fail. But at the higher density, each vine grows comfortably and fruits without undue stress. They shouldn't collapse or suddenly wilt and die during dry periods. And the smaller vine size lets both fruit and wood ripen fully, in plenty of time for winter, giving it a real fighting chance to get through the winter cold without suffering too much injury.

Sugar is the key. A smaller fruitload lets each vine focus its energy not on growing foliage, but on ripening and maturing the fruit. Ripening and maturing aren't necessarily the same thing, as not only sugar but also concentration of flavour and colour and the elusive "somewhereness" only come with time. A lower number of clusters per vine in our short season and on our shallow soil would allow needed extra sugar to accumulate in the wood and canes, acting as a vital anti-freeze during the harsh winter months.

And here endeth the theory.

❧

I marked off a measured rectangle, defining where I'd plant our test plot of vines. In the city, acquiring items needed for planting, I had gone to the hardware store and bought the largest unit of string or twine I could find – costly white mason's roll – to mark the plot; it'd take me a while to learn about farm-supply stores and bulk baling twine. My marked rectangle sat meekly amid a field of barley newly sown by Frank Westerhof, the small sturdy Dutchman who had sold us the land. (As part of the rather low price for the farm, we allowed him five years' free tenancy.)

I started each row at the top of the gentle ridge of our largest field and went south from there. I knew north-south rows intercepted the most sunlight, and with such a tight season I couldn't waste any of it. The first few vines would be in our thinnest soil, then the soil gradually fattened from eight or nine inches to about eighteen inches where the short test rows stopped.

Pounding the corner stakes and walking the string from each to the other, I'd stop occasionally to adjust the earphones on my head. I was listening to the evening repeat of a CBC Radio interview with the brilliant illustrator Ralph Steadman, who was talking to Peter Gzowski about his wine books and his own planting of a small personal vineyard in England.

Steadman had been writing and illustrating brilliant little artistic dissections – I guess they were technically travelogues – of different wine regions, cultures, grapes, and wines for a British wine chain called Oddbins. I remember grabbing every listing flyer I could in the 1980s whenever I managed to get to London. If I recall correctly, he had come to Canada to promote an exhibit of his Oddbins work at a distillery somewhere in western Ontario, and Gzowski's questions to him about his nascent vineyard were the perfect synchronicitous accompaniment to my measuring, posting, and stringing.

(Steadman's work for the chain was recently collected in a volume called *The Grapes of Ralph*. It is probably one of the funniest and unerringly perceptive wine publications to emerge from Britain in the last twenty-five years – and that's no mean feat, as a bewildering number of good to great books stream out of the place each year. Steadman's "Vineyard Diary" is tucked into the collection, and details his progress from eager prospective vigneron to proud, doting, and worried foster parent of a hundred vines, including fifty Pinot Noir.)

The next day, as I started planting my own small company of vines, things were not as amusing.

Each row was lined up, the spacing from as-yet-undug hole to hole properly marked. However, the theoretical treasures of this terroir would not easily surrender. I had good, high-carbon English digging shovels and forks, but after five or six inches no amount of drive and muscle power could get more than a scraping of soil and the odd fragment of limestone. The scratch and ring of the shovel clearly marked the end of easy digging. I had to get the pickaxe and break up the limestone and shale.

Anyone who's swung a pickaxe in stony soil knows that particular striking sound which, in a nanosecond, flashes a warning to the joints and marrow of your phalanges, long arm bones, shoulders, and cerebellum that they might best prepare for a vibrational shock on a scale most of us associate with the spectacular failures of Wile E. Coyote. The first few times it might be amusing, in a head-banging, mosh-pit sort of way, but it gets tedious so very quickly. Most swings with the pick would end with the crunch and grind of steel punching and splitting the thin limestone and shale layers of the Hillier underburden. But every dozen or so repetitions, that *ping* would announce either a slightly thicker band of limestone or a mocking piece of granite. If limestone, a few heartier attempts would crack and pierce it, and the shattered segments could be fished out and the hole continued. The odd time it turned out to be a granite cobble – usually, mercifully, rather small – which had to be traced and pried up whole before going on.

Once a hole was twelve to eighteen inches deep, I'd select one of the new vines shipped to me from Niagara and California from the bucket of water, which kept the roots shaded and moist. I'd trim the roots to about four to six inches, just as in the diagrams, make a small cone of soil at the base of the hole, and set the vine atop it, being careful to fan the roots out around the slope of the cone. Then I'd scrape new soil, pick out large rocks from the shovel blade, and gradually backfill each hole. After two days, I had my hundred Pinot vines in their new home, along with twenty Syrah and forty of the strongest 41 B vines transported to the County by Betty and Garn. The rest of the 41 B rootstock would go into a small nursery row to strengthen for a year and then be dug up and transplanted next to the others in this first test plot.

The 41 B, because they had shoots and leaves, looked green and healthy like plants should. The vines purchased from the nursery stuck up lifeless from the ground, their white-waxed tops (which kept the buds from drying out) making them nearly impossible to distinguish against the white and light grey of the limestone rubble that composed so much of the soil.

The rawness in my arms, shoulders, and legs evolved a day or two later into stiffness, and then disappeared. The salve for painful manual labour isn't a high wage, it is satisfaction with the completed task.

The barley grew, and soon concealed the small plot. A narrow path snaked from the gateway through the field to the plot, showing the route I took from the car as I checked the vines each day.

Crouched down to look at the buds that had just pushed through the wax, proving that I had not in my ignorance killed any vines, I heard: "Hi! We like your woods."

I stood and saw two boys under the age of ten who had materialized behind me.

"It's good for exploring," continued the younger, who stood about a head shorter than the other.

"Ah," was about all that I could say.

I recognized the two. They lived across from the midpoint of our farm on Station Road; the power line ended at their house. I had seen these boys playing with a yellow dog that seemed to enjoy barking energetically whenever it spotted me.

"We lost a rocket over here," said the taller boy.

"Oh," I responded, nodding my head.

For the next twenty-five minutes they filled me full of facts about rocketry, a hobby on which they were obviously keen. I managed to sidetrack them enough to learn the elder boy was Ryan, and his brother was Adam. Van Lune. There was some Netherlandish connection with Frank Westerhof, though what it was I couldn't really make out.

Eventually a woman's voice called out their names, and off they went.

Every few days they'd wander by when they saw me at the farm. I was there most days, because, as the 41 B mothervines were planted green, not as dormant, bare-rooted nursery stock, they required water to settle into their new home. But it was getting drier. At first I'd filled five-gallon pails from our outdoor back tap in Consecon, though all too soon I had to stop.

Andy from next door had shambled over one afternoon.

"First water-load of the summer this morning," he said, nodding toward his house.

I had seen a tank truck in front of their bungalow earlier, and though it was hot out I assumed it was heating oil or something . . . maybe stocking up while the price was low.

"Our well's gone dry. What about yours?" he asked.

"I don't really know." And I didn't. The pump seemed to run a long noisy period every time someone flushed or opened a tap.

Andy went over to our concrete well and pulled open the cover.

"You have a little more than we did this morning. Not much more. If you need the number, let me know."

We put the lid back on.

The next day, I began walking the fifty yards to the end of Bay Street and clambering over a line of large granite boulders extending into the water. Standing carefully astride the one farthest out, I'd scoop up pails of water from Weller's Bay and pour it through a funnel into lidded five-gallon pails. I'd trudge back with two if just watering the garden. When I filled five or six pails for the vines, they went directly into the trunk of the car for the five-mile trip over to the farm.

Lauren's sister Joanne had, mercifully, settled into the upper floor of an old brick house in Wellington not long after I planted our vine plot, and now she let Lauren and me come over with Winona and Jemima every few days for showers and baths. Joanne enjoyed town water. We enjoyed our first County drought.

The dryness, and the hot, bright sunlight, reminded me of something. Walking around the village, clearing my head after working on a deadline for some magazine or newspaper, I realized that, by scrunching and squinting my eyes, the centre of Consecon – opposite the variety store and the bank – in the dust, heat, and light, sort of looked like Gigondas in the Southern Rhône. I imagined this might be enhanced if you had recently taken a blow to the head and had benefit of a minor concussion.

Gigondas was a small, strange little village that produced a wine, made primarily from Grenache, that I enjoyed a great deal; much of what we were drinking with our barbecued dinners this first summer was Gigondas, or, for variety, bottles from nearby Sablet, Vacqueyras, or Rasteau. Lauren and I made our last trip to France in 1990, and I was entranced with

Gigondas. True, we both very much enjoyed the days we spent in Tournon, looking across the great hill of Hermitage, or sitting under the ancient gates sipping breakfast or afternoon drinks. And I loved the smells of recently pressed ferments that filled the air in the strip of small buildings called Mauves. But it was in Gigondas that I believed I had found a place where I might be happy. If it was at all possible to find a place to rent there, I suggested to Lauren it might be a village to keep in mind when I was writing some book.

It was a few years later that I came across Kermit Lynch's passage about the place, in his *Adventures on the Wine Route: A Wine Buyer's Tour of France*:

> Artifacts reveal that the Romans, smart fellows, enjoyed a good quantity of wine at Gigondas. The name is supposedly from Jocanditus, which means "merry or joyous city." While the village as it stands is not *that* ancient, it is old enough. With tile roofs and cavernlike dwellings – the doorways appear to lead right into the hillside – it is an altogether idyllic, surprisingly lazy, secluded spot. What a wonderful place for a wine merchant to retire, surrounded by vines, olive and fruit trees, wild herbs, ruins of the medieval fortified city on the hillside, and a population of only 750 with whom to share it all.

When Lauren and I realized we would have to scrap that dream and create our own version somewhere in eastern Ontario, Gigondas still remained the template. Not the looming ashlar stone châteaux of Bordeaux, or the modern architectural statements of California. Something more modest and human.

I knew I wouldn't be growing Grenache – a very late ripening grape – in Prince Edward County; I recognized the constraints of our terroir. Grenache, in a way, has a silky feel in the mouth very similar to good Pinot Noir, though warmer and deeper in fruit. It in some ways explains why, in decades past, so much Gigondas was pumped aboard bulk tankers and shipped north to the cellars of many a Burgundy merchant to blend with poor, watery Pinots. (Syrah often did the same service for the sellers of Bordeaux.) The Grenache-dominated wines of the Southern Rhône and the Syrahs of Cornas and Hermitage in the north are really my favourites. Authentic, well-made Burgundys and other good Pinot Noirs from around the world are a very close second, so I resigned myself to purchasing Rhônes while thankful our farm promised so much for Pinot Noir. I would, however mad, try some Syrah, which ripened about the same time as Cabernet Franc. Though that was ten or fourteen days later than Pinot Noir, it was not absolutely impossible.

I thought of our vineyard plot as Galets du Nord, which comes from a Rhône word for stones (*galets*), and plays on the idea of growing vines in Canada, which to most of the world is the land of polar bears and hockey.

The real smile in this is that our handful of vines were on a latitude below that of Gigondas, below the old Roman city of Orange, below the market town of Carpentras. Our farm was just shy of a mile south of the forty-fourth parallel; they are all found north of that line.

The mill space is empty
even stones are gone
where hands were shaken
and walls enclosed laughter
saved up and brought here
from the hot fields

• *Al Purdy, "Roblin's Mills [II]"*

alking the narrow, hot, and dusty roads around the mill
pond in Consecon, I would pause and lean over the rail
of the old wooden-decked bridge, watching the giant carp
below me struggle to draw oxygen from the still waters.

I had found an entry on the village in an old atlas of the
County published in 1878:

Consecon – derived from the Indian word "con-con,"
meaning a pickerel, from the great abundance of that fish
along the shore in the days of the early settlement of the
place – is situated at the head of Weller's Bay, five miles
south-east of the Carrying Place; partly in Ameliasburg,
and partly in Hillier; on both sides of the Consecon
River, which empties into the lake of the same name, on

which was built the first grist mill in Ameliasburg, in 1804, by Matthias Marsh, whose son still keeps the Post Office. The situation of the place is very pleasant, and its location is such as will undoubtedly make it one day a place of commercial importance, Weller's Bay being one of the most safe, commodious, and easily accessible (so far as its natural position is concerned) of any harbour upon the lake. The old York and Kingston road runs through the place.

There are a number of very good business houses in the village, including three general stores, one grocery, one drug-store, and some first rate carriage and blacksmith shops.

There are four fine churches, a graded school, employing two teachers, and two telegraph offices.

The village has a daily mail, per stage, to and from Picton and Trenton. It is distant from the former place about twenty-two miles, and from the latter about fifteen. It contains a population of about 400 souls.

I realized that the line of large granite rocks from which I filled my buckets was all that remained of one of the rather large wharves that ran out into Weller's Bay. Over these, County schooners would take on countless bushels of the two-rowed malting barley coveted by brewers in upstate New York. As nearly every farm in the County was four or five miles at most from water, dozens of small ports enjoyed the same success; all were now gone and unremembered.

There was a good premium paid for bay barley – the name given by American merchants to all the brewing grain from the

Bay of Quinte – and the crop brought an unprecedented period of wealth to the County. People still talk of the barley days as if they remember them personally; most of the great mid- to late-nineteenth-century brick houses were built with the money the grain brought. That impressively conservative creature known as the County farmer rushed to become a shipwright too, even if only to avoid paying someone else to take his barley to market. Shipyards sprang up all around the County, and bay barley farmers acted like ancient Greek yeomen, building and sailing their ships to take abundant crops across the water. Hesiod's agricultural poem "Works and Days" advises:

> Admire small ships, but put your cargo in
> A big one, for a larger cargo brings
> A larger profit, if the storms hold off.

If the storms hold off. Many a County ship and crew, trying to get in one last load of cargo before the winter, hit November storms and went down. In County lore, the water and shore between Wicked Point (better known as Salmon Point now) and Point Petre was at times so laden with the barley of ill-fated schooners that it was called Soup Harbour.

Another storm finally capsized the ships, and razed the shipyards and farm fields – a political one. The United States approved the McKinley Tariffs in 1891, and overnight the barley days ended.

It stands to reason that a place with so much shoreline hanging well into Lake Ontario would have a long maritime history. But it has long sunk and been silted over. There are now few harbours left even for pleasure sailcraft in the County.

(The other day in the Picton LCBO, the man next to me in line seemed to have been spirited from a Newfoundland or Nova Scotian trawler; small and greyed, he appeared either phantom or phony in foul-weather clothes for the sea, and it took me a moment to remember there were still commercial fishing boats operating from the County.)

In Consecon, the silent memorial to the days of sail is those exposed rocks from a forgotten wharf.

From where I loitered on the old bridge, I glanced along the length of the mill pond to the west, where a modern concrete bridge crossed the Consecon River (as it is on maps) or Crick (as it's clipped by locals). There was a small dam, silent in the summer dryness. Over it loomed a fairly modern feedmill of green-painted metal siding and new-varnished wood. It was now no longer a feedmill, however; it had just been turned into a bar, Cascades.

The feedmill had replaced a previous large stone mill that was taken down some decades ago. I had seen photos of the Consecon Mill, and it is hard to imagine it in place of Cascades. What a different village Consecon would be with that huge building still on the river (or, if you prefer, creek). In the photos it reminded me of Roblin's Mill, the centrepiece of Black Creek Pioneer Village in the northwest corner of Toronto . . . and with good reason.

I first remember seeing Roblin's Mill as a kid of maybe eight. Its size impressed me, and I loved the greyness of its stone, and the sense of solidity and permanence. My parents had a framed print of Roblin's Mill that dated from the same visit, and it hung on walls in our various houses as I grew up. I knew that Roblin's Mill didn't actually rise where it stood in

Toronto, but it was only much later that I learned it had been dismantled from the centre of the village of Ameliasburgh, Prince Edward County. It was natural that Consecon Mill reminded me of Roblin's: they were separated by only a handful of miles.

The space left by the Consecon Mill had, however awkwardly, been filled by a feedmill that was now Cascades, but a great emptiness spread just south of the new bar. That was where the old Hayes's Tavern once stood. The large wood-frame complex dating from the 1830s, when combined with the stone mill next door, must have made Consecon an impressive little village and would help explain the nearly dozen former stores in the place. Hayes's Tavern was taken apart and moved from Consecon to the other side of the County, just above the drop down the escarpment into Waupoos. It's been saved, while in Consecon it was abandoned and rotting. Yet its removal leaves just a forlorn and dusty little park.

Not far from the park is the old Whittier house, considered a sister building to Hayes's Tavern. A little rough, with weathered green paint, the fine woodwork and Greek revival trim below the eaves of the second storey give this rather large building some elegance and dignity.

There survive a modest number of really wonderful small houses around the various funny little roads of Consecon, roads that cross at the most obtuse, improbable angles, and have names such as Pig Tail Lane, Squire's Street, Mill Street, and Store Street. Lauren, taking Winona and Jemima out for strolls, would come back and comment on this or that building that she hadn't noticed before. We daydreamed that if we had a million dollars one of the best things we could do with it would be to purchase all of Consecon and restore it to something like the village it was and could yet still be.

≈

Though Winona called our rented place on Bay Street Happy House earlier in the spring, it was so small that finding room even for the nickname meant shifting a few things inside. The close quarters made it impossible for visitors to stay for long, but there were a number of people who stopped by: some to see if we were still alive; some to check the vines; all for a swim at Sandbanks Provincial Park.

Steve and Denise — friends of Lauren's from Toronto — came out for a few days with their young son and mentioned that while driving in North Marysburgh, around Waupoos, they noticed a small sign that simply said "WINERY." They couldn't find one anywhere and gave up, but thought it was something I might want to investigate.

I knew that Phil and Catherine Mathewson didn't have a winery. Harold Hossein, weatherman at City TV in Toronto, had told me a few years before when we worked together that, travelling to and from his County cottage at Prinyer's Cove, he had heard of a German fellow near Waupoos who was planting a little vineyard. I corrected Harold, saying that he must have meant South Bay and that Mathewson wasn't German. Harold was absolutely right, however. A fellow named Ed Neuser had put in a number of hybrid winegrapes. But those vines would have been too young, so that couldn't have explained the sign either.

What had Steve and Denise found?

Some weeks later, when Lauren and her sister Joanne were

out for a drive with the girls, they solved it. They came upon one of the signs and followed the trail up a steep sideroad just east of St. John's Church in Waupoos. It wasn't a *wine* winery; it was a cidery. The County Cider Company and Estate Winery. By chance they stumbled across the owner, who said that he wasn't officially open yet but would let them be his first customers. Lauren briefly spun our tale out for him, and he suggested I drop by when I could.

His cider was pretty good.

We went back to Waupoos on an outing some time later. The County Cider Company "store" was set up in the sunroom of a remarkable stone cottage atop a small escarpment. From anywhere up there you had one of the most breathtaking views in the province, as the majesty of Lake Ontario and the eastern parts of the County spread out across the south. The cidermaster manned the tasting bar, and energetically introduced himself. We were his only customers that afternoon.

Grant Howes was a tall fellow, a few years older than I, and bore a notable resemblance to actor Bill Murray. With an M.B.A. from Queen's, he actually lived in British Columbia with a wife and son and worked in finance there, commuting back and forth to save the family appleyard – or at least give it a fighting chance.

Grant's mother, Berva, owned the beautiful house and large orchard, and his brother had more apples on the other side of the ferry in South Fredericksburgh. Apple prices had crashed in Ontario, as local fruit could compete neither with imported apple prices nor with cheap Chinese juice concentrate. Cider, Grant had divined, was probably the only decent value-added product that could justify the continued existence of their orchards.

It was hard to believe. This part of Ontario was famous for the quality and variety of its apples. Apples grew here almost from the moment the Loyalists took up their plots, and County apple growers were especially known for both their skill and their fruit. The County even had its own homegrown Johnny Appleseed, according to a passage in Robert Leslie Jones's *History of Agriculture in Ontario*: "Wallbridge, an old bachelor, originally a Yankee pedlar, it is said, set up headquarters at the mouth of Myer's Creek, in Prince Edward County, where he was the first person to bring in many of the first fruit trees from the States and plant them in various places, often from motives of kindness alone. It has been claimed that all the old orchards in Prince Edward came from his planting."

Whether much of Wallbridge's legacy remains is doubtful. Before the winter of 1933-34, the County had more than 10,000 acres of apple trees and a dazzling array of varieties. After that cruel season, fewer than 90,000 trees survived out of more than 400,000. More of this tiny remnant was disappearing each season, grubbed out by bulldozers and piled in the fencebottoms before being burned or carted away.

That Grant was alone in producing cider surprised me, given the impressively flavourful fruit that still grew in odd corners of the County. As far back as 1852 annual production of cider here was a few pints shy of 50,000 gallons. Cider was the drink of most people in eastern North America, whether American or Canadian. In his book *The Alcoholic Republic*, W.J. Rorabaugh wrote that

The rural North loved cider. The beverage was "omnipresent," with a pitcher on every table and a jug in every field. During the winter, a typical New

England family could be expected to consume a barrel a week. So prevalent was cider that it became a symbol of egalitarianism as "the common drink of . . . rich and poor alike." Even crusty John Adams, who railed against distilled spirits for a half century, drank a tankardful every morning. Cider was so popular that Americans tended to look askance at anyone who chose to drink imported wine instead. Americans heralded their sparkling amber beverage as a cousin to champagne, indeed such a close relative that cider had "oftentimes been passed on *knowing* Europeans." These visitors, alas, were no doubt those who denounced the nation's terrible, sour champagne.

Grant was looking at growing vines too, and was doing a lot of research, reading books, attending seminars, visiting growers and vintners. He filled me in a bit on Ed Neuser's experience with Vidal vines just to the east of him, but said he'd wait a few years before he attempted to grow any himself; he had enough challenges trying to master cider.

Outside, testing the strength of the white fence rails around the horse paddock next to the sunroom/tasting bar, I noted the nice steep slope from the top of the escarpment to the lower shore of Waupoos.

"That should be in Pinot Noir," I said to Grant. "It could work, given the site, and it'd be the most graceful vineyard in the province."

"We'll see" he replied, unconvinced, but well aware of the beauty of the view.

We walked over to a small nursery where Grant had a company of true European cider apples growing. He'd received the cuttings from Albert Piggot in British Columbia, who'd gathered them for his own Merridale Cider Works on Vancouver Island, and Grant had grafted them up and set them out here at Waupoos. I was impressed. I could hardly wait for those trees to take their place in the Howes's orchards. Grant said the hardest thing was trying to blend what are really dessert or cooking apples into proper cider – acids and tannins just weren't there. The new trees would help change that.

If the cider was decent now, I was eager to see what he'd fashion with the right fruit.

❧

This was the summer that the girls first learned to shudder at the word Waupoos. In the car, out on what might seem like a nice family drive, all Lauren had to say was that we were off to Waupoos, and Winona and Jemima (taking her cue from her elder sister) would start to sob and then howl. It meant Daddy would be talking to Grant Howes and then Ed Neuser. For hours.

Ed, as Grant had told me, was a bit like Santa Claus with an attitude. Stocky, powerful, and with a shock of white hair and a carefully trimmed matching white beard, Ed, with his wife, Rita Kaimins, had with time and much expense reclaimed an old apple farm, turning it into a beautiful property. Ed's small, Teutonically neat and orderly vineyard of hearty Vidal and Geisenheim hybrids had survived a pair of cold County winters. That summer, though, the shoots were being stripped of their leaves by something. Ed showed me a container of the largest, greenest caterpillars I'd ever seen.

"Tell me then, what's that?" Ed half barked.

"Ugly. Definitely ugly. But I have no idea," I answered, genuinely puzzled.

"Everyone tells us that! Nobody knows. Nobody can give us an answer. Well, I can tell you, they eat all our fruit and our leaves, and it stops or out come our vines. I'm not growing them for these to eat. For now, we pick them and kill them. Then maybe we get an answer."

⁓

The Mathewsons, Grant Howes, Ed Neuser. It was a small group of people, but more than I had expected. And it had given us a reason to get out and explore. Each trip out to Waupoos was a new excuse to take an untried winding road back home.

Hillier seemed a world away, within the particular insularity of the County townships. North Marysburgh, with its long finger of rock and soil reaching towards Kingston, was the oldest European settlement in Prince Edward, absorbing the first boats of Loyalists. The steep escarpment that pressed on the north of a precious band of south-facing sands and deep clays between it and the shoreline provided the Waupoos area with scenic majesty and a special microclimate. The Lake could either stream warm winds or draw off cold air, which bounced and recycled against the rise of the rock. Whether because of its remoteness or beneficial winds, North Marysburgh still had a good number of orchards. The high ratio of lake to land gave it a unique character in the County – compared to Hillier, which, though well punctuated by bays, felt rolling and very terrestrial, Waupoos seemed dressed as Newfoundland with a modest trust fund.

Nearby, in Black River, sort of the borderlands between North and South Marysburgh, the fields were generous, and the way the houses rose reminded me of Vermont. Farther towards South Bay and Port Milford, the country split the scenic difference between Black River and Waupoos.

The lands about the townships of Athol, South Marysburgh, and the parts of Hallowell around East and West Lakes did not have a landscape of its own as much as it did a calling: it was vacationland. The famed sand beaches of Outlet and Sandbanks meant seasonal cottages, private campgrounds, and roadsides cluttered with commercial signs. The farms and villages appeared to have surrendered their own identity to the greater good of catering to those in quest of sand and sun. Occasionally a comely vista or a pleasing setting of Upper Canadian farm buildings would appear as we drove along . . . and then as quickly be gone, almost a mirage.

Hallowell was all things to all people, with bits of the other township characteristics within its borders, as well as the economic benefits of the artisan's paradise of Bloomfield (where I dare you to cross the street without bumping into a potter, tole painter, or glass-blower) and the County seat of Picton.

Ameliasburgh seemed a little rougher and less fertile than Hillier, with more pasture than cropland; that is, except for the length of Rednersville road that ran on the south shore of the Bay of Quinte. This was formerly prime orchard land, but along the twisting, pleasant drive now rose a massive chain of large suburban houses and faux mansions, broken by one or two of the genuine great old houses and a few hamlets or orchards that easily stood out from the sameness of the parvenu homes.

Sophiasburgh, to the north and east, was *terra incognita*. It always seemed too large and too far away to explore. Its very remoteness meant it held a great treasure of undamaged early-nineteenth-century houses, spread out evenly along the roads and hamlets. And it also provided an immediate language barrier to the outsider. It was So-*fy*-as-burgh, not So-*fee*-as-burgh. The largest settlement was De-more-*est*-ville, and not *De*-more-est-ville, or even De-*more*-est-ville, as you'd expect.

Linguistic secret handshakes were everywhere: *Con*-seh-con, as I mentioned; for Point Petre, *Pee*-ter was right, *Peh*-tree wrong; Huyck's Point Road had to sound like *Hikes*, not *Who*-yucks; Scoharie required the proper emphasis of *Scoh*-hari.

✌

Our little vineyard test plot required only weeding, watering, and watching for most of the first summer. As the shoots grew – and they did so rapidly through May and June, even in the drought – I pounded in wooden stakes beside each vine and laboriously fastened the tender growth to the support with jute twine. I marked each vine-and-rootstock combination with its own copper label so I could identify their particulars in coming years.

As the barley went to head, and then began to turn golden, it made the bare, stony earth of the test plot stand out even more, the clean boundary of the yellow ranks of grain contrasting richly with the white silver of the limestone rubble amid the vinerows.

Portioning out water from the buckets, I was interrupted by a woman who flashed a friendly smile. It was Ryan and Adam's mother, Vicki. She had walked over to introduce herself, and we fell into a discussion about what I was doing.

"Where do you get the water?" she asked at one point.

"I fill the buckets up in the bay in Consecon, at the end of our street, and drive them over here," I told her, while carefully trying to keep the water I was giving a reasonably content 41 B vine from spreading too far from the plant.

"You're welcome to use our hose if you want. Stuart," she said, referring to her husband, "thinks we have our well on the aquifer. We've never gone dry, so help yourself."

I did, knocking on their door each time I needed to fill up, and eventually accepting their offer just to help myself as needed. Stuart was a tall, lanky man with slightly greying hair and a close-cropped beard. An electrical and mechanical trouble-shooter, he worked long, often solitary hours at the Procter & Gamble plant just outside of the County. Originally from the Netherlands, he was quiet and thoughtful in speech, and refreshingly quick to smile.

There seemed to be a never-ending series of projects underway at the Van Lunes, from digging in new plants for the garden to various building improvements and periodic maintenance. Computers and tropical fish appeared to fill out the rest of the family's time and interest; the boys were being home-schooled, and the Internet and computer technology seemed to be important keystones in getting the boys through their requirements.

Before we arrived I had purchased, through Harold Hossein's connections at Environment Canada, all the records I could of different weather-recording stations in the County – most of them no longer collecting data. That helped me read the County and its ability to ripen and sustain Pinot Noir and other vinifera vines. I had installed a small maximum–minimum thermometer in a little shelter in the centre of the vinerows. With this I started to log the highs and lows each day to give me a specific idea of the microclimate of our farm. It was an important advance on the often outdated numbers and somewhat distant locations of the purchased data.

I thought about it, and asked whether Vicki and Stuart would agree to let the boys record the numbers and chart them for me, in return for a very small bit of pocket money. They agreed, and the boys started the task, one or the other getting the readings each day before dinner.

◆◇

The barley around the vine plot was harvested, and the straw baled and carried away. Not all, as a handful of bales were left by Frank Westerhof at my request so that I could cover some of the vines before winter.

The shoots of the vine – which had lengthened so rapidly from small buds hidden under the bone-colour grafting wax many weeks before – gradually began to lose their bright green, and then turn yellow. The vine leaves did the same thing near their margins, and began to show hints of red here and there on the flat of the blade. The yellow shoots were tougher and much stiffer now. Closest to the graft the shoot had actually become a French cocoa brown, and every few inches tiny scales covered a bud that looked like miniature nuthatch beak.

In Consecon, the ancient furnace – one that appeared to be composed of old Spitfire parts scavenged from the Battle of Britain – had somehow been repaired and sparked up by a professional heating man rather than our landlord. The design of the house meant that most of the heat fled quickly to the upper floor; travelling downstairs you could feel a temperature difference of four or five degrees. To bring warmth to the living room or kitchen meant manufacturing an oppressive August afternoon upstairs. At least we would sleep in warmth, however excessive or expensive.

That was a necessary comfort, properly earned after the fall rains had spread indoors. Our roof was reasonably sound and waterproof, but the pipes, in sympathy with the weather, began to send equinox showers. The toilet upstairs was the first to thunder its load upon the unsuspecting. I forget now who flushed, but moments later Lauren and I were both covered in eau de toilette and diving to push tables, chairs, books, and everything else to safety.

The plumbers came, and said they couldn't touch our pipes. Technically, they would have to report it and reinstall everything to a degree of modernity and safety that they imagined our landlord would not spring for. They were right. Lawrence came, and with a relative repaired things to a degree.

Days later the shower drain began to drip and then gush; ceiling tiles were ripped down once again by Lawrence, some sort of fix made, and the ceiling was stapled and glue-gunned back into place.

At the farm, the leaves finally dropped from the canes when the mercury dipped a degree or two below zero Celsius, and as the frost set into the ground I carefully wrapped some straw around the base and graft of each vine. One or two rows I left exposed, and along a few others I banked up soil instead of straw against the graft and lower cane. With a good snow cover blown in from the lake, we'd see how different methods might help the vines survive a County winter.

At Happy House, we snuggled in for long winter naps, and worried about the coming spring rains.

At night in the graveyard
rocking and rocking
he held onto a stone marker
with strangers underneath
not knowing how he got there
but feeling among his own people

• *Al Purdy, "Jib at Roblin's Mills"*

The first volumes I bought that recounted pieces of the County's past were found in my favourite used bookshops in Toronto. A surprising number, really, turned up on those shelves. The history and beauty of this place has always been noted and, if not exactly celebrated, then gathered, stored, and kept from historical invisibility, even as Prince Edward County receded from the province's and the nation's awareness, dwindling from backwater to forgotten and then to unknown, with a population forever unchanging at 22,000 souls.

In one volume I had seen an attractive old photo of the Holy Trinity Anglican Church in Consecon. The book noted that the plain but striking structure, built in 1847, was one of the older "replacement" churches still standing in the County. (The oldest of the surviving first-generation wood-frame ones is the Methodist White Chapel just outside of Picton, raised in 1809.) Rough quarried limestone blocks made up the walls and the massive square stone tower. It was considered Norman in style, and other than the generous Gothic windows, the only real decoration was the octagonal, louvred tower extension with the round "crown of thorns" trim carpentry atop the tower. Before moving to the village, I had always meant to swing through Consecon on one of the early reconnoitres we made in the early 1990s. Though I wanted to see Holy Trinity, I never got round to making that turnoff into Consecon – but then, as I noted before, few ever did.

Now I was sitting in this stone church, as it served as one of Ameliasburgh township's two libraries. Arrayed in front of me was a selection of books, most of which I had never seen turn up in Toronto.

Ameliasburgh's head librarian, Peggy Leavy, would send out my interlibrary-loan request for even more obscure books on Upper Canadian architecture; some requests I dropped with Dianne Cranshaw at the village library in Wellington, just to help liven up her days. As the books came in, I'd read them and pick up little fragments of the past that would change my appreciation of things – even in Consecon.

The large frame Methodist (now United) church across the street from the Norman-style stone Anglican church-cum-library was actually, in one old book, considered a very good example of carpenter's Gothic style and construction. Though it retained the basic shape of the church I could see in the book's photos and illustrations, the building was now covered in aluminum siding, its interesting bell-tower construction and decoration masked by two-tone sheets of metal. I learned that a fire in the building a few decades back was responsible for turning the church into a plainer version of the plain building it already was. And now the pleasing pattern of original tinwork on the previously repaired steeple has been covered in yet more siding, without the rhythm and craftsmanship of what was there before. The worn and decaying wooden-louvred Gothic vents were pulled out, and in their place the roofer crudely fashioned new metal inserts, narrower than before, and not understanding how he might reproduce the curving pointed Gothic arch, or even if it mattered, he decided that an angular point was just as good. I see it every day. I shake my head at the well-meaning vandalism, but luckily I can see it as it is, as it used to be, and as it originally was, somehow all at the same time. All are true, and to me one is not wiped out by the latest incarnation. Maybe that is what attracts me, and impels me to know more about this place, to live in the present and at the same to see the shadows and the highlights – the chiaroscuro that has painted this place richer than most.

I uncovered, in one of those rather overstuffed Victorian histories that were the fashion generations ago, a great truth about the basic natural and historical canvas of the County. In *The Settlement of Upper Canada*, originally published in 1869, William Canniff takes the reader to the height overlooking the ferry that comes to the County across the Bay of Quinte:

We would supplement this just tribute of praise, and interesting statement; and we venture to say, after having viewed many lovely spots in the old and new worlds, that we know of no lovelier panoramic view than that to be obtained from the Lake of the Mountain, not even excepting the far-famed Hudson, and the classic Rhine. Of course we except the rich relics of the old feudal days, which so picturesquely adorn the mountain tops along the swift running Rhine. But even here we are not destitute of historic reminiscences. True, we have no embattled towers, resting on rugged summits; no castle keeps, with mysterious dungeons, upon whose walls may be traced the letters laboriously cut by long retained captives; no crumbling walls and half-filled moats; no magnificent ruins of graceful architecture. We possess no Tintern Abbey by the quiet waters, to tell of the olden time; no gloomy cloisters where comfortable monks did dwell; nor romantic cathedral whose antique window admitted but dim religious light. Still, there is something to be said for the past, in connection with our country. From our position here we may examine the classic ground of Upper Canada, and trace the course of settlement followed by our fathers, the pioneers.

The Bay of Quinte, which serves as the northern border, or moat ditch, of the County, shows the history of this place simply in its name. Quinte is but the English transliteration of the French Kenté. Until recently there were oldtimers who still called it *Kanty*, reflecting a middle ground; their present-day descendants find vowels and the occasional consonant inconvenient and pronounce it *Kwin-nee* in much the same way they shorten Belleville to a lugubrious *Blll-vlll*. (The County, in the same tongue, becomes the *Cow-knee*.)

Kante or Kenté is at best guess an adaptation either of the Iroquois *Yo-ya-da-do-konthe* – approximately "home of the thunderbird" – or the Iroquois for "meadow," and it is part of the same root that gave Kentucky its name in the United States. As

Iroquois affinity to this place is very strong in their legends, and as thunderbirds were thought to reside somewhere on the stretch of the Bay of Quinte near Lake on the Mountain, I tend to the former meaning. In the aftermath of the American Revolution the historical lands of the Iroquois in New York State were taken as war spoils. Though most of the Mohawk and Six Nations who fought alongside the British settled on a special Loyalist grant along the Grand River in western Ontario, a small group broke away and chose the lands of their legends, near Deseronto, on the north shore just east of Belleville. The communion silver given the Mohawk by Queen Anne was divided up between the two groups, and each took their new territories. The Deseronto band is still there and is referred to bureaucratically as MBQ – Mohawk of the Bay of Quinte.

Prince Edward County started to take on a semi-recognizable form in French maps in the early 1600s. A band of Cayugas, southern Iroquois refugees from bitter wars with the Andastes, had settled into the territory, and requested French missionaries be placed among them. Though the Jesuits – especially the flayed, parboiled, and barbecued martyrs of Huronia – are considered *the* archetypal Canadian missionaries, in this case the mission fell to the Sulpicians.

In the last few days of October 1668, two young priests, Trouvé and Fénelon, came into the waters of the Bay of Quinte to establish the Kenté mission among this branch of the Iroquois. It wasn't a particularly glorious success to the Sulpicians, but it limped along, protected under the usual French colonial mix of court intrigue and geopolitics until 1680, when it was finally abandoned. The location of the mission and of the Cayuga village has remained a mystery. A professor of mine at Queen's University at Kingston was intrigued by the problem, and after examining overlooked maps he argued the evidence clearly showed the Kenté mission on Weller's Bay, near the present village of Consecon. And that's where the official blue plaque about the mission was erected by the Province of Ontario, on the site of the old Hayes's Tavern on the Hillier side of the river.

As Catholic missionaries, Trouvé, Fénelon, and their successors at the mission would have brought wine with them to conduct mass in the wilds of Kenté; like the Jesuits, they may even have tried to make it from the wild riparia growing around them. Whether they did or not, however, remains as much a mystery as the precise site of their mission.

The latter of the founding pair of missionaries – François de Salignac de la Mothe-Fénelon – had a younger half-brother sporting the same full name and who also studied as a Sulpician. He's also the better remembered, having become Bishop of Cambrai some years after his half-brother was forced out of Canada and had disappeared into the mists of time. In a book titled *Telmaque*, this more famous of the two Françoise's wrote that "some of the most dreadful mischiefs that afflict mankind proceed from wine; it is the cause of disease, quarrels, seditions, idleness, aversion to labour and every species of domestic disorder." Thank the heavens he wasn't the Fénelon who actually lived here in Prince Edward County those few centuries back; it is not a sentiment that winegrowers here would like to put in their brochures.

ಌ

After the French regime came to an end in the Seven Years' War in 1763, and the lands that were nominally French passed into the hands of the English, the area was abandoned but for hunting and fishing sites – until the next unpleasantness in North America thirteen years later.

The aftermath of the American Revolution, which ended in 1783, impelled another collection of refugees to settle along the Bay of Quinte. Still considered part of the Quebec lands taken from the French after the Battle of the Plains of Abraham, shorelands along the St. Lawrence to Kingston and then westward along Lake Ontario as far as Weller's Bay were surveyed in a rough-and-ready manner to take those loyal to the British Crown: discharged soldiers, their families, and the thousands of ordinary folk caught on the losing side of the revolution. Around the same time, similar preparations were underway in Niagara and at a few other Great Lakes settlements like Detroit.

The original Loyalist townships along the St. Lawrence River and the eastern end of Lake Ontario were given numbers; the County was divided from east to west into Fifth, Sixth, and Seventh Towns. The first batteaux of Loyalists landed on the shores of Fifth Town in 1788; the British intended to keep military groups somewhat intact, and Fifth Town consisted of a number of former British regulars and Germans from the Electorate of Hanover.

Land was distributed by lots, with generous portions for all; grants to officers were often a thousand acres or more, while other ranks received at least two hundred acres. The Loyalist lots provided a basic character of the countryside here. They are all narrow frontage with deep sides – basically long and skinny, like most of the land divisions in the old French colony of New France. This allowed the widest possible ownership of waterfront, so there'd be greater access to Lake

Ontario and the important bays and rivers for travel and communication. Some light settlement took place in Sixth and Seventh Towns, but for the most part these were reserved for grants to the children of the Loyalists, who were also entitled to land of their own from the Crown.

The County finally came officially into existence on July 16, 1792. A proclamation announced new government districts for the Loyalist settlements, and stated

> That the tenth of the said counties is to be hereafter called by the name of the County of Prince Edward; which County is to be bounded on the south by Lake Ontario; on the west by the Carrying-place on the Isthmus, of the Presque Isle de Quinté; on the north by the Bay of Quinté; and on the east, from Point Pleasant to Point Traverse, by its several shores and bays, including the late townships of Marysburg, Sophiasburg, and Ameliasburg. The said County of Prince Edward to comprehend all the islands in said Lake Ontario and Bay of Quinté nearest to the said county, in the whole, or greater part fronting the same.

Fifth, Sixth, and Seventh Towns were bestowed the names of George III's daughters; the County itself was named after his fourth son, Edward. (Other princes provided names for the towns east of the County – with Adolphustown and Fredericksburgh being the closest of these.)

A few short weeks after the proclamation christening the County, Prince Edward actually looked upon his namesake's shore. He sailed past in August 1792 on his way to visit Niagara. Edward was for some reason on the outs with his father and older brothers and had been sent with his regiment (the Royal Fusiliers) first to Gibraltar and then, in 1791, to the garrison of Quebec, where he remained until 1794.

The prince had brought along a mysterious woman, known as Madame de St. Laurent. The unmarried prince's open mistress, she caused some problems for the stiffer British citizens in Quebec, yet was warmly received by the French Canadians. (Two of the greatest stiffs of the time were the lieutenant governor of Upper Canada, John Graves Simcoe, and his wife, Elizabeth Posthuma Simcoe, their middle names no doubt drawing each to the other tight as a death grip.)

Back home in England, dynastic duties forced the prince to marry a German princess in 1818, and in 1819 he fathered a daughter, born May 24. Every Canadian knows that date, as it's the first long weekend of the summer: the daughter was to ascend the British throne as Queen Victoria.

The twist of fate that allowed Prince Edward to gaze upon the land that bore his name is one of those footnotes that seem so well suited to the County: never at the centre of events, but never entirely on the margins.

❧

The County, abundantly served by water routes, prospered after the hard initial years of Loyalist settlement. Eventually the sons and daughters began to take up the grants they were promised, and many settled in the southern part of Ameliasburgh township. Land grants were widened to the population of Upper Canada that had not received them as Loyalists, and Joseph Forsyth, one of the powerful merchants of Kingston, petitioned for many large blocks, and, not surprisingly, got them.

Forsyth's County grant doesn't appear in his entry in the *Dictionary of Canadian Biography*, though his grants of land in Clark, Cramahe, Haldimand, Percy, Scarborough, and Thurlow townships do. In 1796 this well-connected Scottish emigrant received a 1,200-acre Crown grant in Ameliasburgh from which our farm and little house were eventually carved. It's doubtful he ever saw it. The land was instead settled by American Quakers who flooded into the County just before the nineteenth century dawned, following their relatives who had arrived in the crush of Loyalist settlers. Forsyth was to die in Kingston during the War of 1812, respected and rich. (He was said to have been the first in that town to learn of the American declaration of war, through private business correspondence, and informed the military of the American aggression.) His County properties were sold off by his heirs to the Quakers, who hacked back the ancient forests upon them, their steady arrival aided by a good stretch of the Danforth military road. American contractor Asa Danforth took on the construction of this improbable highway from York (Toronto) to Kingston, and felt ill-used and underpaid doing it, but his road across this section of the County was good, and it is still in use; part of it, made obsolete by the Loyalist Parkway between Hillier and Wellington, is but sixteen feet wide, twisting and peaceful. During the War of 1812, Americans travelled this stretch of Asa Danforth's road as footsore prisoners-of-war trudging eastwards to Kingston.

The War of 1812 left the County unharmed; it was a safe military supply route. A few residents served in the militia companies, but most of the men, it appears, did service moving munitions and goods through the Bay of Quinte or along the Danforth. The closest danger came when Commodore Isaac

Chauncey and his American fleet were slowly trolling the north shore of Lake Ontario. Aboard was a potentially dangerous detachment of American regulars. Dr. W.K. Burr wrote in his *Historical Sketches of Prince Edward County* that one of the oldest families settled there recounted how

> early in the morning in June of 1813 Mrs. Rose stood on the verandah of her home and saw the American fleet lying at anchor near Timber Island and at the south end of Point Travers.
>
> The people of Marysburgh from Waupoos to Indian Point were very much excited, fearing the Americans would come ashore in search of food and supplies. Especially were they alarmed, as all the men were away helping transport munitions of war by water. . . .
>
> It was, no doubt, in view of what might happen that morning that Sergeant William Carson donned the Revolutionary Red Coat, shouldered his flint-lock musket, and marched back and forth, up and down the road on the brow-side of the hill in sight of the American fleet, to give them the impression that the place was defended by a garrison of British soldiers.
>
> Sergeant Carson at this time was seventy years of age and too old to engage in active service.

And indeed there was a Sergeant William Carson who died in Marysburgh in the 1820s. According to Dr. Burr, his regiment was at the capture of Quebec in 1759. He was a soldier all through the American Revolution, and was "appointed 'Captain of a Company' in the Battalion of Militia of

Adolphustown, Marysburgh and Sophiasburg in 1788, one year after arriving in Prince Edward County."

I've always been fascinated by how much influence is wielded by a generation in an important military struggle once the conflict ends, how it claims the succeeding age as its own. The men of Wolfe's army and Saunders's navy before Quebec in 1759 included so very many like James Cook; the Second World War generation has only recently stepped aside from running our world. In the early 1800s it was the time of the Waterloo men.

While the War of 1812 was but a sideshow of first the Revolutionary and then Napoleonic Wars, the officers with the Duke of Wellington at that famous battle in June 1815 returned to administer Great Britain and her empire. Two such Waterloo men landed in Upper Canada: Lieutenant Governor Peregrine Maitland and his secretary, George Hillier. Maitland was made famous in the final repulse of the French columns at Waterloo; Hillier was also in the campaign, seconded from his regiment and serving on the staff of the quartermaster general.

In the early years of the 1820s, the residents of the south part of Ameliasburgh found the township too large and petitioned to have it divided; they obviously were in the debt of Major Hillier when the division was granted in 1824, for they named the new township after the fellow. And while Hillier was but a junior staff officer at the Battle of Waterloo, his is one of three names from that battle that were bestowed upon the County. Picton, the County seat, took its name from Wellington's general who was slain that day. The village of Wellington needs no explanation.

The County apparently even holds a real Waterloo man in its soil. Again, Dr. Burr, who liked to preserve these odds and ends of history before they passed from memory, notes a

William Massey who died in 1863 at the age of eighty-one and lies near the Bowerman Church. "Mr. Massey was a soldier in the British Army at the Battle of Waterloo in Belgium in 1814 [*sic*]. I believe he is the only soldier who is buried in this County who took part in gaining that famous victory."

Unlike Sergeant Carson, Massey has a marker, on which this verse is engraved:

> Here in my silent grave I sleep,
> Freed from all pain and grief;
> Though my disease was long and sharp
> God sent at last relief

❧

Graveyards are part of daily life here. They are everywhere, a part of the landscape. I can barely count the number, though a map of their locations produced for amateur genealogists lists more than one hundred. Starting from the one that lies behind the house we rent in Consecon on the shore of Weller's Bay and then driving on to Picton, I can pass a dozen or more, depending on the route. Many are small, neglected, forlorn. Some, though tiny, can be seen from the road, surrounded by aged Victorian metalwork, their white stones weathered but still bright. Many more are those burial grounds – some still soliciting custom – which are mowed and manicured, but suffering in other ways. In these, the thin white marble headstones so popular in the nineteenth century are almost all gone, especially if the buried have living descendants. The old marble is plucked out, and a thick slab of black or pink granite etched and machined by a computer-driven tool is stuck in its place. Many of the most visible cemeteries along the Loyalist Parkway look more like giant chess games, with squat ugly pieces of black and pink fighting it out. In Bloomfield's main boneyard, the imposition of a modern relative's tastes upon ancestors who actually knew and loved the dead they buried is depressing, especially under the magnificent white pines that rise there.

As we are a few centuries on in County history, the number of graveyards is naturally large. Yet the County has always had more than most areas. William Canniff embellished and romanticized this feature in his *Settlement of Upper Canada:*

Sometimes families would prefer to have a private burial ground, some conspicuous spot being selected upon the farm, where the ashes of the family might be gathered together, as one after another passed away. The Dutch are particularly attached to this custom. This may be seen even yet in those old sections of New York State, where the Dutch originally settled, especially at Hoboken, opposite New York City. Sacred spots were appropriated by each family upon the farm, in which the family was buried. The descendants of these Dutch who became such loyal subjects, and suffering refugees who settled around the bay, followed the same practice. These spots may be seen along the Hudson, and the Bay Quinté, which may be regarded as the Hudson of Canada, and are indicated by the drooping willow, or the locust or cypress. Some from whom reliable information has been received, state that the spot selected on the Bay Quinté was often that where the family had first landed – where they had rested on the bare earth, beneath the trees, until a hut could be erected. This spot was chosen by the refugee himself as a suitable place to take his last rest.

Individual family gravesites gave way to community cemeteries after a generation or two, as villages, with their many churches, matured. The changes in fashion and landscaping continue to work themselves out in garish ways on County burial plots and graveyards, but occasionally one can get a glimpse of the ephemeral, a chance to see into the past through the eyes of someone who now, too, lies in the ground.

John Coleman was an artisan in Ameliasburgh who lived from 1819 to 1900 – a cabinetmaker with a specialty in fancywork and hand-carving. He later left and took up photography in Niagara Falls and Ottawa. He was twice married, but childless. Photos of his cousins and other family members in the village, and of general village life in Ameliasburgh, are a delightful look into the nineteenth century in Prince Edward County. (Coleman's nephew Isaiah also set up as a professional photographer, and Colemans seem to have been as thick on the ground as Roblins in that village.)

There's a particular photo I like, of John Coleman at the grave of his wife Mary. There's a simple round-topped tombstone, maybe even of painted wood, which simply states:

Mary A.
Wife of
J. Coleman
Died May 8th 1873

Coleman is alone, a top-hatted figure in a bright clearing of long summer grass. He's reclining on the ground, leaning on his right arm behind the marker, maned with a grizzled beard and long white hair. A pot, maybe two, of flowers sit in front of him. He looks almost as if he's picnicking; he could be Walt Whitman. Well behind him are scattered a few other markers; the trees visible are about thirty-five to forty years old.

It's hard not to feel kindly towards him, looking at that photo, a faded glimpse of an aesthetic and a pace of life no longer found.

during the fall plowing a man
might stop and stand in a brown valley of the furrows
and shade his eyes to watch for the same
red patch mixed with gold
that appears on the same
spot in the hills
year after year
and grow old
plowing and plowing a ten-acre field until
the convolutions run parallel with his own brain

• *Al Purdy, "The Country North of Belleville"*

It was in *Belden's Atlas* that I found some of the references Phil Mathewson had first mentioned to me a few years before while chatting in the organic market in the shadow of Honest Ed's in Toronto.

In the back of the atlas was a list of inhabitants of the various townships; in the Hillier township section an unusually long entry stood out from the others:

"Dorland Noxon, Allisonville, Farmer, Vine-grower and Wine Manufacturer, medal and diploma, International Exhibition, Philadelphia, U.S., 1876."

The man, based on his age in the atlas, would have been sixty-nine years old during the Philadelphia Exhibition. And this was an important world event: it celebrated the centennial of the American Declaration of Independence. This was where, for example, Fleischmann's dry yeast was introduced to the public. It was no township fair!

Dorland Noxon was born in Canada, the son of a Loyalist. The whole Noxon family were Quakers, or more properly members of the Society of Friends. One County historian comments that Dorland "was a man of culture and refinement." If being a Quaker winegrower isn't the sign of an open mind, then I don't know what is.

The Noxon family is still spread throughout Prince Edward communities, and they've provided various glimpses of this man to the County archives. One of the most startling is a page from a receipt book printed for Dorland's winery. On it is a picture of an overflowing fruit bowl. The text says "Canadian Native Wine, Allisonville." In ornate Gothic script runs "Bought of D. Noxon," and tagged in italics is "*From Noxon Vineyard, Prince Edward County.*" No one in the family knows what happened to the medal or certificate Noxon won in Philadelphia, and I haven't been able to discover what varieties of grapes he grew.

In a family history there's a photo taken about ten years before Dorland Noxon's death in 1895. He stands in front of his Christian Street home, elderly, yet straight and strong. He is thoughtful looking, with a white beard and wearing a black suit, with a few of his sons and their families behind him.

I find it amusing that this Quaker gentleman farmer grew an international-award-winning wine in Hillier more than a hundred years ago – and did so on a Hillier road that legend has it was named Christian Street because barn raisings there were – to the horror of County neighbours – free of whisky. (More likely, as with most roads out here, it was named after a family who settled along the same road.)

Bits and pieces of the County's viticultural past turn up now and again at the archives, or somehow end up in the hands of someone like amateur historian and archivist David Taylor. One that surprised me was something he found in *The North American*, which was published out of Toronto. On December 14, 1865, in the section called "Ameliasburgh Advertisements," this one-column announcement ran, set in various types:

G R A P E   W I N E

The Subscribers are manufacturing a PURE GRAPE WINE, from Grapes grown on their own premises, and they desire to call the attention of the Public thereto, as it is in every way

S U P E R I O R

for Medicinal Purposes to the adulterated and drugged mixtures daily exposed for sale.

It is highly recommended by the best judges in CANADA, and the manufacturers feel a pride in presenting a

GENUINE ARTICLE

to the Public.

ALL the materials used are of the best possible description, and all who use it, especially

I N V A L I D S

may rely on its purity.

They would particularly call the attentions of CHURCH AUTHORITIES to it as being very suitable for

SACRAMENTAL PURPOSES,

much more so than the Wines ordinarily used.

The price, quality considered, is very low.
SEND ORDERS to the Manufacturers.

J.H. MORDEN & SON

Rednerville P.O.

Co. Prince Edward

December 8th 1864

R.S. ROBLIN Agent

So Dorland Noxon was not the only County winegrower and winemaker. What others there might have been in addition to the Mordens and Noxon remain unknown.

The earliest mention of viticulture here that I've found dates to 1854, in the *Report on the State of Agriculture in the County of Prince Edward*. In it the member of Parliament of the day wrote that "Several varieties of grapes were exhibited by farmers; but they have not, as yet, been cultivated to any degree of perfection, although many persons are sanguine of succeeding in their culture in the open air in this county."

In the same report, it's mentioned that the County Agricultural Society had quite a good library, which in 1853 saw 312 volumes taken out – including "six volumes treating specially on the grape vine." This was a few years before the famous, foxy Concord grape was developed in Massachusetts and spread widely across eastern North America. The mix of grapes listed for Ontario around this time included some native hybrid grapes now long forgotten, and a handful of European vinifera that didn't survive long, because methods of protection against disease and winter had not been discovered yet.

I haven't been able to learn the titles of the vinegrowing books that were in circulation in the County at that time, but I imagine that two Canadian pamphlets were later among them.

Written by Justin M. DeCourtenay in 1863 and 1866, these publications encouraged and profoundly influenced the Upper Canadian grape-growing boom in the last three or four decades of the nineteenth century. Although it is common knowledge that Niagara grew grapes as far back as the 1850s on a commercial scale, it's forgotten that all along the Lake Ontario shore other farmers grew grapes, for both wine and dessert use. At a fruit-growers' meeting held in Trenton in 1881, there was almost a brawl as an argument raged over what grape was for Canada: the Concord or other less pungent varieties that could make more elegant, potable wine. It seems grape-growers have always been partisan, passionate, and given to feuding.

The County, and southern Ontario generally, like much of North America, was in a grape-growing boom in the mid-nineteenth century. Every province and state had breeders, and hundreds of new varieties were introduced by them. Most quickly disappeared. In 1901, U.P. Hedrick wrote the monumental *Grapes of New York*, which listed many of these; the book itself is a valuable rarity, and many copies have been broken down and the prints of the different varieties individually framed and sold.

The books by J.M. DeCourtenay – unillustrated and highly opinionated – were quite prophetic. He has made appearances in some of the brief histories of Canadian winegrowing, but going through the text first-hand is always better than getting a summary and a few clips.

In Toronto, during the years I was doing research and planning to become a winegrower, I was able to read – and photocopy – both publications at the main reference library on Yonge Street. There are so many little passages that are useful even now, and many prove to me that there really is nothing new under the sun.

In his first work, *The Culture of the Vine and Emigration, Quebec, 1863*, DeCourtenay makes a strong argument that oil, wine, and silk produced great wealth and were missing economic elements in Quebec. I find it impossible not to smile at one of his more contentious sketches of the Canadian farmer:

> A combination of unfortunate circumstances have ever tended to drag down this country to a standard far beneath its natural position. . . . Our farmers and agricultural labourers have emigrated from more northern latitudes.
>
> The Norwegian, Scotchman and Northern Englishman may feel at home during our winters, but no class of emigrants arriving in the St. Lawrence are prepared for the *heat* of our summers, and none know how to profit by the *wonderful wealth* of that heat, which appears to our populations only as an inconvenience, and to be apologised for.
>
> Had we endeavored to obtain even a limited emigration accustomed to the broiling summers and rigorous winters of the slopes of the Jura, the Alps, Pyrenees or Appenines, or to many similar climates, from Hungary to the Crimea, we should long since have discovered that our lands had other resources and other riches than could ever be extracted from them by the *Ne plus ultra* of our agricultural imagination, a Scotch farmer.

DeCourtenay's proposals and examples (such as using native nut trees like black walnut and butternut to get "100 francs or $20 worth of oil every year, and without labour") still seem sensible to me, and a century and a half later they may yet take hold here in Prince Edward County.

Not surprisingly, after reading DeCourtenay I found I had marked a number of passages where he refers to that great viticultural touchstone, Burgundy:

> In Burgundy, the Vine flowers on the 11th of June, colours on the 15th of August, and ripens late in October. . . .
> Our amount of heat during a season of vegetation of 135 days is *far superior* to that of Burgundy with its 174 days. Notwithstanding, that our contrasts between the temperature of day, and night, are much greater.

The information he provided is roughly accurate and remains useful; it helped me in my early research, when I found Prince Edward County in the 160- to 170-day period. However, his conclusion in favour of Quebec's climate – specifically, on the shores of the St. Lawrence – I found a little dodgy, and indeed the region proved not to be fertile ground for DeCourtenay.

He went west, into Upper Canada, purchased the old vineyard west of Toronto once owned by pioneer Johann Schiller. DeCourtenay called it Clair House, and maintained thirty acres of vineyard there.

In 1866 he published *The Canada Vine Grower: How Every Farmer in Canada May Plant a Vineyard and Make His Own Wine*. In the preface he made a simple plea: "Indeed, any ten householders who will purchase *each* of them *one* acre of land, and employ *in common* one labourer to cultivate the ten acres and manufacture the produce may, by following my instructions both recover their outlay, supply their wants, and obtain a genial and healthy recreation; and I am encouraged by the hope that these instructions may succeed in rendering *practically* possible the realization of theories for which I have so long struggled, and which after many years of scornful incredulity are finally accepted as probable, and examined with attention and respect." As in his book for Quebec, he makes one or two references to Burgundy as a model.

A short-lived wine boom did take place in Upper Canada (soon to become Ontario), though it didn't take root as deeply among farmers as DeCourtenay had hoped.

Although DeCourtenay appreciated the benefits of stony ground, he wasn't a fan of close-spaced vines, planting his own at 350 vines to the acre, or about four yards by four yards, and was scornful of the Cincinnati folk who planted "at distance of two or three feet, pruning of course accordingly. By my estimate of their climate, I should judge *at least eight yards* as the distance to be preserved." I found that odd, given that in his earlier book DeCourtenay describes a number of benefits to close-planting:

Another reason may be discovered from the recognised fact "that the closer the plants, the sooner the fruit arrives at maturity."

The action so produced, is because the stronger the vines, the later they blossom, and therefore they have time to develop more branches, and leaves, than are necessary.

An isolated plant, blossoms, and ripens, long after those that are crowded together, and have therefore less vigour.

The first ripe grapes, are never to be found on the borders of a vineyard, and old vines planted on poor soil, are considerably in advance of those, younger, and better manured.

The debate on density is never over, and is rarely civil and tidy, but in DeCourtenay there was an intelligent, experimental mind at work, and at least he did recognize that density should vary according to climate and soil.

Even though there are parts of these old books I delight in, I know very little about the man himself. In some places he's referred to as a count; from whence he came I have no idea. I do know that ultimately his hopes to turn Canadians into wine drinkers failed.

In Volume XIII of the *Dictionary of Canadian Biography*, DeCourtenay turns up just in a footnote in the entry on Father William Flannery, an Irish-born priest who at one time served in Streetsville: "An unfortunate dispute arose between Lynch and himself [Flannery] over the canonical validity of the mass wine used in the diocese. Justin DeCourtenay, the manufacturer and one of Flannery's parishioners, vehemently protested Lynch's judgement that his product was impure and thus unsuitable for sacramental purposes. Flannery took DeCourtenay's side and, according to Father Denis O'Conner in November 1867, 'spoke his mind freely' during the quarrel. His indiscretion cost him the support of yet another bishop, and he was obliged to leave Streetsville."

Not long after, so was DeCourtenay. His Clair House vineyard was sold, and eventually it disappeared.

✌ৈ

The question of what happened to the handful of vineyards and wineries in the County is a small mystery. I often wondered why Dorland Noxon, Prince Edward County's first (and so far only) award-winning commercial winegrower, gave it up. Other than winning a medal and certificate in the 1876 Philadelphia International Exhibition, nothing further can be discovered about his vineyard and wines. At first I thought the vines died of disease, but that was not the case. The early County historian W.K. Burr writes that "George L. Werden came into possession of a fine grape arbour and trellis when he bought the pioneer Noxon farm on Christian Street."

So what was it that wiped this devout Quaker gentleman farmer's winery from memory?

It seems it was an equally devout group of Methodists who, unlike Noxon, did not see the civilizing benefits of wine; it was, like all alcohol, a horror to be stamped on.

Letitia Youmans died in 1896, a year after Dorland Noxon. And that Noxon should predecease her she probably saw as another small victory for the Women's Christian Temperance Union. (She did live twenty years less than the Quaker gentleman farmer, though, and spent her last eight in bed.) This woman founded Ontario's second WCTU, in Picton, in 1874, became the first Ontario president of the organization in 1877, and the first Dominion WCTU president in 1883. In photos she looks like a young Orson Welles.

Mrs. Youmans believed that Canadian women had three inalienable rights: "the right of every woman to have a comfortable home; of every wife to have a sober husband; of every mother to have sober sons." Not exactly the American "Life, Liberty, and the Pursuit of Happiness"; by comparison, it even makes Canada's unofficial motto of "Peace, Order, and Good Government" soar like Shakespeare. Yet she had a following, and worked tirelessly for the cause. According to a former president of the organization, "Letitia Youmans did more than any other one to make the WCTU known in Canada."

Another Methodist, Stephen M. Conger, owner and editor of the *Picton Gazette*, was an earlier standard-bearer of the temperance movement in the County. In the late 1850s he wrote numerous editorials demanding that the province bring in "a stringent prohibitionary liquor law." Richard and Janet Lunn, in their book *The County*, say Conger "never let up. His paper never failed to carry the most sordid and sad tales of drunk, defeated people – not only from Picton but from anywhere he could find them – Toronto, Kingston, Montreal, Birmingham, Alabama."

Now there's no doubt that hard drink – mainly cider and whisky – was a problem in Upper Canada, and in the United States. There's an eye-opening book amusingly called *The Alcoholic Republic: An American Tradition*, by W.J. Rorabaugh, which describes alcohol and American society in the eighteenth and nineteenth centuries. Much of it also applies to Upper Canada during the same period.

Rorabaugh writes, "One can only conclude that at the root of the alcoholic republic was the fact that Americans chose the most highly alcoholic beverages that they could obtain easily and cheaply." And the reason? "The taste for strong drink was no doubt enhanced by the monotony of the American diet, which was dominated by corn." With little ability to preserve food, diets usually consisted of about one pound of bread and one pound of salt pork a day. And generous amounts of cider or whisky to get it down.

Lunch-bag letdown aside, the Lunns point out that Susanna Moodie, the author of *Roughing It in the Bush*, called drinking "the curse of Canada" and blamed it on the very low price of whisky – about fifty cents a gallon in 1851. Back then, there were a hundred distilleries in Upper Canada, producing 1.7-million gallons of whisky about half as strong again as the modern stuff. By comparison, there were only forty-nine breweries, so whisky was king.

The high consumption of alcohol, and the low price, fuelled numerous scuffles, fights, and near riots all over. Early judicial assessments noted "Seventh Towners were the most notorious fighters in the whole Midland District." (Seventh Town, remember, was the name given to the western part of Prince Edward County when it was first settled. It was renamed Ameliasburgh, and Hillier was carved out of the southern part of Ameliasburgh.)

Letitia Youmans's first moment of glory came after the 1874 battle to get the town of Picton to ban alcohol. She lost that attempt, so she aimed at getting the County to accept the Dunkin Act. This law, named after Judge Dunkin of Brome, Quebec, had been on the books since 1864, and allowed municipalities and townships to go dry. No Ontario county had adopted it until Mrs. Youmans led a successful campaign in September 1875. A special campaign song was even composed. It went, in part:

The girls will sing, the boys will shout,
When alcohol is driven out,
And we'll all feel gay when Canada is free. . . .

From Quinte's Bay to Wellington
Hurrah! Hurrah!
From Marysburgh to Consecon,
Hurrah! Hurrah!
The struggle now is going on
And when the mighty victory's won
We'll all feel gay that whisky's reign is o'er.

Shortly after this victory, the Dominion Parliament sponsored a convention in Montreal to discuss alcohol. Mrs. Youmans attended and was well pleased. "Prince Edward County," she reported, "that had voted only one week before, was held up as a beacon light. One delegate from the west stated that the steamer on which he came contained one hundred delegates, and as they passed the Prince Edward shore, the delegates all came on deck and gave three hearty cheers for the prohibition county and the women who led the van."

It doesn't seem as though things changed right away in the County. It wasn't until 1878, for instance, when the Canada Temperance Act succeeded the Dunkin Bill, that Thomas Faughnan, owner of Picton's Victoria Hotel, and a former British colour sergeant in Queen Victoria's army, was finally forced to close his establishment. The prohibitionists had won.

In his autobiography, Faughnan wrote that temperance came to the County because of the efforts of "a few fanatics [who] in order to get their names before the public as great temperance advocates, not knowing of anything better to preach about, like the Turkish Dervishes, tried to make people believe that they were all saints and everybody else sinners; although the temperance saints generally had a bottle in the garret or the cellar which they used when not observed."

I believe Dorland Noxon's Canadian Native Wines also disappeared for the same legal reasons. The description of Noxon as "Farmer, Vine-grower and Wine Manufacturer, medal and diploma, International Exhibition, Philadelphia, U.S., 1876," was published in *Belden's Atlas* in 1878. Unfortunately, that was the year prohibition finally took hold in Prince Edward County "from Marysburgh to Consecon."

Letitia Youmans is buried in Picton's Glenwood Cemetery. A blue provincial plaque honouring her was unveiled there in 1974.

There is no plaque to Noxon, nor to the Mordens. At least not yet.

> — the bird's blue shadow racing
> over the earth and our local
> heartbeat matching its wingbeat

> • *Al Purdy, "Birds Here and Now"*

One day they just arrive, and you know spring is but days away.

At first you mistake them for a piece or two of ice, floating in a tiny unfrozen puddle on West Lake near the liquor store in Wellington. A day later you drive by, and instead of one pair you see ten or a dozen, majestically riding the surface, the puddle now a small pond, the ice beginning its inevitable retreat.

The swans have returned.

The tundra swan – formerly the whistling swan – is this first promise of spring. The more practical locals will say it's when the ice huts are pulled back to shore each year from the Bay of Quinte and from all the inland lakes and bays of the County. As that's mandated by the government for the last day of February each year, it requires no special powers of observation. And, as so many ice fishermen will complain, the ice can remain thick and hard for another month, maybe more after a rough winter. Spring seems no closer then than it did in December.

Yet the return of those pure white swans means the ice is on the verge of breaking up. In mere days the gathered dozens near Wellington harbour will spread out: a pair or two to the mouth of Consecon Creek in front of our house, a handful to Pleasant Bay, and most to the reedy east end of Consecon Lake. To step out of the house and go trotting off to the post office is damn near a festive occasion with a pair or two of the swans fifty yards away, gliding and periodically up-ending to grab a nibble of something within that long reach of body and neck.

It's the necks that are so distinctive. Unlike the European mute swan, with its elegant S curve, the tundra swan keeps its neck ruler-straight. Not always, for there are moments when they will flex and bend them, and for a moment look like the European breed. However, it is only a momentary affectation; the stiff-neck look returns. They would have been a perfect symbol for the ancient Hebrews, tribes so proud and pure, and so often chided by the prophets for being a "stiff-necked people," unwilling to bend or show thanks for the gifts they enjoyed.

In Britain, the swan has long been a symbol of status. The Queen maintains swans on the Thames, with keepers assigned to them. I seem to recall Ottawa receiving some of these creatures as a gift from Queen Elizabeth, and they were later within a feather of being extinguished by bureaucrats of the amalgamated capital city madly looking to pare costs; a public outcry saved those birds, though I've not heard anything more about them these past few years.

Other than the monarch, just one other group was allowed to keep and tend swans on the Thames – the Worshipful

Company of Vintners. To distinguish the monarch's birds from the vintners' birds when they were counted each season, a system of nicking the bills developed. The vintners' swans had two nicks cut in them. As the vintners also owned public houses in England, this led to a corruption in the name of premises christened in the birds' honour: "Swan with Two Nicks" became "Swan with Two Necks." The latter, fantastic creature – like an escapee from a modern genetics lab – was depicted on pub signs.

The link between swans, London's Worshipful Company of Vintners, and our own vineyards in Hillier (I honestly don't know if swans are seen to the same extent in other parts of the County) I find irresistible.

Tundra swans weren't part of the landscape in our first few years of County life. They seem to have sprung up like the vineyards. About five years ago a pair was spotted in Wellington, and it was big news. The next year a dozen or more pairs put in at Weller's Bay. Presently we're up to three, four, or five dozen. Now they no longer just pay a short visit, awaiting the thaw farther north before they fly off again. A few pairs stay the summer through, building nests and raising cygnets before they head south again to escape the worst of winter. A breeding pair or two spent the summer where Dorland's Creek empties itself in the reedy end of Pleasant Bay. And a number stayed in the shallow end of Consecon Lake, raising their young, visible through the trees some days if you cared to look while speeding along Scoharie Road.

I never paid much attention to birds before I came to the County. Yet living out here hasn't turned me into a birder either: I don't own a single bird guide. It is impossible not to notice them, though, and, after a season or two, mark and note their arrivals and departures as natural, important parts of the year.

A few weeks after the swans return, another familiar shape will cross the sky. The brief glimpse you get of the first great blue heron of the season can create doubts: "Was it, or wasn't it? It's too early. I must be mistaken." Then, a day or two later, you'll spot one crossing the horizon in front of you. It looks prehistoric, like a pterodactyl, with its slow, steady, majestic wing sweeps and long trailing legs. The neck is folded upon the body in a way that to my eye mimics the bow of a Roman trireme galley. There are so many great blue herons in Prince Edward County that most people barely notice them . . . or not enough to bother remarking on them. There are numerous heronries here, in the treetops of the large swampwoods that cut across the County. The adults keep regular hours and routes, commuting from their nests to their different fishing spots. You can almost set a clock by them.

The only great blue heron I had seen before settling here was a tatty specimen that hung out near the duck pond in Toronto's High Park. It in no way prepared me for how beautiful a healthy great blue actually looks. The woodsmoke grey-blue of the feathers, their patience standing in the shallows looking for small fish or frogs or garter snakes, and their complete unconcern for people nearby I find marvellous. There is almost always a heron or two to be found if you look carefully from the bridge over Consecon Creek. If I don't see one on my way to the farm, I am clouded briefly in disappointment.

Soon after the herons, on the first sudden warm day that sneaks into mid to late March, up to a dozen huge spans of motionless dark wings appear in the sky, swirling effortlessly around an imaginary centre. The turkey vultures are back. Many mistake them for hawks, or even eagles, but as someone pointed out to me, if the wings remain fixed like that, they're turkey buzzards. If I have my glasses on, I can make out the light trailing feathers under the wings that otherwise appear dark and ominous. Looking up from hoeing or vine-tying on a warm day, you can catch one . . . then two . . . then seven, eight, maybe eleven, twirling into your field of vision. On the updrafts across Hillier, above the stony fields and rolling ridges, they'll start at one end of your horizon. In a minute, without a single wingbeat, they are circling and interweaving overhead. A minute later their sky ballet has moved almost out of view, for someone else to enjoy, someone who is blessed with the peripheral vision of peaceful work, rather than the circumscribed box of drudgery.

It is not only the birds that mark the change of season. Once the ice is breaking up, I find my morning walk to the post office widens and takes me onto the bridge over Consecon Creek.

The bridge hangs like a private sports-arena box over the broken limestone bed of the creek, providing a perfect view of the pickerel, or walleye, spawning ground. Each morning, looking over one rail, then the other, I hope to glimpse the first returning fish. A car or two will often stop, and someone else will get out and do the same thing.

It's a remarkable sight. From the bridge you look down at the mass of huge, blue-grey pickerel labouring against the hard current to hold their place. About once a minute, a slash of scarlet gill breaks the surface of the water as some fish gets jostled out of position and fights to hold its spot. The spring runoff over the dam creates a sound somewhere between a steady roar and gentle far-off thunder. Watching them, it's easy to see why "Consecon" derives from the Mississauga word for big fish or pickerel. The fish have been gathering here for centuries.

The first time I saw the Mohawk spearing pickerel was a Friday night in April a few years back. Returning to the hamlet from Wellington, Lauren and I could see in the distance eight or nine flashlight beams waltzing over the water. Occasionally, one of the lights would stop and linger for a while. As we drew closer we could see they were Mohawk kids, one of whom, with the water just over his knees, was thrusting his long homemade spear into the fast-running water. If he was lucky, he'd pull it out with a pickerel the size of a man's leg in the prongs. Then he'd drag the fish up the riverbank and heave it into the back of one of the vans or pickups parked on the bridge. One van had a large Warriors flag – a banner Canadians saw a lot of during the 1990 confrontation in Oka, Quebec – flying from its open window.

To get around the temporary snow fences and the array of no-trespassing signs that the locals had put up to block access to the river, some of the Mohawk had lowered themselves from the bridge by ladder. Others had gone to the mouth of the river about three hundred yards away and waded upstream, safe on Crown land. From behind the large windows of the Cascades bar, perched above the mill dam and overlooking the pickerel spawning area, a few patrons glared out silently. To hinder the Mohawks' efforts, they'd turned off the bar's outdoor lights, which usually shine on the river below.

While I was there I witnessed only quiet muttering and angry stares, but later in the evening tensions escalated, punches were thrown, and in the aftermath one or two Mohawk took a few of the locals to court. It's not quite April on the Ormeau Road in Belfast, but it's an embarrassing, legally tolerated display of in-your-face tribalism from both sides. And there are worries every spring that "this year might be the year someone gets killed."

A few years back the authorities were obviously worried. Just before pickerel spawning season, about fifty people from the neighbourhood crowded into the Legion Branch 509 – it's a two-tavern hamlet – for a meeting called by the Ontario Provincial Police and the Ministry of Natural Resources. Sport fishermen and their sons and grey-haired locals, many of whom have lived here their entire lives, listened as the OPP officers talked earnestly in a dry Canadian manner about trespass law and citizen's arrests, cautioning everybody in the room against doing silly things.

"Don't take the law into your own hands," warned the OPP representatives. "Hopefully, we'll prevent bloodshed." An older woman in the crowd cracked, "You gotta put that no-trespass sign in Indian language," and a local politician talked about how the Mohawk's hunting in other areas of Prince Edward County had made things "like the Wild West down there."

Apart from the spear fishing in Consecon, there were other problems. Presqu'ile Provincial Park, a few miles west of Prince Edward County, had to be closed for a few days in the winter to prevent people from getting hit by the gunfire of deer-hunting Mohawk. Gary Brown from the Ministry of Natural Resources also confirmed that a number of Mohawk had been charged with selling contaminated fish in Toronto. "They should all have mercury poisoning," somebody in the middle rows helpfully pointed out, to much laughter.

Brown calmly explained the Supreme Court ruling that allowed – no, actually forced – provincial and federal governments to remove impediments to aboriginal harvests in traditional hunting areas, such as the Consecon, even if the spot was a posted fish sanctuary, protected each spring so that the pickerel could come and spawn, as they always had.

We must be "liberal and generous" in our dealings with the Mohawk, Brown reminded the crowd. He was reinforced by the OPP staff sergeant, who caustically added, "Some people have more rights than others."

Some of the older people in town have told me that as kids they could have walked across the river on the backs of pickerel during spawning season. I believe them.

Even in the nine springs I've lived here, the numbers of spawning fish have decreased dramatically. This past year there was but a handful, outnumbered many times over by the suckers looking to hoover up loose eggs and fry. Many locals are certain that the decrease is due to the Mohawk kicking loose all the eggs and tiny fry in the spawning bed during their fishing trips. But there are other theories.

It could also be because the riverbed was carved open the previous year to install pipes to carry safe drinking water from Trenton. Or it could be that the yearly catch by sportsmen, such as the ones at the Legion, are significantly adding to the pickerel depletion. According to three MNR scientists, the increasingly sterile water of Lake Ontario, filtered by invading zebra mussels, is forcing the pickerel to go farther away in search of the murkier water they prefer.

The first pickerel returned a few days before Easter this year. Seven days later, the river was full, but certainly not as crowded as in the previous run last April. Coming back from Betty and Garn's on a Saturday night during the run, I spotted a loose knot of people at the northwest corner of the bridge. Paula Roblin was there with her son Joey, who rides the same school bus as our girls. They were talking with Bert and Pauline, who'd just come from the Legion. A fellow with a nineteenth-century face wearing a red Mackinaw tottered over to where we stood. He had already spent a long evening at Cascades. The Mohawk had been here the night before, they said, pointing to the blood and roe sprayed across the bridge, as if it had been tagged by a Toronto graffiti artist. The guy from Cascades sputtered incoherently with rage as he unburdened himself of what he really thought of the Mohawk.

He staggered off, and the rest of us stood silently near the bridge. We could hear the river in front of us and in the distance the low rumble of aircraft engines at Trenton air-force base, readying themselves for a trip to the Adriatic. There was singing coming from somewhere, and when I looked around I noticed all the lights were on in the apartment above the hamlet store. The Korean owners live up there. As long as they've been in town, I've never seen them smile, but that night they were having a party: it was their singing that led Paula and Joey to think that the Mohawk had returned to the bridge.

We stood there as the sounds of Korean karaoke drifted down to us, talking about what might happen if the Mohawk returned. Bert and Pauline said they were worried that the Mohawk would be there late one night, when the local guys "come out drunk from the bar, and drunk from the Legion, and drunk from their houses," and things would get out of hand. Before we went our separate ways, a patrol car drove by, the first police presence any of us had noticed in weeks.

That night, I went into Cascades to wait and see what would happen if more Mohawk arrived. I talked for a while with Nick, the owner, who told me he was one of the people being dragged through the courts by the Mohawk. (I later learned he had initially taken me, with my long dark hair, for a Mohawk come to spy on his patrons.) As the small crowd of regulars, huddled along the bar, continued their regular conversations and regular drinks, Nick said he just didn't want to see anyone get hurt, and freely admitted he was responsible for putting up the unsuccessful snow fences last year, and for the numerous private-property signs posted around the bridge. With a bit of regret in his voice, he said most of the Mohawk seemed to blame him for the problems each spring.

But then he also recalled an incident several years ago just after the Supreme Court decision, when an old Mohawk came to the river to show his grandson how to spear-fish. The bar emptied immediately when the man and the boy were spotted, and by the time Nick got outside someone had slashed the tires on the man's truck. Nick and another guy got into the river and made sure the Mohawk got to their truck safely. He was still ashamed of how that frightened old man had to burn out of Consecon on his rims.

I wasn't happy to hear the story. But neither was I happy to see the mess of blood and roe on the bridge and all over the limestone blocks along the riverbank. Nobody has been hurt this April, but the dead fish the Mohawk couldn't bring to shore floated around in the river for days. One abandoned pickerel lay on the grass next to the bridge for weeks, mummifying in the sun. Even the birds wouldn't eat it. They must have read the *Ontario Guide to Eating Sport Fish*, which recommends a very limited intake of Bay of Quinte pickerel.

❧

Somewhere in all of this excitement, the clerk at the bus depot in Trenton phones to announce another spring arrival: my first vine cuttings of the season have come in.

Carried by Greyhound coach from Naramata, British Columbia, the cuttings are destined for our vineyard later this spring – some for planting out on their own roots, some for grafting and then planting. Kathleen Nichol cut them while doing her March pruning, then soaked them for a night and packed them up in two large boxes. I pay ten cents a bud, which gives her what was the commercial-nursery price a few years back, for her effort. They always arrive in great shape, well bundled and healthy. Kathleen and her husband, Alex, are not getting rich selling me wood, but I'm sure it helps when I get my usually tardy cheque out to them. The two of them operate a very small vineyard and winery – a cult winery – and that's not making them rich either.

Before we left Toronto, I had compiled a list of a few of the obscure winegrape varieties (out of the hundreds of choices available) I'd like to try planting in Prince Edward County one day. These were varieties that, based on what I had read, might do well in the County, apart from the Pinots and Syrah I had already determined I'd try.

At the top of the list was a very scarce Austrian variety called St. Laurent. I first stumbled across references to it in, *Larousse Wines and Vineyards of France*.

"This vine originally came from the south of Alsace," read the *Larousse* guide. "It gives full-bodied wine of an attractive, dark-red colour. An unclassified variety, it is very little grown in France."

The grapes' early ripening and thick blue-black skins looked attractive, and the description of the wine quality in this write-up was much more encouraging than those of some of the other early-ripening grapes listed in *Larousse*, which often had descriptions like "a repellent raspberry-like flavour when fully mature" or "is of passable quality, although some-what flat." This entry was from the French perspective, and so I looked up a few other sources. All were very positive and noted that St. Laurent ripens about ten days earlier than Pinot Noir. It seemed made for Prince Edward County's growing season and winter.

The name had a certain appeal too, as it evoked Canada's past. The St. Lawrence River was the central artery of the nation, or rather nations, as it also divided the Canadas into the English portion farther up the St. Lawrence (Upper Canada), and the French one lower down the St-Laurent (Lower Canada). A person might argue, after a few glasses of wine, that Prince Edward County is, heading towards the Atlantic, the first and largest of the famed Thousand Islands in the St. Lawrence. From the air it seems plausible as you look at the string of islands that start at the County and trail off eastward. Only another County person with a few glasses of wine in them would agree; most put the river's beginning just east of Kingston.

However, the synchronicity of Prince Edward and his mistress, Madame de St. Laurent, sailing up the St. Lawrence in August 1792 and setting eyes on the County named after the Prince a few weeks before seemed too perfect. Excellent wine quality; early ripening; a coincidence of storied names. It only remained to find some.

Tony Aspler is one of Canada's pioneering wine writers and columnists. In the second edition of *Vintage Canada*, he listed the varieties each Canadian winery grew. In the entry for the tiny Nichol Vineyard (4.5 acres), Aspler began, "Alex Nichol, a former symphony double bassist, has long been the conscience of the Okanagan. As a writer he has documented its history in *Wines and Vines of British Columbia*, and has worked tirelessly to import its wines." He and his wife, a former corporate librarian, sounded like my kind of people. And there, the last of six varieties that they grew (including Pinot Noir and Syrah), was St. Laurent.

The Nichols were given their first seventy-four St. Laurent vines by a British Columbia grape scientist named John Vielvoye, on condition that they provide cuttings to any grower who wanted them. St. Laurent made its way into Canada from Germany, as part of a large varietal trial conducted there in the 1980s. The year I contacted them was the first that anyone had asked for cuttings: both a Niagara nursery and I were finally interested in the variety.

The Nichols make a tiny amount of St. Laurent, fifteen to thirty cases a year. Until recently, all of it was purchased by one restaurant in British Columbia; the last three vintages have been made available to a handful of customers. It is a cult wine, even more so than the modest quantities of Syrah, Pinot Noir, Cabernet Franc, and Pinot Gris they grow and vinify. They've single-handedly established the variety, which has now spread to Prince Edward County and to other new vineyards in British Columbia. Through some writings I've done about St. Laurent that hit the Internet, the Nichols have even sparked interest in the Central Otaga region on New Zealand's South Island. A grower there contacted me, stating that the Otaga — which is getting a pretty decent reputation for Pinot Noir — was looking for another variety. Based on what I had put together about it, St. Laurent seemed to fit the bill. They got government funding for a study, paid for micropropagation of clean vine stock from B.C., and it's simmering away down there. The Kiwis have even had precious bottles of Nichol St. Laurent and Pinot Noir air-freighted to them for comparative tastings with some of the best Austrian examples.

It's hard not to smile at how all these little chance events and contacts around St. Laurent have reverberated. Wine writers have recently "discovered" how good Austrian St. Laurent is, along with a few other reds made there. If it also takes hold in Canada and New Zealand, it might achieve that critical mass that will make it easier to market.

Certainly, the taste will only help. It fits somewhere in the mouth between Pinot Noir, Merlot, or *really* good Loire Cabernet Franc. Pinot Noir is nearly always priced dearly and is in short supply, so that means there's some room for an entry-level wine of similar quality. And St. Laurent is a serious but still affordable and pleasant wine very close to Pinot.

Joseph Umathum, a passionate Austrian grower of St. Laurent, believes that the grape is a clone of Pinot Noir developed in Austria by medieval monks. The religious name came because growers noticed that this early-ripening winegrape began veraison around the feast of St. Lawrence, celebrated on August 10. (It does. Canadian wine writer David Lawrason wrote after touring my own test plots that "on August 12, one St. Laurent vine under which Heinricks had piled stones to reflect heat, had fully changed colour [gone through veraison], and was almost sweet to the taste.")

Safely at their journey's end in Consecon, the new vine cuttings will sit for a few weeks out in the cool shed, and then the first of the real spring vineyard work begins – grafting.

The canes I cut in late November from my rootstock mothervines are about to be roused from their winter sleep; they've been stored in garbage bags conditioned with a few handfuls of damp peat moss to keep them from drying out. The numerous bags of various wild riparia-vine wood I'd harvested from different parts of the County – primarily in Hillier, on dry, stony areas – are readied for the same purpose.

I was discouraged from doing my own grafting by other growers, who saw it as a waste of time. And yet, working at the table in the kitchen, or out in the garage, I take pleasure knowing there are others around the world doing the same thing, because they care about their vines so much they don't trust them to anyone. There's a small photo I like of the owner of Domaine Confuron-Cotétidot in Vosne-Romanée, sitting at his grafting table, in Remington Norman's book *The Great Domaines of Burgundy*; the caption reads, "Jacky Confuron stamping out his grafts – most vignerons buy them in." (Confuron also uses a riparia rootstock, Norman points out.) Buying a one-year-old vine from a nursery is somewhat like assembling an army of mercenaries to stand in the field for you. Being responsible for the vine from the beginning to the end of its life seems only right. And maybe a bit fanatical, I'll admit. But I believe it brings a great understanding of the vine; your thoughts and hands are there from the beginning.

There are a few other reasons why I do this, which go beyond stewardship and craft. I realize not everyone has the temperament or the time or the skill, let alone the desire, to do this. I do. Now, a few others in the County do as well. The cost of purchased vines adds up, especially at densities of 3,630 an acre, the number required with the spacing of four feet by three feet I and a handful of others use. At $2.50 a vine, that's a lot of capital. Other vineyards out here cover three or even four acres with the same number. If I were rich I might not have bothered learning to graft, though I'm not certain of that. I probably would have just bought better tools and facilities.

The most pressing reason I do my own grafts is to get the rootstock and scion combinations I want for my plots; I can't buy County riparia from a nursery. (Though I could pay Martin Gemmrich in Niagara to custom-graft it for me, even as he'd shake his head about the wisdom of doing this instead of using a commercially popular rootstock.) It not only allows me the choice of grafting combinations, it gives me control of the length of rootstock. Vines produced in nurseries tend to use very long pieces of rootstock. On the shallow soils in parts of Hillier, it can be hard, if not impossible, to dig a hole deep enough to seat the vine and its roots properly, with the tender graft union close to or an inch or so below the soil level, to allow banking with soil in fall to protect against winter damage. Hand-planting these to the proper depth eats time in a way that mocks the long daylight hours. Yet machine planting – the most common method across North America – means that a lot of vines are "popped" high out of the ground by changes in the bedrock or a large stone affecting the tractor and machine. All too often, these vines, with their grafts riding up to six or seven inches out of the ground, are not replanted by hand. They are doomed, sure to be killed, if not by the coming winter, then by the following one. And what works in one region is not necessarily useful in another. The French vines I've purchased can be anything up to six inches too long. California vines I've brought in, grown in their deep, fertile, and dry soils, have been almost a foot too long. These vines can be successfully planted in the deep soils of the County, if done so with care, but in many parts of Hillier – especially our own – shorter-grafted vines are the best option.

I usually begin grafting in the first week in April. The rootstock I remove from its bag as needed and dry it gently with a towel to remove any peat moss. I cut the lengths into smaller sections of about one internode long – from just below one bud to just below the next one. The scion of fruiting wood I cut into short, one-bud pieces – from just above the bud, to an inch or two below it. From this one bud will grow the future fruit and all the wood above the ground. The trick is basically to replace the excised top bud and node of the rootstock with one of the scion's. As the wood is dormant, it will awaken in the right conditions, and both cuts will produce cells that form a white callus. If the cells successfully intermingle, the vine will heal together as one. Maybe a half to a third of Pinot grafts will take in this manner.

The first skill in this is getting the green tissue under the bark of each piece to line up. This is the cambium, the layer of growing cells in the vine wood. How to select a piece of root-stock and scion that are nearly an exact match is learned through thousands of repetitions. The first tries were slow and agonizing; now, years later, I can pick a rootstock portion with my left hand, and then look at the tray of cut scions and feel with my right for one that matches. A quick check to see that they line up is usually all I need; the pieces are ready to cut and fit together.

The first few springs in Consecon I'd clear the kitchen table after everyone was in bed, cover it in plastic, and begin to prepare rootstocks and scions in piles. I'd use a nifty little pair of pliers from Hungary that cuts a small omega shape (Ω) in the wood; first you slice a male cut in the scion, then make a female cut in the rootstock, in effect making a negative of the first cut using the same blade. Then you slide the two gently together like jigsaw-puzzle pieces. The tip of the graft you dip in wax, to cover the join and protect it from drying out during the few weeks before the callus forms. I was using the stove to melt the wax, getting drips everywhere. After a few hours of grafting, I'd clear off the table, sweep the floors of debris, and try to scrape the wax off the floor and stove-top. Lauren was pretty forgiving, as long as I cleaned up thoroughly.

Things changed for the better when sympathetic Niagara vineyard managers and new friends Deborah Paskus and Marek

Maniecki dropped off a large weather-beaten wood table early one spring morning. Deborah offered me the loan of her grafting machine – something that now costs about $1,500 new. She had done some grafting in the 1980s while conducting her early Chardonnay field trials in Niagara. She eventually lost interest in grafting, because of the time it required and the high failure rate, but offered me the use of the machine as an alternative to the slower hand-grafting pliers.

It has become the centre of a small grafting room I have at the back of the large garage/outbuilding next to the house. I now melt the wax in a pair of electric crock-pots, instead of messing up the stove. It can be cool outdoors in April, but using the machine has sped up the process. On a clear spring day I can sit out there with the door open and look over the blue water and distant tan stretch of the sandbank across Weller's Bay. On rainy days, if the wind is right, I can open the door and watch the rain fall without getting wet.

There is a smell to the wood that I find pleasing. One rootstock – good old 41 B – has an almost spicy, musky fragrance. Riparia has a sweet, vinous quality that smells of good wine. The different viniferas – really only St. Laurent and Pinot Noir, though I'll usually have some small quantities of Syrah and Melon de Bourgogne to do each year – have much less of a wine-like aroma. It's subtle and not as sweet, more fruity. Yes, fruity. It throws me every year. The vinifera can smell of melons, caramelized apples, or sometimes even bananas or overripe strawberries. I cut and sort a day's worth of the different components for faster grafting, and breathe the first viny smells of the season.

Hands reach left and right for uncut pieces. The scion goes in the groove to the right, and the pedal is pushed forward. The blade cuts the male omega shape into it and holds it suspended. The rootstock is set in the groove to the left, and the pedal is pushed forward again. The blade slices the female, and the scion is moved down into the cut at the same time, in one motion both cutting and uniting. Every twenty-five grafts or so I stand up, to help fend off cramps from working the pedal and to dip the newly cut joints in wax.

Slowly the number of grafts builds up. Hundreds eventually become thousands. For the next three or four weeks they sit in their callusing boxes, suffering through my primitive attempts to keep humidity and warmth at the levels required to ensure the callus gradually swells at the joint, intermingling the cells of both scion and rootstock. One of the most exciting days is the day you see that the callus has burst through the wax; they are healing together. A short time later the good joints are either started in pots for planting out in late May or through June, or they're placed in nursery beds for the summer, to grow good roots and a shoot or two from the scion.

⁂

As April exhausts itself, a mild panic usually sets in, especially if there is lots of wood still to graft. Other vineyard tasks begin to beckon and then, if neglected, holler like ignored children.

When the temperatures rise and the soil begins to dry out, winter insulation over the vines in the fields has to be removed. Straw must be peeled off and most hauled out of the rows, though a bit can remain to help open the earth. The banks of earth must be moved back from the graft unions and spare parts protected through the winter. If done too early, and winter cold returns, the buds may freeze and die; if left too late, the buds may start to swell under the soil and rot if it's wet, or more likely get knocked off when the soil is pulled back. Timing is important, but as the days tick off, time becomes scare. Any schedule can be trashed, because the fickle and dangerous April days have the last say.

A given day may be like summer, spring, winter, or fall; a brief span of three or more days can combine the weather of all four seasons. Flexibility and hope are the coping mechanisms, for once the snows have disappeared, tasks left over from last year show themselves again too: a trellis that needs mending, frost-heaved posts that need repounding, stones that were not there before now pitched to the surface, areas that require hand-forking and weeding . . . it's not that there is always something to do, it's that, in the last two weeks of April, there are constantly ten things to do.

The key task of pruning I won't undertake until the buds have begun to swell on the vines. I look carefully at the canes through the latter half of April, and usually during the last week or few days I'll see the slowly growing buds, slightly furry and doe-brown in colour, pushing back the protective scales. On the mature vines I look for two canes, one on either side of the small central trunk, of about four buds each. In the centre I keep maybe another three or four buds as insurance and to renew some of the older trunks that are beginning to flirt with inevitable winter damage.

The first time I had to prune our grapevines, I started one white February day, as I'd read I was supposed to. I'd been devouring all the books I could about the mysteries of vine pruning – there are hundreds of pruning and training methods in use around the world – and I had decided on the future shape the vines would take. Fortunately, the kind of sculpting required would not be necessary for another year or two, when I hoped I'd be more competent. Some simple cutting was all I had to do first, just snipping back two or three buds near the ground.

I had never done anything remotely like working with pruning shears and saws, unless you count felling saplings as a boy, or cutting and pasting in public school, but I cut away with no problem, with brand-new, razor-sharp bypass shears (anvil shears crush the wood). No mishaps. No terrible errors. While walking back to the car, I was trimming the dried tendrils and dead wood off some of the canes I had just pruned, intending to plant those cuttings in the spring. I wasn't paying attention, and the blade bit midway into my left thumb. I still remember the sound of the tissue being sliced. It didn't bleed as it should have, because my hands were numbed with the February cold. I drove the five miles first to Consecon to show Lauren, cheerfully told her I was going to the hospital, then travelled the ten miles to the emergency department.

The flap of the wound was closed up with a few stitches, and it healed well, leaving nothing but a small ridge of scar tissue. I recognized I well might take to vineyard work, because the injury didn't dampen my enthusiasm for being out among the vines that day, or any other. But every year, when I start pruning and tying for the new season, I can't help but think of it, and focus my attention if it has wandered even a little.

And although it was that late winter cold that kept the blood from pouring out of my thumb, it was the last time I did any pruning in Arctic conditions.

Each vine is an individual; at every one the growth made the previous season, the extent of winter damage, and the likely strength for the coming year must be divined quickly, and the cuts made sure and clean. This late in the spring, sap immediately seeps out of the wound and begins to drip, drip, drip. There's one school of anthropomorphic thought that says causing such injury robs the vine of vitality and vigour – I guess in the mystical way some sports coaches proscribe sex before games. Another says that the vines are less likely to become infected with disease if the sap is flowing out, and there are some particularly horrible infections that like to crawl into pruning cuts. I go with the latter theory; I really don't have a choice, because pruning too early is silly before winter injury is known and the weather settles down. Temperature swings between 15 and -15 degrees Celsius are not unknown in late March and April in the County, and can do more damage than January cold to vines that have come out of deep winter dormancy and are starting to plump up their tissues again with water.

Besides, it is sweet indeed to bend and prune these low vines in a warm, bright sun, with the soil comfortably dry underfoot. And it's so much better to return home with a slight sun- and windburn in April or early May than to speed home in February, cursing the decision to do one more row and trying to recall the danger signs of frostbite.

Orioles, robins and red-winged blackbirds
are crayons that colour the air;

- *Al Purdy, "Interruption"*

There is a traditional Burgundian word that has a lot of meaning for me at this time of year: *ouvrée*. I first saw it in Matt Kramer's *Making Sense of Burgundy*, in the entry on the vineyards of Volnay.

"An *ouvrée*," Kramer writes, "is an ancient and still commonly used term in Burgundy. To this day, the size of vineyards for sale is expressed in *ouvrées*: .0428 hectares or one tenth of an acre or 428 square meters. Dating to the Middle Ages, an *ouvrée* was the amount of vineyard one man could work in one day."

For me, to borrow a term like this from the Burgundians is only natural. In fact, I've borrowed a lot of things from them. Our shallow, rubble-strewn soils are much like theirs, and our similarity of season has dictated that our major variety is Pinot Noir, the famous red-wine grape of the Côte d'Or. Our vine density is 3,630 vines per acre, spaced three feet between vines, with rows running four feet apart, close to the metre-by-metre spacing most commonly found in the original home of Pinot Noir.

And given that Canadians (at least ones my age) have this bizarre mixed system of imperial and metric measurement, where people spend their day thinking in ounces and pounds for cooking, litres for milk and for gas, miles for distance, and kilometres per hour for speed, why should I not add a medieval unit to my measurement of the physical world?

Basically, it comes down to manual labour. Caught up in the romance of imagined vineyard life, most people forget or wilfully ignore the bloody hard toil required to coax out and ripen a healthy crop of grapes. I believe there is an unshakeable farming gene that still exists in us, even though about 95 per cent of Canadians are now urban dwellers. How else do you explain the hours of drudgery men spend pushing lawn mowers or riding back and forth on tiny tractors most Saturdays? It's the faint impulse of vestigial DNA created by generations of following a plough. Those most likely to act on their fantasy of owning a vineyard are probably in a financial position to hire staff, but if one is not from this genteel class, the desire and dim instinct are not enough: you need to work hard. And if you really intend to get your hands dirty, you need a strong back. I inherited one from my father, and helped it along with a few years of university football.

It's an ache I now remember well: the overall stiffness and soreness that haunts you the first three or four days of training camp. It's something I had quite forgotten in the twelve years or so after I gave up football, and it only flooded back to me in 1995 – the year I planted our first plot of vines.

Very swiftly I found that when you have thousands of Pinot Noir vines to dig and weed with a spading fork, you soon learn just how much you can do in a day before collapsing. Strangely enough, it turns out to be about a tenth of an acre. An *ouvrée*.

Each day at the task, I constantly, painfully, relearn what an *ouvrée* is. It's the work I get done before my legs go wobbly and my back and arms start to stiffen. Within a day or two, the muscles slowly begin to knit and heal up; in a week or two, some of my winter flab will start to disappear. Forget the protein diet; there's nothing like peasant viticulture to whip you into shape and consume unwanted pounds.

The work season began relatively quietly, with the intellectual challenge of pruning, but now I feel lost in the spine-crunching job of turning over the ground under the vines, pulling up the large weeds, aerating the soil, and loosening it for regular, gentler hand-hoeing through the season. After hand-forking and weeding between vines, there is still about three feet of untouched ground between the rows. That can be handled mechanically, either by a small Rototiller or a compact tractor. Both options are massive improvements on digging every square foot by hand with a large two-handled garden fork. This large tool is basically a two-foot-wide shallow U of metal, with tines welded to the bottom of the U. A handle on each side allows you to grip it comfortably. With your instep, you drive the tines into the ground, and then draw the handles down, lifting the soil. It's an intelligently designed fork that in small gardens eliminates the necessity for a gas Rototiller. Eliot Coleman, a famed New England organic market gardener, thought highly of this device and tweaked elements to create his own model, which is sold through Johnnie's Selected Seeds in Maine. The one I have is a version from Lee Valley Garden

Tools of Ottawa that I customized myself. It came with sturdy but heavy metal handles that made it a trial to work with for any length of time. I replaced the steel shafts with wood, and now it is more comfortable to use. Coleman wrote that a garden fork could be used for up to an acre (let's see, that'd be ten *ouvrées*), though that would be in well-maintained market-garden soil that has been lovingly aerated and generously provided with humus. In our clay gravels, taking on an acre with a garden fork would require some degree of madness. Attempt even a tenth of an acre and you really learn what an *ouvrée* is. It is a lesson I will never forget, and never wish to repeat – and something university medievalists should try some time.

Yet, when it is all done, the look of the clean, tilled soil underneath the new season's green growth does make you forget a month of absolutely brutal work. With attentive hand-hoeing, those horrible weeds are kept down, and a light machine cultivation between the rows each week is a pleasure compared to the first tilling of the year. One can proudly show off the vineyard again to visitors, and actually talk to people intelligently at dinner, rather than collapsing into sudden deep animal sleep whenever the conversation lulls.

᪥

May brings a seasonal flood of new visitors, and of visits by others who once were sojourners but have now settled down into vineyards of their own.

I first met Deborah Paskus and her companion, Marek Maniecki, on New Year's Day 1997. I'd arranged with one of the owners of the famed Thirty Bench Winery, on the Beamsville Bench in Niagara, to buy some Pinot Meunier cuttings; he put me in touch with the winery's viticultural manager, who at the time was Deborah.

Deborah had been vineyard manager at Thirty Bench since 1991. An attractive, strong, and wilful woman now in her late forties, she graduated from the University of Guelph with a degree in agriculture, and then did work on a master's degree in oenology while employed at Cave Spring Cellars, also on the Beamsville Bench. Not long after joining Thirty Bench she met Marek, who is burly, amiable, sports a moustache and hair queue, and has the same deep field tan as Deborah. He's the voice of caution in their relationship, has viticultural skills at least the equal of Deborah's, and is likely her equal in will too. Marek has taken over as vineyard manager of Thirty Bench; the two live in a very tiny white cottage on the grounds.

While I was making arrangements with her to get the Pinot Meunier, Deborah had volunteered that she often visited Prince Edward County to get away from things. She offered to bring the cuttings with her, curious to meet someone who was obviously quite mad to be attempting to grow vines so far from the confines of Niagara. When Deborah and Marek turned up, Deborah immediately offered this helpful suggestion as she pulled two bundles of sticks from the back of her blue Toyota truck: "Why don't you just burn them now, and save yourself a lot of trouble? They'll die out here anyway."

"Maybe," I replied.

"Well, here you are," she said. "Knock yourself out."

We talked and had coffee, and I wrote out a cheque for the vine wood, as Lauren's parents looked on, bucked up by the sudden appearance of others who doubted my sanity. Deborah grilled me on climate and soil details, and so I unfolded a map to explain my theories on Hillier and the County, and why winegrapes could grow here, thrive, and produce spectacular wines. Somewhere over the span of an hour, Deborah stopped laughing and shaking her head. A few minutes later she vowed to return in the weeks and months ahead to check out my research.

And she did. Three or four times a year she was back in the County, driving around in her small truck, going over records and old newspapers and books, visiting our plots and the more substantial ones Ed Neuser had on his lakefront farm in Waupoos. Then one summer day in 1998 Deborah pulled up in Consecon to drop off some maps and research material I'd lent her. She got out of the truck and said, "You know, you're right. Hillier is the best place to grow grapes. Marek and I had our heart set on Waupoos."

Like everyone, the pair had fallen in love with the view of the lake from the escarpment along the Waupoos road in North Marysburgh. Before they met me, Deborah and Marek had toyed with the idea of retiring out there. After our first discussion, they modified that to retiring and maybe planting a few vines. Now Deborah had decided she would buy land in Hillier for a serious vineyard. Some months later she acquired partners from the top echelons of Alliance-Atlantis, the Canadian movie and television power, and bought a property on Chase and Closson Road, about four miles west of our farm. Marek and Deborah also found another acreage for themselves on a ridge east of the ragged little hamlet of Melville I'd pointed out to her.

I have to admit that when Deborah conceded I was theoretically right, I felt pretty good about things. Here was someone whose talents and abilities and knowledge I greatly admired, and she'd come to the same conclusions I had. Suddenly, others in the wine world – especially journalists – began to look seriously at the County. That day took a decade off the struggle, the day when Deborah decided to try the County.

Serendipity. It seems to happen now and then in our lives since we moved out here. Deborah's interest in Prince Edward County sparked the curiosity of Stephen Temkin, the other eponymous half of her celebrated Beamsville Bench Cuvée Temkin Paskus. Soon Stephen Temkin arrived in the County to investigate things for the *National Post*.

It would have been hard to come up with two better patron saints for a new region like Prince Edward County, a place whose only real chance in the vastly overcrowded world of wine is to tease from our rocky soils and grim climate a battalion of brilliant, top-tier offerings.

In the *Globe and Mail*, writer David Lawrason had declared of their 1993 Chardonnay that "Temkin and Paskus should send a bottle to every winemaker in Ontario. Those who view it with excitement, admiration and hope will themselves advance the quality reputation and commercial success of Ontario wine. Those who dismiss it as the unrealistic musings of dilettantes will likely never make anything like it themselves, to the detriment of all."

Drinking the 1995 Temkin Paskus with dinner one summer night out on Deborah and Marek's cottage patio left me speechless. This wine absolutely deserved the accolades and cult status. It was one of those moments that clearly shouts out the reason why one toils away in the vineyard. And it was also the cause of mild terror – how completely absurd to even dream of being able to achieve the same sublime quality. For a moment, shame, fear, and embarrassment start measuring your ego for new drapes.

Starting off with a citrusy, almost ripe Riesling note, this Chardonnay continued to open up with new layers, showing licks of light honey and grape-blossom one minute, a bit of gentle, stony, mineral depth a few moments later. The balance in the mouth made it feel smooth as the finest silk, and somehow both rich and light as a feather at the same instant. The finish went on for days, with the mix of previous flavours and aromas taking repeated little curtain calls, and with delightful glimmers of butterscotch footlights shining through it all. Any oak had perfectly assimilated, and was undetectable as such.

The wines of the Temkin-Paskus partnership trickled out of a chance meeting in the vineyards of Cave Springs in 1991. Stephen Temkin, a small, gentle man, with a quick humour and an artist's sensibilities, had his own wine newsletter at that time, and was examining the vinerows with Cave Spring owner Len Pennachetti. Deborah Paskus had recently changed her life, having fled the Toronto advertising world and an unsuccessful marriage. She returned to university to do graduate work on vinegrowing, and was working on a research project on Chardonnay clones at Cave Spring. Temkin and Pennachetti found Paskus amid her test plot and fell into a discussion of Ontario Chardonnay. Temkin doubted that anything really worthwhile would be achieved in the province because no one was really trying, and said so.

A few weeks later, Paskus showed up at Temkin's home in Toronto with a handful of experimental bottles of Chardonnay that had been cropped at different levels. Temkin, with a laugh, now modestly says it was "pure and utter luck," but he correctly ranked each wine from highest to lowest crop level.

With no capital, no vineyard of their own, and unencumbered with a winery licence, the pair cobbled together a label.

They would work together to fashion two barrels of Chardonnay, combining Temkin's ideas on what might best be tried in the struggle for glory with Deborah's field and cellar skills. Money was raised among friends and relatives in exchange for the promise of wine from one of the barrels, while the other barrel was reserved for the Toronto restaurant Scaramouche.

Having no legal existence as a winery, Temkin and Paskus travelled a circuit of facilities along the length of the Niagara region, camping for a time at the Reif, Cave Spring, Thirty Bench, and Thirteenth Street wineries – a pair of true gypsy vintners.

The clever use by Temkin and Paskus of their "landlords'" licences to make and sell wine was a profound moral problem for the mighty Liquor Control Board of Ontario. When the monopoly was desperate to secure a tiny parcel of the 1993 Beamsville Bench to offer customers in 1996 in their elite LCBO Classics catalogue, there was internal bickering over whether this sent a dangerous signal that would encourage other "dilettantes" to find ways of skirting somewhat arbitrary government regulations.

In the end, the LCBO's catalogue listed a handful of cases, and Beamsville Bench Chardonnay Cuvée Temkin Paskus nonchalantly rubbed shoulders with the top tier of wines from around the world.

The prime reason the Temkin Paskus wines get mentioned in the same breath as great white Burgundys is because they do exactly what the few top domaines in Burgundy do: ruthlessly chop the crop of fruit each vine carries. Most Chardonnay vines in Ontario are harvested at four to six tonnes per acre; the yield of grapes harvested by Deborah Paskus is closer to one or two tonnes.

In August, when the green Chardonnay berries start to soften and edge towards a golden colour and enter those final hair-raising weeks before full maturity, the excess clusters are cut off – dropped right on the ground. This allows the vine to concentrate on ripening a smaller load of fruit and increases the maturity, sugars, and flavours. Think of having three wailing newborns handed to you, rather than the one you were expecting, and you'll have an idea of the stress suffered by an unthinned vine.

It's expensive to do this, because most farmers are paid by the tonne; if you cut the weight before harvest, you hack away at your income.

Many winemakers self-servingly question whether thinning is necessary, and argue that a Chardonnay cropped at four or five tonnes per acre is just as good. But it isn't. The best white wine at the 1993 Cuvée – the Ontario industry's annual black-tie competition – was a declassified Beamsville Bench Temkin Paskus that had been sold off in bulk to another winery because it didn't meet the pair's exacting standards. The concentrated wine – though unsuccessful in their eyes – beat out the standard overcropped Chardonnays of the other Niagara wineries.

Temkin Paskus started as a brave experiment to push the boundaries of wine quality in Ontario. It has done just that, and though the industry did its best to ignore the pair for years, there is an agonizingly slow change to produce wines that rise to the pure hedonistic, almost spiritual delights that great – truly great – wines achieve. Stephen and Deborah are not business people, and they admit it; they rely on a small circle of dedicated partners for that. But they have precisely the intelligence, enthusiasm, artistry, and bloody-mindedness needed to blaze a trail of glory, showing what might be accomplished if only more of their peers would look up and follow, instead of remaining bent over, counting their money.

శ్

To forget about the account books, persistent bills, and shrinking lines of credit is one of the hardest things to do. And yet that is probably what underlies most people's fantasies of owning a vineyard. If you are not out in the rows yourself – at least for a large part of the day – working with your own hands, then I'm not sure any personal benefit comes to you. In the field, for those hours each day, the press of numbers has no meaning. Nor, often, does time, or at least not in the way we normally quantify it between 9:00 and 5:00.

Weather and daylight are the only real boundaries on time in the vineyard. It slows down during the performance of a necessary task, and is measured more in the arc of the sun than by the tick of a clock. Or at least so I try to tell Lauren when I've forgotten to make the jump back from vineyard time to that of the outer world and am late for something. I muse on this, lost in my digging, trying to remember if I promised to be home before dark this evening.

A familiar rough, dark-coloured farm truck has pulled into the lane across our main field, promising a break in my toil. I've hired Ron Alexander at times to plough and cultivate our vineyard expansions. He's a burly bachelor farmer and shepherd who lives a few miles west of our farm on the road to North Beach in a large brick farmhouse at the centre of a spectacular example of agricultural entropy. Ron is bearded, in his forties, perpetually in a pair of coveralls, and gentled by the quiet tones and accent of an eastern Ontario farmer. He's one of the few people still actively working the land near the hamlet of Hillier, and was recommended to me as someone who might be willing to hire himself out, with his larger machinery, to prepare our land for spring plantings. Ron became curious about vine-growing a year before I contacted him after the real-estate agents started coming by his farm, inquiring if he would be interested in selling to eager vignerons. He admitted to me he'd already walked our rows before I called him, curious to see for himself what the fuss was about.

In the truck with him I recognize Jack Mountenay, who lives in the hamlet of Hillier with his mother, Dorothy, sister of Edith Taylor Ashton, author of a history of the hamlet. Jack may or may not be related to Ron – I can't keep these things straight. Almost every one else in Hillier seems to be connected somehow. Anyway, Ron takes Jack into Wellington a few times a week for groceries and beer, and the pair often skulk around together like high-school kids. One fall afternoon, while driving up the slope to Ron's farmyard, I noticed in the front pasture a goat with a large pair of deer antlers on its head. Near one of the outbuildings, Ron, Jack, and a few other friends were cleaning a few deer they'd shot and hung up, and were clearly tickled when I commented on their unique goat.

"We duct-taped them on," Ron said with some engineering pride.

I know Ron provided a reason for the practical joke – I think to tease someone – but I'm damned if I can recall who or why. I only remember their mirth when I noticed their efforts, and thinking to myself that, thankfully, at least they didn't nail the things on.

I leave my spading fork and walk down the gentle grade to where Ron and Jack have parked and are opening a couple of beers. When I get to them, they hand me a can. "We're going exploring," Ron announces. "Jack's going to show us where we can find stuff."

By "stuff" I know Ron meant Iroquois artifacts. We have been talking about them for months. Spring is the best time to look, after the cultivated fields have been sitting out over the winter and the elements have exposed and washed pieces of pottery and stone pried loose by fall ploughing. Our lot and the Taylor farm next door are considered good sites – a secret kept from most people, though many know about the collection of pipes, stone tools, arrowheads, spear tips, and pottery shards that Jack Taylor and his sons have put together over the years. Edith Taylor Ashton has photographed part of the collection for her history of Hillier, and the items are going to be turned over to the Wellington Museum at some point. A few archeological surveys were done in the 1950s, but I've never seen any of the reports or summaries.

The County, being so well constructed and furnished by nature, was an attractive place for different periods of Native settlement. The many dozens of significant archeological sites are a closely kept secret, as officials strongly fear that they'd be raided by gaggles of amateurs or set upon by professional thieves. I've seen a general map of the different County sites only a few times, and briefly at that, during meetings of the Prince Edward County Heritage Advisory Committee. The municipal planning-services department keeps it from the public, and refers to it to determine if land use and planning decisions might impinge on anything important.

Jack knows where to look, because as a boy he went out with his uncle Jack Taylor to scout for new acquisitions. A few beers later, after being filled in on the local Hillier gossip, we walk over sections of the field where Jack thinks he remembers walking decades before.

The gentle swells of the stony Hillier fields are warm, and the opening leaves along the fencerows add a cheery new green border to the brown and grey of the limestone rubble. Three abreast we walk up and down, listening to Ron talk, with our eyes cast to the ground, looking, poking, picking up anything that breaks the monotony of grey and red-brown. In a few sections the soil changes to a softer, sandy texture, and treading on it feels like padding along on a generous goose-down duvet, unlike the firm return of footfalls on the Hillier Clay Loam. Noting the difference under my feet, I recall the woman I met in Wellington one day who, after hearing that I had grapes on Hillier soil, said, "Well, let's see your boots," and motioned for me to show her the soles. Authentically wounded and worn from rubble fragments, my footwear met with a nod of approval, and she agreed that, yes, she recognized the pattern of damage and I was definitely out in the fields, not on a tractor.

The sandy patches are well larded with granite cobbles and stones of all different hues and sizes. Travelling over these sections means a lot of bending and fruitless examination, and on this occasion, other than a few pleasant hours of light exercise and beer, little is gained. Ron has an armload of unnaturally rounded, smooth stones about the size of five-pin bowling balls, which may have been tanning or grinding tools. No pottery shards or arrowheads or hand-axes or pipe fragments. Ron and

Jack leave, and I try to work off the beer before sunset, getting back to neglected rows that still have to be weeded.

I'm surprised that nothing really turned up. It seems that nearly every time I decide to walk the same fields I add another three or four pieces of pottery to my collection. The fragments aren't Etruscan or Minoan or Mesopotamian, but still I find these crumbs of history and prehistory enthralling. The thick-walled red pieces are often blackened slightly on the smooth inside; some interiors end in a carefully indented diagonal band of marks on the inner lip. On the outer surface are the distinguishing diagonal lines combed into the surface. One piece has fractured just below this combed, angular motif where a border of horizontal indentations has created a pattern like the perforations of a magazine subscription card.

The shards date to a period of Iroquois design used around the fourteenth and fifteenth centuries. I like the connection to our land, feeling the cool fragments, the smooth or incised sides, the jagged exposed edges of the breaks. One pipe stem I have is made of a grey clay. It probably was acquired by trade, as everything else is of the usual terra cotta colour. The oldest item I have found is a black granite hammer, which dates to about 5000 or 6000 B.C.E. – badly worn, but still showing the tool marks that created the grip that still fits so comfortably into my right hand. I managed to find the same tool in the collection of the Royal Ontario Museum, a less-weathered example, down in the basement where the Canadiana exhibits were kept.

I hold in my hands things that were made centuries ago within a few yards of my vines, in use on the land we temporarily tend, created and valued at the same time the great cathedrals were rising in Europe, the monks and lords of Burgundy were clearing parts of the Côte d'Or, sorting out the good vines and vineyards, establishing the foundation and reputation of the most seductive and rarest of wines.

≈§

While someone like Ron Alexander is just curious about what his neighbours are up to, and may flirt for moments here and there with the idea of planting some vines on his slopes, if he were to find a partner to finance and run it, there has been no shortage of prospective growers with more serious intent. Late in 1999 I received an e-mail from one of the first of these would be vignerons, a man named Dan Taylor:

> Hi Geoff, you were referred to me from the growwine internet group. I'm seriously looking into Prince Edward County as a place to establish a vineyard (I hope to grow grapes and start up a winery one day)....
>
> From what I understand about the County and Hillier in particular is that the growing season is as favourable as Niagara, soils possibly better – good drainage, limestone – winters are harsher. What can you tell me about wintering vinifera vines especially on a commercial scale? ...
>
> A bit of background on me – who is this guy e-mailing me and asking all these questions????
>
> I'm an avid wine appreciator, ran winery tours to Niagara for 4 seasons '94-'97, have been making wine from Niagara grapes since '92 and wine starting with kits since '90. I am particularly interested in Pinot Noir, I made a low yield Pinot (1.75 tonnes per acre) from

Funk's vineyard in '98 – it's Big!!! Maybe too big – 25 brix! I'm not sure, we'll have to see how it ages. . . . Funk did their thing in the vineyard and I came down several times and further thinned "my" row to get the lower yields. . . . I have looked at land in Niagara but it's just too expensive and from what I understand soils (though not winters) may be better in PEC and the price seems to be right. . . .

Any help would be greatly appreciated. . . .

Thanks,
Dan

I answered him in painful detail, and a few days later received a reply from him that made me ponder not only my sanity, but his:

You're my hero . . . no seriously. Wow, you've gone whole hog. That's great! (You must be the only wine grower in Ontario doing that?) I assume you are about a metre by a metre spacing? You don't have a tractor, do you? How do you work with such tight rows?

I met with Dan, who wanted to throw over a marketing career in Toronto while only in his mid-thirties, because he had fallen tragically under the spell of Pinot Noir. Dan averred that his wife, Carrie, with a career of her own, was not opposed to leaving the city, though I warned him that it required far more than non-opposition, that he'd need his wife's goodwill and faith to survive the move, let alone the years of toil.

After a number of talks about Pinot Noir and growing philosophies, Dan managed to persuade me to let him work with me some key days through a season.

A few weeks later, I received another e-mail from someone else in Toronto:

Geoff,

. . . I'm also one of those who is interested in getting into grape growing in a bigger way in Prince Edward County. I have wanted to for the past 8 years, that is, ever since my wife and I discovered Prince Edward County and bought a country retreat in Wellington. Currently, we live and work in Toronto.

We now want to go ahead with trying a vineyard in PEC. However, although we are wine enthusiasts and have the desire, we don't have the technical knowledge required to establish and maintain a vineyard on our own, nor do we know that much about all the other issues involved, for example, VQA requirements, the potential market for grapes, etc. Also, currently we don't have the equipment or time to do the required work ourselves. Therefore, we need help.

Are you interested in consulting us, or could you recommend someone, or could you point us to someone or some organization who could recommend a consultant or whatever? If necessary, we are prepared to pay for consultation.

We will need advice and guidance, as required, on everything, starting with site selection and the feasibility of options.

Our objective is to grow grapes that can eventually be sold. Currently, we have no intention to get into vinification. We want to get going ASAP.

Regards,
Ken Burford
Yvonne Millman

When I met Ken and Yvonne, I found they were a quiet, pleasant, and intelligent couple, and to some degree their gentleness seemed at odds with the pioneering vineyard they desired. Both of them dark-haired with a few wisps of grey, they appeared younger and fitter than I expected. Ken had already revealed his engineer's mind in the simple, rational questions he raised, and in the methodical manner in which he campaigned for their vineyard. Yvonne, working in the Ontario Ministry of Education, was clearly too practical to embrace a delusion. Their calmness and balance was so constant that I was surprised when Yvonne told me that Ken could be emotional and was not above flashes of temper; I still have not seen it.

Over the course of the year we managed to find small pieces of Hillier – a pair of farms under fifty acres between the two – that both Dan and Carrie and Ken and Yvonne could start planting the next season. With them, the missteps and disasters I had thoroughly embraced and made my own in our first years were unrepeated; for both these vineyards I was able to start anew, with the knowledge I had pried from the Hillier Clay Loam. Both Ken and Dan had championed Pinot Noir, so the benefits came swiftly: spacing, trellis designs, and the very plants themselves were done correctly. The last element – the all-important vines – had been solved.

The lack of a wide, commercially available range of good Pinot Noir clones meant that most of my plantings were self-rooted cuttings. By the time Dan and Ken were ready to plant their first vines, two nurserymen in Niagara, Martin Gemmrich and Lloyd Schmidt, had established commercial relationships with a few key French nurseries that Canada permitted to export vines into the country. My client vineyards were able to purchase, at about $2.50 apiece, the new officially sanctioned French clones of Pinot Noir on rootstocks that could not be secured in Canada. Our federal rules had gradually been changed as bureaucrats recognized that the French vines were not going to ravage the Canadian countryside with unstoppable viruses and pests, and so a handful of vineyards in Ontario and British Columbia made their own successful arrangements with the French nurseries to import scion-and-rootstock combinations on the approved government list. However, those vineyards were importing thirty, fifty, or a hundred acres' worth of vines at a time, and that made it worth the trouble of the French order clerks. Small vineyard plantings such as Ken's and Dan's – barely three acres between them each year – invited a high risk of Gallic indifference. So Gemmrich and Schmidt appeared at just the right time as nursery middlemen and became minor heroes to small Canadian growers.

From box to small vineyard was only a matter of hours, thanks to the newly available selection of French vines, and to the planting machine of Abe Wiens.

Abe and his brother grow a few hundred acres of grapes in Niagara. He also has a custom machine-planting business, using a laser-guided mechanical vine planter. On a soil that has been properly deep-ripped and cultivated to break up clods and compaction and create a nice, crumbly structure, Abe's large John Deere tractor pulls a self-correcting device that digs a trench then buries the vine roots. Keeping the vines loaded on a cam-driven chain that feeds the planter are two workers seated behind like trotter jockeys. Abe uses two small Mexican men, who have been with him for some years; the driver is Abe's nephew, part of a large family of German Mennonites that still, for the most part, lives in Paraguay.

It's hard not to envy the way things can go from box to planted vineyard in a blink, especially when you are swinging a pickaxe or smashing down a steel bar to create a hole while hand-planting. For about 35 cents per vine, plus $30 per row set-up fee, Abe's machine and crew will take those boxes of imported French vines and have a vineyard in the ground a handful of hours later. By hand, in rocky soil, getting 100 to 150 vines planted per worker per day is a pretty spectacular pace. It's easy to see why nearly every vine planted in the County now goes in by machine. Abe has learned to appreciate the different soils in the County, compared to the cold, deep clays of Niagara, and managed to work with a fair degree of success in the shallow Hillier Clay Loam and its load of rubble and threatening basement of limestone. He hates the climate here – those ten degrees lower we go most winters unhinge him. But as for the soils, he has told a number of people, "I'd like to take a hundred acres of this back with me to Niagara."

The first planting Ken and Dan did on their sites went smoothly; the next year was a complete mess, thanks to weeks of ill-timed rains. But now, thousands of new Pinot Noir vines have a home in a pair of new sites in Hillier, and both Ken and

Dan and their wives have made impressive leaps from e-mails to true vinegrowers.

Spring seems to end with the third straight week of asparagus on the dinner table. The first spears are welcome – anticipated, in truth, with a salivating hunger.

On the Ridge Road just southwest of Picton, well along the high, sandy esker that gives the road its name, is the largest asparagus farm in the County. As soon as the word is out that the crop is being picked it spreads quickly. Wait half an hour, and almost everyone you know in the County is likely to turn up; it's as busy as a Tim Horton's donut shop as everyone hops out and buys large bags of first- or second-grade spears. In the morning, the field behind the sorting shed is grazed by large picking machines lazily flying at ground level, their shade-giving canvas awnings spread out above them like wings. They look like inventions by the British cartoonist Rowland Emett. If you come in the afternoon, they've stalled in one spot, waiting for dawn for the harvest to continue.

Mario Batali, the famed New York chef, has written of asparagus that the Italians have a fitting word – *scorpacciata* – "describing a full attack of eating a particular ingredient in copious amounts and very often in its evanescent period of local perfection." By the third week, I think most people in the County live up to that concept most faithfully. The sheer over-abundance of asparagus eventually bores the taste buds. It is still tender and sweetly green at the end of its season, but familiarity does breed contempt. It doesn't freeze well, becoming grassy and tough and nothing like the delicate fresh spears of spring. Asparagus is trapped in a feast-and-famine cycle.

Other fruits and vegetables take over the plate when they come into season in the coming weeks – strawberries, salad greens, peas, raspberries, corn, new potatoes, garlic, tomatoes – but they don't dominate it in the way asparagus does as the sole performer in spring.

In the same way, everyone anticipates the lilacs that bloom at about the same period; they are everywhere in the County, around old houses or marking the spot, with their pale mauve flowers and heady perfume, where an old house once stood. The perfume from a distance I find pleasant, though it hits me like a solvent when it is too close. The eruption of those bunches of small blooms against the dark-green leaves raises everyone's spirits, for a week or two. The tall lilac hedges that line the south part of Station Road by the railway bed are beguiling in the first few days, and Lauren always makes me drive that section of hard-angled turns so she can take them in.

A year after we moved to the County, Lauren's parents followed, trading their tiny old house in Weston for a much newer one in Wellington. I can remember their first day rather well. Garn was driving with Lauren, me, and the girls along the Danforth Road as we showed him the alternative route along that forgotten old highway from Hillier into Wellington. He spotted lilacs blooming along the route, finally could contain himself no longer, pulled the car to the shoulder, and armed with a penknife cut six or eight bunches, giggling like a boy rather than the grim seventy-nine-year-old he often was.

It still makes me smile. He couldn't wait to plunk those flowers into a vase to show Betty.

It was a strange incident, because any time since, if someone shows up with lilacs, Garn will launch into a routine about how they are full of earwigs and give the flowers the bum's rush to the deck outside.

the Big Dipper the North Star the
planets dangling like grapes
in a galactic vineyard
and even the home galaxy I'm standing on
all vanished
and words lost their connectives

•   *Al Purdy, "Barn Burning"*

Intoxication. I really think that's the only way to describe those first few days when summer takes hold each June, and the scent of vine flowers wafts across the fields.

The vines have grown with a vigour and speed that always seem remarkable. It takes only a few weeks to go from bud swell in the first days of May, where the emerging vines looked like the tip of a child's finger enveloped in a blanket of doe-coloured hair, to the appearance of the flower structure about three or four leaves above the starting point. Inside each bud is the basic vine – flower clusters included – up to a height of maybe a dozen leaves. When the bud pushes, the shoot expands and grows, taking advantage of the starches stored in the roots and older wood. It's a fact of vinegrowing that the quality of vine shoots and clusters each year is in large part determined the summer before; one bad year can often mean a poor start the next spring.

The wild riparia vines in the fencerows are tl e first to flower. A handful of days on, and the St. Laurent starts to bloom, and then a week later, near the anniversary of the Battle of Waterloo, on June 18, the Pinot Noir is usually underway.

I doubt if there's anything as insignificant – and yet, for its size, so heady – as a grape blossom. The scent is a lemony lime and honey signal. At first you catch it out of the corner of your nose. You turn your head instinctively to widen the intake, and it begins to intoxicate. How? I don't know. Sometimes I think, once your life becomes entwined with vines, a special, more sensitive pathway is beaten from the nose to brain; visitors never seem affected the same way when the smell is pointed out to them.

To me, the scent is powerful, which is surprising, given that grape flowers are probably the most disappointing fruit flower you can find. In fact, when you see a nascent cluster in bloom, you really aren't looking at flowers at all, but at a display of small yellow pollen-coated anthers, the male sexual parts. The petals of a vine are fused together into a small green calyptra, or cap, and actually open from the base, dropping completely off when bloom starts, like little parachutes.

Winegrapes are nearly all hermaphrodite, with both male and female functioning sex organs; their wild-riparia relatives have one superior primary set or another, and usually must cross-fertilize between plants. With the self-fertile winegrapes, it's suspected that in many cases each floret's own anthers may provide the pollen needed even before the cap drops off completely and exposes the pollen to the efforts of breezes and insects.

The cluster structure is a fuzzy yellow while blooming, and if conditions are still and warm, fertilization takes place with uniform rapidity. Cool temperatures, rain, and winds, however, can inflict a ragged burst of flowering among the developing clusters, staggered over one to three weeks, meaning that individual clusters and even berries will ripen at painfully different times. Pinot Noir fruit will mature about a hundred days after flowering, so a rough and uneven *floraison* starting, say, on June 18 may mean some fruit will be ready for harvest around September 26, with other clusters or berries from later fertilizations straggling to ripeness in early or mid October.

With the perfume in the air and mental calculations of when the harvest, or *vendage*, might be expected to begin comes another treat – the wild strawberries. At the foot of the fencerows the tiny fruits are ready to be devoured. Sampled, I guess, would be more accurate, as there are never enough to really gorge on. Usually they reflect the conditions of flowering: delicately flavoured, tender, and almost translucent ripe red strawberries fit the sunny and warm days of a good *floraison*; berries almost half white, dense, and bland and nutty with seeds proclaim the grey and cold days of a disappointing year.

At the top of the small hill where my minute plot of Syrah vines grows, there has sprung up a carpet of wild strawberries. Cultivating the soil, and so destroying them, before their fruit ripens seems unwise. Fortunately, they spread low to the ground, so I can get away with leaving them until I've gleaned a few handfuls of fruit. This year I've also noticed canes of wild raspberries growing in the few inches between the Syrah and the stakes they are tied to; the seeds must have been deposited by birds visiting the vines, perched upon the steel and wood supports, and my less-than-attentive weeding allowed them to establish.

Constant weeding and perpetual grooming of the growing shoots take up most of the vineyard day. I think the best description of this activity comes from David Andelsheim, who wrote in the *Oregon Winegrape Grower's Guide* that "training young vines . . . is chronic work; in my mind, it is very much like doing the dishes. The work is not terribly difficult, but no matter how much you do, there is always more." The lengthening shoots have to be placed so they are supported by the wires, or else they will flop on the ground and form an unruly prostrate bush, a growing trait that is very pronounced with Pinot Noir and gives rise to one of its common French aliases, Pinot Tordu, or "twisted." Spacing the shoots out into a hedge allows each leaf to capture every last possible ray of daily sunshine. The other major benefit is that a well spaced and groomed vinerow allows sunshine and breeze to inhibit disease.

A handful of particularly distressing vine diseases originated in our part of North America, and for centuries, if not millennia, they reached an understanding with our native vines. When they crossed the Atlantic in the mid to late nineteenth century, however, powdery mildew, downy mildew, and the louse phylloxera ravaged European vineyards. The European wine vine, which had a much smaller natural set of pests and diseases, was genetically unprepared for the arrival of our native vitis nasties, and each presented a dire crisis. In the case of powdery mildew, the problem was fixed with sulphur sprays; downy mildew could be prevented by spraying a copper and slaked-lime solution that came to be called Bordeaux mix.

Sulphur and Bordeaux mix are still the backbone of any spray program that is considered "organic." Most vineyards use an array of potent modern fungicides, insecticides, and weed killers, and have left sulphur and Bordeaux mix behind. The questions about spraying have disappeared from public discussion in this age of agribusiness. Sure, a problem like alar on apples hits the headlines once a decade or so, but for most people, agricultural sprays are a non-issue.

When you move from the city to an agricultural area like Prince Edward County, it's hard not to notice the accoutrements of farm spraying. Most farmers contract out spraying to one of the local farm centres. Their amazing tractors seem to spring from a George Lucas storyboard: huge ten-foot tires, a chassis and cab suspended five feet above ground, and giant spray booms folded back like insect wings. My favourite intergalactic version has a perfectly spherical tank behind the cab instead of the more boring rectangular one. These vehicles straddle the vast acres on which the old Loyalist fencelines have been torn down, and crawl along the soybeans or corn, blasting the plants with whatever planet-saving salve Monsanto or some other corporation is pushing that season. There is a terrible beauty to it all, when you see it.

Before we moved out here, I knew I couldn't entertain this approach to farming. I didn't want to work with the highly toxic chemicals, or lie awake in fear at night because I discovered a tear in my ventilated chemical suit after dosing the vines and our land, or because I thought the girls had gone into the vineyard before the required time had passed.

I believe the health of people who work with the sprays – and the health of the land – will become a big concern one day. For consumers it is an invisible problem, because in a store one sees only the stacks of glorious produce. In the rural world, you're reminded of it every time you pass one of these Star

Wars technomonsters roaring along the shoulder or at work in the field, or when you go into the Co-op and see the shiny posters for Roundup Ready® soybeans and corn.

Even if you don't spray modern pesticides yourself, that is not the end of the problem. As I walked along the western hedgerow of our Pinot Noir plot one summer I checked for phylloxera galls on the wild vines a dozen yards away. The galls can be found every year, but what stood out this time was the number of them. I looked closer and noticed something strange: many of the wild-grape leaves were deformed. Some were growing extremely long teeth, almost like long strands of green hair. Others mimicked a gingko leaf shape, with veins arrayed like fans.

I knew it was herbicide damage. There must have been 2,4-D drift from the fields on the other side of our hedgerow, for the deformations were clear symptoms of the herbicide hitting new grape tissue.

I quickly made for the row of mature vines closest to the hedge. There it was, the same damage to the Pinot Noir, a few badly affected leaves taking on that gingko shape, others with distorted leaf margins, and some with a surface that appeared bubbly and crinkled. Judging from the growth above the damaged leaves, the 2,4-D would have hit about six weeks before. The new leaves were normal, or so it seemed.

In the standard work *Compendium of Grape Diseases*, under "2,4-D" it says, "Vines are very sensitive to long- and short-distance aerial drift. A few isolated affected leaves can be tolerated, but vines are damaged by very low levels. Volatile forms of 2,4-D should never be used in vineyard regions."

Though it was late when I got home from the farm, I called one of the Kamink brothers. The Kaminks worked the neighbouring farm for Frank Westerhof, the farmer from whom I bought our land. Ben said he didn't know anything about the spraying and doubted it was his problem anyway. When I asked who his contract sprayer was, Ben said, "Warren McFaul."

The McFaul family are sort of kings of the old township of Hillier. The main trunk of the family farms about 8,000 acres, a mix of land they own and rent. There's a vegetable-freezing plant at the core of the operation, and a fairly substantial egg barn too. Warren is one of the sons of the patriarch, and has his own contract spraying company, servicing farms all over the County and into the country north of Belleville. Given the huge increase in the use of pesticides and herbicides by large farming operations, most use specialists like Warren to do their fields rather than invest in the expensive equipment themselves.

I phoned Warren and explained what I'd found. We made an appointment to discuss it the next day.

Warren pulled up in a van and made his way through the clover to the plot rows. I pointed out the affected Pinot Noir and Meunier leaves, and then the wild-grape damage in the thick hedgerow. Warren admitted that they had sprayed a weak 2,4-D formula herbicide about six weeks before on a field of wheat next to our farm, but he didn't believe the drift could travel, and certainly not through such a thick hedgerow. I told him I had never used pesticides or herbicides other than Bordeaux mix and sulphur in our vineyard, that there was no other working farm close, and that the damage was on the rows close to this hedge, while the others farther east and north were almost unaffected. The drift had to have come from the field to the west of us.

He wanted to see if there was evidence of the direction of the drift on the other side of the hedge. We found it, as the wild vines on that side were much worse.

I showed Warren the texts about 2,4-D damage and vines, and noted that there were now hundreds of thousands of dollars invested in winegrapes in the County; other problems were likely unless something changed. I promised him a map of the different vineyards so that he would know where not to spray the volatile 2,4-D mix, and left it at that.

I have taken the required provincial pesticide course myself, and got my green Grower Pesticide Safety Course card, even though I'd only be purchasing sulphur, copper sulphate, and lime. The day-long session and exam had me calculating nozzle rates, volumes per acre and hectare, and demonstrating proper toxicity awareness. I found myself giggling as I worked out flow rates and passes per field while thinking of the contrast to my friends accumulating billable hours in law offices, or typing away on teleplays or magazine articles. But I was also unnerved by a few of the other, older farmers who began to complain they couldn't use DDT any more.

So technically I'm licensed, just like my neighbours. If I wish, I can buy and apply Dikar, Phaltan, Captan, Polyram, and Dithane like any viticulturalist in the province. I haven't had to.

I'm not a hippie or New Age kind of guy. We buy our groceries at Loblaw's, IGA, and A&P. In Toronto, I did go into a couple of health-food stores, but was spooked after being hit on a few times by women asking earnestly, "Do you work with oregano?" I am concerned about some of the food we're eating, but that's as far as it goes. However, when it comes to mixing up a batch of deadly chemicals that can shuffle my genetic code with the swift indifference of a Mohawk blackjack dealer, I have better things to do. I've learned when to spray Bordeaux mix to head off downy mildew and cut down on black rot and cane phomopsis. I've recognized when the threat of powdery mildew takes over, and when to switch to wettable sulphur. Other than a faint whiff of Dantesque fumes on my work clothes after using a battery of backpack sprayers, all has gone well. (Lauren tells people I smell like farts for weeks.) The vines have a decent population of ladybugs preying on aphids. I see lots of tiny parasitic wasps on patrol. And the leaves are the proper green and free of insect damage. From time to time I have to pick off horrid, fat sphinx moth caterpillars before they begin to dine on the greenery, and I scan the clusters and pluck off the odd berry that may be infected with black rot or macrophoma before it infects others. Sure, it'd be nice to have the weeks of absolutely neat, weed-free soil under the vines you'd get by spraying Roundup rather than just the few days provided by cultivation. It is my choice, though, and it's working out fine, both for me and my vines.

I've dithered about joining a certified organic program. These folks squabble and splinter more than Methodists did a hundred years ago. I believe I'd qualify for transitional status with most of them, and would willingly allow testing of our soil and plants for residues. I'm a classic Nonconformist in religious matters, and similarly I don't know which, if any, of these organic churches to join. I've continued to read a lot about all aspects of organic viticulture, including biodynamics, whose practitioners look upon other organic farmers as Jesuits do Protestants – as poor, well-meaning souls misguided and fundamentally in error.

A good, simple summary of this sect of organic farming is given in Jacqueline Friedrich's *A Wine and Food Guide to the Loire*:

> Biodynamics can sound New Age zany but it embodies a wealth of folk wisdom. Homeopathic vine treatments replace synthetic fertilizers, insecticides, and herbicides. Planting, pruning, and so forth are scheduled according to the positions of the planets. Farmers have always sown grain and vignerons bottled wine by phases of the moon. And while those traditions may have fallen into disuse, some impressive wine people (Lalou Bize-Leroy of Burgundy and the Huets of Vouvray, for example) are reclaiming them in biodynamics.

I've noticed others, like the Chapoutiers of the Rhône, and the Humbrechts of Alsace, have also started using biodynamic methods, which are adapted from an agricultural approach created by Austrian philosopher Rudolph Steiner about the time Hitler was a minor pain in Bavaria. The quality of these producers forced me at least to poke around and see what the fuss was about. In another part of Ms. Friedrich's book, describing her classification of producers, she notes that for her outstanding rating producers must be "among France's 'artist-vintners.' . . . They are exigent in the vineyards and in the cellar. Yields are low; many practice either organic or biodynamic viticulture (although this was not a criterion)." It's an observation that crops up repeatedly in other recent books by such wine writers as Clive Coates, Patrick Matthews, and Andrew Jefford.

Reference material on biodynamics in the vineyard is sparse, and most of it is in French or German. There are some

American consultants taking client wineries and vineyards through the system, but mainly in California, where such practices barely register on the state's loopy scale. Basically, I'd sum it up as treating a farm as a living entity and keeping it self-sufficient, using slightly bizarre compost techniques, a regimen of homeopathic sprays to enliven soil, plant, and atmosphere after lengthy vortex-inducing mixing, and a sensitivity to lunar phases and the position of constellations. Oh, and a lot of German Romanticist philosophy. The planetary and star stuff and the philosophic rambles don't do much for me. But there's no doubt the cycle of the moon does affect living things, and there are centuries of cellar observations that note changes in wine clarity tied to its phases, so who knows? Some of the methods of making the sprays – packing and burying cow horns, using animal skulls or bladders as containers – unnerve me quite a bit.

I do use a few of the natural potions suggested by bio-dynamics. One is a tea of *Equisetum arvense* (horsetail), for use as a fungicide; another is a fermentation of stinging nettle used to help stimulate green growth and to work against drought. Nothing horrible has ever happened, and the results have always been positive.

There definitely is a good feel in my vineyard plots, which I've worked hard to establish. Above me the other day I noticed a strange aerial dance taking place. There were two distinct layers of creatures darting at random above the old rows of Pinot: the first layer, up to about twelve feet, consisted of dragonflies; above them were dozens of swallows. It looked like a miniature theatre of war, the dragonflies like helicopters, the fork-tailed birds racing above them like fighters supplying protection. The enemy were mosquitos, which have been insufferably thick this year. I had noticed while working that they had eased for some reason, but bent over as I was, pulling weeds like a peasant with my head a few inches from the stony soil, I hadn't realized why.

Moving to the edge of the vineyard for a better view, I was surprised to see that the birds and dragonflies were contained within the boundaries of the acre and a half of Pinot Noir. They turned almost magically at the edge and flew back above the vines. Had I somehow managed to create on this plot of land a harmony and balance that drew creatures and order into it? I had to wonder, as there were far more mosquitos in the clover fields and hedgerows all around. One can be bled dry crossing the clover, and to go into the hedges is almost to tempt death. Establishing such peace and order is one of the reasons for farming without dangerous chemicals, close to the real purpose of growing the healthiest, most flavoured, balanced fruit possible. Curious. Something else to file away, in the same way I take note of the leopard frogs I surprise every day hiding under the vines, or the large snapping turtle I spied last week parked in the shade of a row, a good half-mile from the nearest water.

That turtle I discovered from the back. I went to edge it out with my boot, thinking it was a granite boulder I'd forgotten to haul out. Luckily I glimpsed the armoured tail and stepped back as the business end whipped to the side and snapped at the air.

Moments of wonder like that are spread out here and there through the long hours among the vines. The gain in daylight until the equinox only adds to the temptation to put in more time. Not every vinegrower can or will allow it to happen, but enough do that it's considered a telling vigneron characteristic. In her memoir *Tender at the Bone*, Ruth Reichl writes: "'Don't take it personally,' put in Madame de Montille gently. 'He is the strangest man. They say that even when he goes to mass he runs in putting on his clothes. And as he leaves the church he is already undressing so as not to lose time. He is devoted to the vines.'"

◆

The work eventually tails off for a few weeks – at least in actual hours spent in the rows, though my mind is never clear of tasks I *could* do, like trellising the new plantings, or getting a jump on the next round of weeding. The demands of young vines and of a young family are at war during the daylight hours this time of year. The last weeks of June are the worst, as soccer games for Winona and Jemima begin.

Fetching the girls from school in Wellington, getting to swimming lessons, synchronizing dinner, and meeting the game schedules for two different teams in Picton is as taxing as any corporate executive's day spent constructing a labyrinth of shell companies or fiddling revenue streams. Lauren has been slowed and wearied by Keziah, the County-born sister to Winona and Jemima, who joined the brood the first day of the ice storm that ravaged much of the country east of here in 1998. Now Keziah is on toddler's legs and dangerously attached to the delights of anarchy, and Lauren's ability to marshal the parade is hampered by our refusal to resort to a dart gun more than is absolutely necessary.

With three daughters, I find myself keeping notes on other examples of daughters working successfully in their family vineyard as future enticements to get the girls interested in our own. I started when I first came across Remington Norman's entry in *The Great Domaines of Burgundy* on the Domaine Alain Michelot of Nuits-St-Georges. "Alain," Norman writes, "exudes 'joie de vivre.' He eats and drinks well and occasionally hunts for the pot. One sphere, however, in which he has had no influence is on the eventual succession: he has three daughters ranging in age from 19 to 25. Apparently there is a Michelot gene which favours girls – his cousin Bernard Michelot has three daughters and he himself was the only boy among several sisters." Among my two sisters and me there are nine daughters and one son, so I was amused by that.

Norman's entry on Alain's cousin Bernard, in Meursault at Domaine Michelot-Buisson, notes that Bernard is assisted by *his* three daughters, Chantale, Odile, and Jean-François. Another trio was added to my list from Andrew Jefford's book *The New France*: Denis Durantou's "three talented daughters, Alix, Noémie, and Constance," at L'Église-Clinet in Pomerol. Besides examples of sisters, I have a mass of clippings and notes on female winemakers: Deborah Paskus and Anne Sperling in Niagara; Lalou Bize-Leroy and Annick Parent in Burgundy; Helen Turley and Merry Edwards in California. Those are just a ready fraction. If Winona, Jemima, and Keziah want to take on the vineyard one day, I want them to feel confident that they can, and that they're not alone.

Lauren's parents have provided babysitting when I couldn't give up a day in the vineyard. Lauren's sister Joanne has also generously helped, especially on the days when two games were under way at the same moment on different soccer pitches, allowing me to continue working until dusk in the Hillier fields.

The pulls and juggles required could make mornings in Consecon the most fraught moments of the year, as Lauren and I tried to sort out what needed to be done that day, and how to arrange it all. Too often it ended with me barking and Lauren fighting back tears of fury and frustration.

The toughest of these mornings is usually the one when I notice the clay pots of wedding ivy have nearly dried up; the vines in Hillier have taken my attention from the handful right here at home.

My Scottish-born great-grandmother had somehow passed on the tradition: a cutting of ivy was taken from Lauren's wedding bouquet and it was thought important to keep that evergreen alive. As the tradition sprang from my family, and I was the one supposed to have an affinity for plants, it fell to me to take the original piece and make it root and thrive. My mother said that Great-Grandma Lane had kept various cuttings of family ivy alive, including that from my parents' wedding. When she died at 102, the ivy lost its caretaker, and though it had no direct bearing on what happened, my parents divorced not long after. It's irrational and thoroughly superstitious. But glancing to the windowsill and seeing the gasping, shrivelling vines makes the hair on the back of my neck stand up in horror.

I've somehow managed to revive two particularly woebegone pots in two different difficult County summers, my actions probably not noted by Lauren. Each fall I now take more cuttings and carefully ensure I have many pots of ivy growing at any one time. When we settle at the farm, I hope to fill areas of garden with it too, a way of betting across the board, and one future day perhaps providing a source of ivy for the wedding bouquets of my daughters. Ivy was also an emblem of Bacchus, but that is a mere footnote to the role it has in our house.

Lauren has her own superstitions, and if I know hers, then she most likely has observed mine. On the kitchen windowsill over the sink she has a toy shepherd, a lamb under his left arm and a crook in his right hand. Behind him lies a plastic ewe, at the moment bowled over by a handful of beach pebbles the girls put there for safekeeping. The shepherd has the most generalized, bearded features – like a Hans Holbein Old Testament woodcut – and Lauren has told me the little toy has meaning for her, ensuring the safety and health of our family.

Once I settle down into the delicate but necessary balancing act, I remember that the time lost ferrying the girls around in the car is not as irredeemable out here as that lost traversing a suburb. Travelling in the car, with Lauren and some or all of the girls, was when I noticed that the hamlet of Rosehall is Rosehall on the sign approaching from the north, but Rose Hall coming the opposite way. It was also in the car one June, when the first cut of hay had been taken, that Jemima pointed at the large white-wrapped bales lying in the fields next to the lake and urgently announced, "Marshmallows." Or there was the small marvel one morning of seeing four swans just out of the waters of Pleasant Bay flying next to us for about a quarter-mile . . . capped by Winona refusing to look at them because they were not the mute swans she liked most.

In the evening, the stars over Lake Ontario light in their true uncountable numbers, and the girls thrill at the richness of the sky. Black, clouded nights are unmistakably so; when it is clear, the moon looks down on them through all its phases, and when it is full they can see its intense light cast shadows everywhere. They wonder at the furnace glows of Rochester on the nights when it is reflected a deep red and orange across the water, and note when the smaller humps of orange-pink from Trenton and Belleville assert themselves before we reach Consecon.

For months they could see the comet Hale-Bopp for most of the drive home from Wellington, and would marvel at the clearer view from their own back yard when we emptied the car to spill into the house. The faint shimmer of the northern lights made Lauren ask that I stop the car one evening. The girls were unimpressed, but now, a few years later, they're quick to point them out to us whenever they spot a display as we drive along Scoharie Road. They are as delighted when they luck on a falling star, though it can raise from those who missed it a wail of outrage that smothers the joy of the others; it's as if we've bought a gift for one and left the others empty-handed.

They've seen a doe gallop alongside at night as if trying to outpace the car, then turn to disappear down the ditch and over a hedge. Foxes and rabbits are caught by headlights in the dusk, healthy and as beautifully coloured as any Jan Brett illustration in our copy of *The Mitten*. Families of whitetails hold still for them too, pausing as they glean the fields in broad daylight. Uncounted legions of fireflies give command performances, dancing in the dark right angles of Station Road. These are the things our daughters take as their spoils. I suspect Lauren and I enjoy it all more than they do. It makes up for the uncountable times I've heard *The Disney Princess Collection* cassette and the other back-seat tape requests they also see as their due for enduring time in the car.

Sure, they squirm with delight whenever a trip to the mall in Belleville is planned, and covet and enjoy acquiring Groovy Girl dolls the same as any girls their age. Yet they recognize they have rare things about them. Lately, after a deer or a fox or a falling star or brilliant moonrise breaks the routine of a car ride, one or all will chirp, "I'm glad we live here." Sometimes it may just be brave young ladies talking, but once in a while Lauren and I sense it tumbles out truthfully.

❧

The last few weeks in June might flip me an afternoon or two when I can collect Winona and Jemima from school. I stand somewhat awkwardly on the fringe of the loose huddle of mothers and babysitters waiting on the front walkway; one or two I recognize well enough to smile at and greet by name, though Lauren knows them better, having the pass-key of motherhood.

The school in Wellington is well sited, set back from the main road at the end of a long, pleasant green alley. It has a clean, well-proportioned design from the 1920s, of tan brick and with grey stone accents, and a clock frozen at 1:17 high above the main doors. The modern expanded wing of dark brick is tucked to the west, and for the most part is hidden from view until you are halfway up the front lawn.

The staff nearly all live nearby the village, or somewhere else within the County; the students see their teachers not only in their professional roles, but run into them as part of the community, even if it's only while shopping or at the theatre. Though the resources of a small community are fewer than in a large centre, and there are gaps and strains in the school system, for the most part the teachers seem relaxed and unstressed, much like everyone else in the County. Some staff were local County kids themselves.

It is hard to be anonymous, either as a teacher or as a family, which is uncomfortable for some who come here from the city, but the benefit is seeing some good teachers take our small parade of girls in succession. There must be an advantage for the staff too, because there is little turnover.

As agreeable as the school looks and feels, it is on leaving the building that its true fortune and beauty reveal themselves. Coming out the main door and standing in the portico at the head of the steps, you look down the elegant lawn at a breathtaking view: it hits you all at once in the afternoon sun. First you see St. Andrew's, the old small brick Anglican church, to your right, and then the larger brick United church across Main Street. Setting them off like tawny gems is the glorious Prussian blue of Lake Ontario, broken by gentle whitecaps. To the left of the grass alley, across the street separating the school from the lake, are the soft limestone and granite colours of what are among the oldest stone houses in Ontario – certainly built before 1800, though exactly when is not known. Through the trees, the sun's rays set off the beach of the distant Sandbanks Provincial Park as a luminous strip of white gold. Anyone willing to stop for just a moment and soak it up will immediately find their breathing has slowed, their cares have receded.

I hope, like everything else they enjoy out here, that the unequalled charms around their school fill the girls' eyes and their hearts. I hope it all gives them a sense of home and binds them to Prince Edward, wherever they go in life.

❧

Before you know it, July has vanished, consumed easily by the days in the vineyard and swimming lessons and soccer – and maybe a precious afternoon at North Beach.

Winegrowers here in the County, as difficult as we find the juggle, have a distinct advantage over the many other growers here who still live in Toronto and zoom down every week or so and try to get caught up. And that group has it easy compared to Jeff Connell.

Jeff lives in Manhattan, and if others are juggling tennis balls, he's attempting to keep a chainsaw and an axe in the air. He commutes about every other weekend from New York, then returns home. If he can take a string of days as summer or fall holidays, he does so. It hasn't been as successful as he had planned.

I first heard from Jeff when he called and asked for my opinion about some properties on the market in Hillier. The one I told him I liked best was a long seventy-acre strip beside the Loyalist Parkway, with a very nice slope of well-cobbled gravelly sand overlooking Pleasant Bay. It had been for sale for two or three years, and I told him if I had the $70,000 they were asking, I'd have bought it already.

A few weeks later he purchased it, and negotiated to buy the seventy acres next to it.

Jeff had already come to the same conclusions about density and organic viticulture I had, the result of his own research and of his being a well-travelled, card-carrying wine geek. He had looked at Nova Scotia, where his parents were from, as a possible site for what he wanted to do, and had also explored the established vineyards of both the Finger Lakes and Niagara. He even toyed with buying a property in the Loire Valley in France, the wine region at the centre of his love of wine. Jeff's father, until recently deputy minister of agriculture in Ottawa, had learned about the pioneering efforts in the County, and spread the word to him.

Jeff was one of the first in the County to take advantage of mechanical planting that first year, putting in tens of thousands of vines in eight acres. I found the speed of the laser-guided mechanical planting machine and crew stunning. The first day of work at Jeff's farm, in mere minutes I saw nearly two rows go in. Ed Neuser stopped by while I was there, and I introduced him to Jeff, who was busy snipping roots and putting the waxed vines in a water trough to rehydrate them after months of cold storage. Ed didn't say much, pointed out a few irregularities in the first rows, and then went off to Toronto, impressed by the pace, though convinced such a machine couldn't be used in his rockier new plots.

Jeff had to return to New York that afternoon. His father would take over. When I met the senior Mr. Connell, he was all alone. Rain had ended the day's work almost before it had begun. The crew departed for Niagara, to return in a few days once the soil had dried. Mr. Connell looked like John Huston in *Chinatown*; it was hard to imagine him dressed in the uniform of the high-up civil servant he was. When planting did resume, a few people came by to help him; I heard that Deborah Paskus was there at some point and did some root trimming alongside Mr. Connell. Twenty-one thousand vines had to be prepped for the crew working the laser planter.

To that original eight acres, Jeff added another two acres the next year. It was planted as a large experiment, and a costly one.

I've got to know Jeff very gradually over the years. It is obvious he's not your ordinary vigneron. An intensely thoughtful fellow, dressed in tweeds like a country gentleman, he has a capacity for hard work that betrays the reason for his taking up American residency. He went to New York to pursue a Ph.D. in experimental psychology, and after earning his doctorate he continued living in Manhattan, where he has subscribed to three or four complete Ring Cycles and, until vinegrowing intervened, seemed to attend the annual festival in Salzburg more than I get to the dentist. Where I recognize I can be intense or laconic – or at awkward times both at the same moment – conversations with Jeff have been punctuated with long pauses and silences, whether from guardedness, boredom, or natural reticence I still can't unravel.

His wine tastes and enthusiasms are too subtle for many in the County, but he has the tremendously generous nature that is the mark of an honest connoisseur and follower of the vine. He has provided countless bottles for collective tastings for County growers, and has opened up wines that I needed and hoped to try but would not have encountered otherwise, such as Jean-Paul Brun's Cuvée à l'Ancienne from Beaujolais, the delicate Henri Goyard Chardonnays, and an intelligent array of bottles from Muscadet Sèvre-et-Maine growers like Marc Olivier and the Luneau family.

The wines are not chosen by price or magazine rating, and in many cases, such as Brun's Gamay and the Melon de Bourgogne from Muscadet, they are made from very humble grapes. Instead, they've been gathered for the story they tell – of the terroir, the variety, the maker. In fact, most of the wines have been shockingly inexpensive for the quality and care they evince, averaging I imagine in the range of fifteen to twenty dollars U.S., though not exclusively. They also tell much about why Jeff has planted as he has, and what he is striving for.

I've returned the favour when I could from our nearly extinct Toronto cellar, such as a 1986 Chave Hermitage Lauren and I brought to a dinner he hosted for us a few years ago, but I will never be able to match the generosity. So instead, we cellar the bottles and cases Jeff has brought up with him over the years, allowing him to have a County cellar, though distant and minute compared to his New York collection.

For the moment, Jeff inhabits a near-permanent camp at the top of his front slope, which he has named Two Tents at Once Beach, referring to the sandy fields angled down to Pleasant Bay. Tasting with Jeff always makes me think of the old *Punch* cartoon of two old-school British wine snobs at a cleared, polished table in evening dress. One is considering the cloaked wine at hand, commenting, ". . . and trodden, I should say, by Jacques Dupont fils." Though our setting, in a screened tent, with summer stars filling the sky over Pleasant Bay, is as far removed from that world as imaginable, there's always the fear the conversation isn't.

Without the full attention of their owner, Jeff's vines will never prosper as they should. He knows this, and it must eat at him every fortnight he spends in New York between visits. Unreliable labour in his absence has been his undoing. Jeff says he is planning his escape from midtown Manhattan, though it can't be soon enough. When I ran into him recently he was particularly dispirited by the lack of progress in trellising his rows. The delay had allowed diseases to attack the vines, which couldn't be properly sprayed until they were firmly tied up. With a sincerity only Jeff could pull off in these parts, he said, "I let St. Lawrence cry for my vines last night."

The day before was August 10, the feast day of St. Lawrence – or St. Laurent in France, San Lorenzo in Italy. Jeff was referring to the shower of meteors that has occurred on or near that day since the tenth century. They are better known today as the Perseids, because they seem to fall from the August sky where the constellation of Perseus lies.

St. Laurent is also one of a band of saints that European vignerons look to for various reasons, but he's at the tail of the list.

St. Vincent is considered *the* patron saint of vinegrowers. His feast day of January 22 is cause for big celebration in France, especially among Burgundians. And for no readily identifiable reason. He didn't transform water into wine at a tricky moment when the wedding guests were just about to learn that the open bar was not quite as open as they had hoped. And he wasn't miraculously preserved in the desert by a vine issuing forth from a pip dropped by an angel or raven.

Nope. Nothing like that. The French drafted him because of his name: *Vin*-cent. Or, in the deeper explanations, *vin-sang*, wine and blood, a mnemonic for part of the menu at the Last Supper. (Such a manufactured association is not unusual; the sea-going Bretons adopted an obscure martyr called Phocas because his name sounds similar to their word for "seal.")

In a book composed by Benedictine monks, more than thirty Vincents are listed. The one most publications cite for January 22 is Vincent of Saragosa, or Vincent the Deacon. And most put the date of his death at 304 C.E. The Benedictines write, "Details of his martyrdom are lacking but the fact of it is indisputable. He is depicted as a deacon holding one or many ewers and a book; or with a raven or ravens defending his martyred body; being torn with hooks, or holding a millstone."

Turning to the amiable authority of Sean Kelly and Rosemary Rogers's *Saints Preserve Us!*, we get the uncomfortable details:

Still a boy when he was ordained a deacon by Bishop Valerius, Vincent was arrested with his mentor in the year 300, by order of Dacian, the cruel Roman governor of Spain. Because the elderly bishop stammered, it was up to young Vincent to argue their case in court, and he was fearless and forthright in declaring his readiness to suffer for the Faith. Impressed, Dacian dismissed all charges against Valerius, but prescribed a course of tortures for Vincent unique in the gory annals of martyrdom. . . . He was stretched on the rack, and torn with iron hooks. He was forced upon a bed of iron spikes, set over a fire, and salt was rubbed into his wounds. He was finally rolled in broken pottery, then locked up and left to starve. (The faithful would visit his cell, and dip cloths in his blood, any of which precious relics are still venerated in Valencia.)

The *Oxford Dictionary of Saints* adds that in addition to being imprisoned and starved "he was commanded to sacrifice, but he refused. Then he was racked, roasted on a gridiron, thrown into prison, and set in stocks." With spartan understatement, the writer comments, "He died as a result of his sufferings."

That, of course, was not the end. In *Signs & Symbols in Christian Art*, George Ferguson adds that "Dacian ordered the body to be thrown to wild animals, so that it might be devoured, but a raven came and protected it from all attacks. The body was then taken out to sea in a boat and thrown overboard, with a millstone tied round its neck. It was miraculously washed ashore, and then the waves of the sea hollowed a tomb for Vincent in the sands. Many years later, his body was discovered and buried in Valencia."

Not all of him remained in Valencia. Somehow, Abingdon in Britain acquired "substantial relics of him in the 12th century."

Even Vincent's old gridiron was appropriated by those fond of St. Lawrence, and who needed to pad his story, and not unnaturally believed poor Vincent could spare an instrument of torture or two.

With all this detail, it's hard to tell Vincent from dozens of other saints in art. He's usually young, wears a deacon's dalmatic, carries the palm of martyrdom, and may have protective ravens or even crows (who, it seems, moved his relics from Cape St. Vincent to Lisbon). There can be a whip, a chain, a gridiron, a grill with hooks, a millstone, ewers, and books, and, of course, a bunch of grapes.

Vincent's defence of Valerius should have made him the natural choice of lawyers, or the gridiron and the dipping given him favour with clients of Swiss Chalet. However, Sean Kelly says Vincent looks with favour on roofers, schoolgirls, and, paradoxically, both vinegar-makers and vintners.

᛬

If summer for me starts with the vines flowering each year, it draws to a close with veraison. Even though there may be more than a month until the *official* change to fall, the visual signal that ripening has begun seems most appropriate. Work in the vines has pretty much been suspended by August, and it is not unusual to find winegrowers sneaking in a conference vacation like the International Pinot Noir Celebration in Oregon, or maybe just time with their family again. It's often only in August, sadly, that I can manage a day or two at North Beach or Sandbanks with Lauren and the girls, and maybe entertain some visiting relatives or friends.

The individual grape berries have transformed themselves in the past month, like Robert DeNiro packing on pounds for his role in *Raging Bull*. A few weeks ago you could pop an entire berry into your mouth on a hot afternoon and crunch it pips and all for a refreshing, tart taste. Now, the two to three pips inside have matured enough to be loaded with bitter, harsh tannins and must be spat out. The seeds have nearly reached their full size and are yellowing, the first step towards their mature brown. The green shoots they hang from are now turning yellow then cocoa brown, transforming into ripe canes.

The skins of certain individual berries — first on the St. Laurent, then the Meunier, the Pinot Noir, and finally the Syrah — turn a smoky, clouded colour here and there, and then rapidly darken to a blue-black. It is always a tense time, as small annual ravages of black rot also cause berries to darken, then collapse and shrivel. These berries must be picked off the clusters, to prevent a buildup of spores and a disastrous infection that will suddenly stop only when the berries naturally change colour and have reached a certain sugar level. The day veraison takes hold can cause a wave of nausea and depression, as it looks as if black rot has suddenly become an epidemic. I might pull a berry or two in this funk until I realize they are healthy and soft and juicy.

It isn't disease, but rather the final, short interval before harvest.

I am thinking what the grapes are thinking
become part of their purple mentality
that is
    I am satisfied with the sun and
eventual fermenting bubble-talk together
then transformed and glinting with coloured lights in
    a GREAT JEROBOAM
that booms inside from the land beyond the world

·   *Al Purdy, "The Winemaker's Beat-Étude"*

T he grapes. Nothing in the world seems as important as
those tiny Pinot Noir berries.

People like to visit in the fall, because the fruit is what all
the fuss is about. Ninety per cent of winegrowing is fruit quality
– at least if you ask an honest winemaker. Dan Taylor has admitted to me that he has snuck into my rows at this time of year to
look at (and sample) the deep black-blue berries in clusters
about the size of soap bars. The small berries, thick skins, and
full flavours are unlike anything he's purchased from Niagara
vineyards. "It's the real deal," he says. I know he's kept some fruit
on his first-year vines this summer, when he really shouldn't.
Ken Burford, if he's hiding any clusters, is much better at it. But
I understand Dan's eagerness to try something from his own
patch of earth, to begin to get a taste for *his* vineyard, to try to

imagine what *his* vines will provide in bottle. It unduly stresses the young vine, which should be growing roots for two or three years rather than fruit, but a few here and there . . . well, I did the same thing too. We all do.

Veraison is the anglicized term for the French *véraison*. On paper there's but an accent's difference, but when it rolls off the tongue of a grower in California, Oregon, New Zealand, or Australia, the pronunciations are worlds apart. However it's said, "veraison" is much more elegant and mysterious than "berry softening" or "colour change."

It is beautiful to see how in just hours the individual berries on a cluster will change from green to a dark black violet in Pinot Noir, or a smoky, bluey, reddish pink in the Pinot Gris. Inside, the pulp softens and becomes translucent, and for the first time is perceptibly sweet. The first berries to start this final push to maturity are usually those that were fertilized first and which have enjoyed slightly warmer microclimates on the vine, likely nearer the rock-strewn ground or one of the steel trellis posts, which absorb and radiate heat.

About half the berries in our St. Laurent plot have darkened now. The thirty or so Pinot Noir clones I have from around the world lag far behind. Which is about right, as St. Laurent usually ripens before Pinot Noir by as much as ten days. The Pinot Gris is maturing at the same pace as the Pinot Noir, though from experience I expect it to race ahead of the Noir any day now.

I finally have some clusters on the few rows of Melon de Bourgogne I've been growing. This variety originated in Burgundy and is, in the words of Brit wine writer Oz Clarke, "a vine long since kicked out of Burgundy as having no class and lowering the tone of the place." Melon is the grape responsible for the Muscadet wines from the mouth of the

Loire. I've always liked Muscadet Sèvre-et-Maine, so I gathered cuttings from scientific collections to propagate. Apart from enjoying the wine, I was intrigued to learn in a Cornell University study that Melon is one of the most winter-hardy vinifera vines, and that a few wine writers consider it capable of some pretty good wines when given a chance.

Veraison is not the only change in the vineyard plots. When the vines change colour you'll also see the shoots that emerged from the buds in May begin to turn an attractive woody brown. The French call this *aoûtement* – the "Augusting" of the canes. Further growth at the shoot tips at this stage isn't a good thing. It consumes sugars and energy the vine should be using to ripen the berries and the canes. And that new green growth is certain to be killed during the winter, because it won't have time to ripen before our first leaf-killing frosts come in October.

Last year I lost about 80 per cent of my Pinot Gris and 60 per cent of my Pinot Noir clusters. I ended up with a fraction of the wine I thought I would have after such a glorious growing year. I estimated we'd harvest just enough to start trying a number of different experiments with yeast strains and vinification techniques – important lessons before we apply for a commercial winery licence. Instead, I saw much of the crop vanish, admitted defeat, and picked the remaining grapes early, in the first few days of September. In the Pinot Noir I had achieved only about 18 Brix (or 18-per-cent sugar) in the berries. Usually I would prefer to wait for about 23 or 24 Brix, if we can keep the grapes on the vines that long before the balancing acids drop.

I had expected some problems with birds, particularly with the Pinot Noir. Birds – especially robins – zoom in on black berries. When I first noticed large numbers of ripe berries disappearing from one day to the next, I ordered rolls of bird-netting from Frensch's vineyard supply in Beamsville. I laid it over the rows of ripening fruit and expected my problem to end. It didn't. I was shocked. The fruit kept vanishing. As soon as berries hit 18 Brix, they'd be gone next day.

I didn't know what kind of super-intelligent birds I was dealing with – until I spoke with Phil Mathewson. When I mentioned the disappearing grapes, Phil asked me to describe the damage. I told him I was finding just bare stems when I checked each day. No ragged skins or punctured berries. Everything ripe was clean gone.

"Those are voles," he said nonchalantly. "They climb up, push all the fruit off, and roll the berries to a spot where they'll open them up for the seeds. You'll find a pile of skins and pulp someplace nearby," he added.

I did. The voles – short-tailed, plump grey meadow voles – were seeking out the ripe seeds to store for winter. At about 18 Brix the seeds have browned. These tubby, fairly slow-moving creatures were partying all night, pushing off berries and rolling them away *just for the pips*. The bird-netting made it even easier for them, because now they didn't have to worry about owls or other birds of prey.

Only after learning the truth from Phil did I read that low-trained vines are favourite targets of voles. In Burgundy, where the vines are also trained low to the ground, there are problems with the little rodents too. The trouble goes all the way back to ancient Rome, according to William Younger in his classic book, *Gods, Men and Wine*: "There was one great disadvantage in that type of low vineyard where the grapes lay on the ground for, as Varro says, 'the foxes often share the harvest with man in such vineyards, and if the land breeds mice the yield is cut short unless you fill the whole vineyard with traps, as they do in the island Pandateria.'" Overall, I knew the benefits in Hillier of lower vines far exceeded the problems, though when I looked at the bare stems it took great concentration to remember that.

It was too late to bait the voles that season, and the piles of seeds I left to lure them away didn't keep them from taking the grapes as well. Finally, these furry little thieves forced me to pick before everything was gone, otherwise I'd have no wine at all. Never again, I vowed.

As much as I am reluctant to poison the voles, I do have bait stations set up. I'm worried their corpses could poison other animals, however, so I've also put out large multiple live-capture traps. That, I hope, will solve the problem. Unless birds inflict a lot of damage this year, I'll try to leave the netting off, to allow birds of prey to swoop on the voles who get through the defences. If this doesn't work, I may find myself spending a lot of sleepless September nights protecting fruit from the little furballs.

Awaiting this year's harvest, a few other chores can be squeezed in during those tense four weeks. I was in Joe's, the small café in Hillier, with my work crew recently. Actually, it was just my father doing his annual gig as the human piledriver, putting in trellis posts. I made a bit of an ass of myself.

For the first few years I didn't have the courage to go in, because I felt like such an outsider. But I noticed that all the locals went in there. One cold day I rode my bike from the vineyard to the café and bravely went in for a cup of coffee and a plate of fries. There was only Joanne, who owns and runs the place, and me in there, and very little conversation. The work area behind the counter opens onto the house, and the dividing line is pretty informal. The place used to be an inn and tavern at some point in the past, and judging by the pavement outside I suspect even a gas station a generation or two after that.

Gradually I went in more and more, and relaxed. I brought in other winegrowers too, and pretty soon it was not merely the *only* place for a break in Hillier, it properly became *the* place. I've learned more from Joanne and others, conversing or just listening, than I could possibly have imagined. It's probably the only way, short of being raised here, to understand the place and its people.

Because Joe's is the centre of news and gossip, and provides the best breakfast in the County, soon everyone in Hillier will learn of my error.

My father, in from Toronto, asked Joanne if she had green tea. I jumped in, somewhat embarrassed my dad would ask for something so urban in Hillier, and tried to head off the request. Joanne just looked at me, and said, "Geoff, you never know what I might have." Then she smiled at my father and replied, "Yes, we do have green tea. I bought it for the house but didn't like it."

It's all just a diversion though. A state of war exists in the vineyard.

Stretches of metallic red and silver Mylar flash-tape, strung loosely down the vinerows to unnerve the enemy, undulate in the breeze. It's not exactly the Maginot Line, though it provides a similar feeling of reassurance. Overhead, like barrage balloons, bright yellow beach balls hover above the Pinot Noir, staring out with large red and black raptor eyes finished with shiny silver Mylar pupils. So much for those feathered Stukas and Messerschmitts known as robins.

The obstacles against the meadow vole Wehrmacht have been out for a few weeks: bait stations constructed of black plastic pipe fixed at strategic approaches to the soft underbellies of the waiting grape clusters. These PVC defences have been reinforced by galvanized-steel windup traps, positioned to mop up and detain any vole patrols that avoid the bait stations.

So far, it's a phony war. The black berries can be spotted at a great distance by the robins and other birds. The enemy is massed and waiting, all the different scenarios have been war-gamed endlessly, and there's nothing to do but fiddle until the other side attacks.

Apart from what they take themselves, the birds set off a whole chain of woes when they begin to strike. If they are kind enough to leave any fruit, what they do leave can be filthy and full of unpleasant surprises. Their droppings, loaded with dark grape juice and pips, cover the vines, including the fruit they haven't got to yet. In their exploratory peckings to see if the berries are to their specifications, they leave behind a seeping mess if they don't find them appealing. The exposed grape pulp then begins to rot, and the whole bunch can be lost if the damaged bits are not removed quickly. The same holes also draw in wasps and yellow jackets attracted to the sugars. Before you know it, a cluster with a few half-pecked grapes – broad-casting the allures of glucose and fructose – can be a writhing mass of humming yellow and black.

There are two other insects that are unwelcome in the vineyard right now. The consperse stinkbug didn't mean anything to me until last year. I saw these funny, shield-shaped bugs about the size of my thumbnail climbing on the grape clusters but didn't realize right away they were responsible for what I thought was particularly clumsy bird damage. Ragged flaps of skin would be left where the ripest berries had been the previous day. The stinkbugs puncture the berries, and because they usually choose the ripest ones, the sweet juice and pulp seeps out onto the rest of the cluster, making a sticky mess. Now I seek these insects out and crush them, leaving their remains nearby as a lesson to other stinkbugs.

The other hated insect at this time of year is the sphinx-moth caterpillar, which looks very similar to the familiar tomato hornworm. These fat, vivid-green pigs can defoliate a cane in just minutes. I noticed them first because I could hear them eating. The munching sound really threw me, as did the way this caterpillar reared up on its hind legs, squealed, and puked out green goo when questioned about its responsibility for the missing vine leaves. Even late in the season, losing leaves is a serious problem, because they are needed to keep producing the sugars to ripen the fruit and harden the wood off for winter. Too many lost leaves, and the vine could end up too weak to survive the cold months ahead. These creatures are brilliantly adapted to stripping canes, and can be found in two colours at this time of year – green and mahogany. The usual green for most of the season blends in with leaves and shoots, while the reddish brown assumed by late arrivals closely matches that of the mature canes. Like the stinkbugs, the caterpillars are quickly dispatched whenever spied, or overheard.

Apart from the birds and the voles and the bugs, another natural threat is getting to me right now. The rain. Prince Edward County is nearly always in drought when veraison hits in August. That is perfectly acceptable to a wine-grape grower, because mild water stress at this stage in the vines' season helps keep their attention on ripening and wooding up. Instead, we've had far too much rain for my liking. The ground is damp, and the vine tips are threatening to come alive again, diverting energy from clusters and the *aoûtement* of the canes. The fruit are also dangerously swollen.

When too swollen, the grape skins can split, sending out party invitations to rot and wasps. The usual fungal diseases that are quite under control in drier weather revive, and are in the mood to gate-crash. Now that we're into the last few weeks before harvest, the usual sprays of sulphur and Bordeaux mix can't be applied without adversely affecting wine quality. It's a tricky time, and all the gains made through the most perfect growing season can be undone; as the French say, September makes the vintage.

᪥

"There's a fair!"

"Yeah, there *is* a fair!"

Or so my two elder daughters squealed when the car pulled into the farm to pick me up. Their younger sister echoed their excitement. And I guess it does look like a fair. Bright yellow balloons hang over the Pinot Noir, and metallic red and silver tape flashes brilliantly in the sunlight. It all lends an undeniably festive air. Though mildly disappointed there *wasn't* a fair at their farm, they still seemed pleased with the idea that it looked an awful lot like one.

I have been tying together the sections of bird-netting that I have finally hauled out. The outer rows of the Pinot Noir have been picked pretty clean. If I am going to take complete advantage of the glorious ripening weather we've finally been enjoying and get the potentially excellent sugars and flavours out of the grapes, I have no other choice. The yellow scare-eye beach balls and the tape deterred the birds from trial maraudings, but now that the sugars were 18 Brix, the siren call of the berries overwhelms natural caution and fear.

Crows caterwaul to each other in the hedgerow as I work, telling their comrades to wait but a few minutes until I am gone. Cleverly out of sight, too. Following the string of calls down the trees, I finally spot one crow, sitting atop the highest maple. That is the only one I can see.

The next morning, I finish covering the Pinot Noir with the netting I purchased last year, along with more sections bought this fall to cover the new fruit-bearing rows. It's a nice, light black plastic mesh that doesn't break down in sunlight.

I have also bought my own affordable refractometer from Watson's Barrels & Winemaking Supplies in Niagara-on-the-Lake. It's not a toy. It's a fairly costly piece of equipment that's invaluable out in the vinerows right now. It looks like a small collapsed telescope, with a little hinged lid at the end opposite the eyepiece. By squeezing a drop or two of juice from a berry on a glass plate and closing the lid, a system of prisms and temperature compensation devices calibrate the sugar of the sample in degrees Brix. Looking in the eyepiece in the direction of the sun shows one the reading on the Brix scale. It's an amazing, easy-to-use tool. Last year, Phil Mathewson lent me his expensive, older, French model. This year it was definitely time to get my own, and, luckily, cheaper ones made in China are suddenly everywhere.

The refractometer is a good teaching aid. As in all things, constant repetition, in this case plucking, squeezing, tasting, and then looking at the reading, helps train the taste buds to recognize the sugar percentage. Most of the time I find I'm within a few tenths of a degree Brix. The next phase of tasting comes only with more experience: the ability to recognize whether the acid is in good balance with the sugars, and whether the skins and the grape taste "right." Even with good sugars, a grape can still taste green and underripe if it comes from a vine that is too vigorous and out of balance. That kind of judgement may take quite a few harvests to develop.

At this point the samples in the refractometer are reading 20 or 21 Brix, and the grapes ripen fast in the intense sunshine and 30 to 31 degrees Celsius heat we enjoy for a few key days after the rain. The nights drop quickly into the teens, which helps keep the grapes from losing too much acidity.

The voles have started to help themselves. Some ravaged and even undamaged clusters show the signs of nocturnal visits: mud on the berries. The cool nights have caused very heavy mists and dews to settle all around Hillier for the past few weeks. The moisture on the fruit turns the dirt on the fur and paws of the voles to mud as they clamber over them, and so each morning there are streaks of dry clay on the berries. It ruins that wonderful heavy grey-white waxy bloom on the blue-black Pinot Noir. And it's just plain annoying, like waking up to find graffiti tagged on your house or store.

Do I have the character to let our Pinot Noir hang for another week or so, to get the raw material I need to make the wine I *tell* people I want to make?

I debate that each morning when the weather turns wet once more. Grey days and steady drizzle from the remains of a hurricane have kept the ground and fruit sodden. So far the Pinot Noir is free of disease. Their thinner skins and tight clusters make Pinot susceptible to botrytis, or grey rot, which leads the disease parade now with the rains and the mists and heavy dews. Our grapes are healthy, the skins tough. Unfortunately, I'm not the only creature that has noticed.

Every night the ripest clusters, with berries around 21 to 23 Brix, disappear. Or they are obliterated, left nearly naked on the stems, with a paving of plucked but forgotten berries around the vine trunks. The voles mock me not only with what they take, but with what they leave carelessly strewn about.

That little detail is bothersome. The voles, it seems to me, have to work too hard to abandon fruit without taking the seeds. Also, some of the windup traps I put out to thin the population have been batted about, even after I weighted them with chunks of limestone.

I decide I'd better make a surprise night visit to the vineyard. What I find is a patrol of raccoons stalking the edges of the netting. One, an immensely fat creature, is leaning against the netting, helping himself to grapes from the outer row.

I scream and yell like a madman, and they slowly waddle to the hedgerow. I pull the netting away from the clusters where the giant raccoon has pushed in, and add more stones to anchor it. My heart sinks, and I know that the share taken by voles and birds is nothing compared to what I now recognize as the worst thieves.

The next night I come to spend all the hours until dawn guarding the fruit. I have a gun – an air rifle, because, after all, this is Canada, and I haven't done the paperwork that would allow me to own a shotgun or proper rifle. It will at least get their attention. And I have a few good clubs as backup.

These are some of the hardest hours I've put in among those rows. I patrol, then crouch down and wait for half an hour or so to set up an ambush. The cool evening temperature, so good at holding acidity in the ripening fruit, forces me every hour or so into a lawn chair to drain more of the tea and coffee I've brought, and to fume about wasting my time.

Not a single raccoon shows up.

When the darkness gradually begins to lift, I walk towards the car. The sound makes me jump: the fenceline is suddenly filled with clicking, the strange *tcchk-tcchk-tcchk* raccoons make. The damned things have been watching all night, waiting for me to leave so they could get down to work. I just shrug, and when I get to the car, my sense of defeat is complete. I've locked the keys inside. I'll have to wait another three hours before I can knock on the Van Lunes' door to use the phone.

I stop by to check things again, after some breakfast and a shower, and startle two raccoons at work. They turn, and without much haste make their way down the unnetted young rows, where they have been helping themselves to the odd cluster that wasn't worth protecting. The only signs of their displeasure are the purple turds of skins and seeds they leave, either to hasten their taunting, sauntering escape, or to let me know they didn't much enjoy being put off their schedule last night. I have the air rifle with me, but of course the tin of lead pellets is in the trunk. I peel to the car, but by the time I run back the raccoons are nowhere to be seen. I scream in frustration, and ping off a few shots into the trees like a fool.

There are only three things to do. The first is to ensure that next year I put up electric fencing around the perimeter. The second and third are to hope for a return to fashion of coonskin coats and a worldwide Davy Crockett revival. Roadkill for me is now one less mouth to feed. I have not hit a raccoon myself yet, but cheer whenever I spot the good civic work performed by another driver. The turkey vultures can have all they want.

◆

I'm still hoping I can improve on last year's harvest. The specific gravity of the must (grape juice) reads 1.082, or about 11 per cent total alcohol. (Refractometer readings at this point are not as accurate as floating a hydrometer in a sample of the must.) The heat of the summer means that more of the acids might have been saved in this first harvest. If all the grapes were at 22 to 23 Brix in the field, and they came in at once, the acids might be too low. Because Pinot Noir has thinner skin and less tannin than other red-wine grapes, it relies quite a bit more on acids to preserve it in bottle.

Just how to make wine out of Pinot Noir is one of the darkest circles of winemaking hell. There are countless theories and approaches, though everyone says they just try to do what the Burgundians do. The problem is there is no uniformity in Burgundy either. So the whole Pinot Noir debate is disorderly and loud and partisan, with accusations of betrayal and oafishness issuing from every corner of the world where the stuff is made.

Wading through the bewildering number of books and articles on Pinot Noir over the years, I've set upon an approach that seems to make the most sense, given both the characteristics of the grape and the track records of the best producers. As I pick the clusters, any damaged berries are removed, and only good and healthy grapes go into the picking buckets. Each picking is cooled for a few hours. Later I manually de-stem, though this will be the last vintage I'll do *that* without a machine. Gentle hand de-stemming provides unbroken berries, and to these I add a few selected whole clusters complete with mature stems for extra tannins and flavours. Keeping the berries and some clusters whole helps to release sugar slowly and stretch the fermentation out for a week or two. Then I put all into sterilized food-grade buckets before cooling them again to around 10 degrees Celsius. (The buckets will give way to stainless steel over the next year as more vines mature and bear fruit.) Some of the grapes are gently crushed, to get the sugar-rich juice out, and then samples are taken of the must and various tests are done for sugar and acid levels. Finally, I cover the buckets lightly with cloth or plastic to keep out fruit flies, and leave the must alone to gradually warm up and start bubbling.

Wine yeasts are a subject of earnest discussion that often ends in winemakers taking swings at each other. Most wines are made using commercially prepared, preserved wine yeasts, selected from wine regions around the world. Last year I used tiny amounts of some bought yeasts once fermentation had been going for a few days, hoping a "safer" strain would kill off any undesirable natural yeasts that might have been lurking in the must. This year I decided to let the first batch of Pinot Noir start on its own and allow it to ferment out to dryness without using a commercial yeast. It is an intensely debated strategy. It is risky, because there are different types of yeast (and, of course, bacteria), and not all of them are suited to helping the process of alcohol formation. Some can leave downright filthy tastes behind and completely ruin a batch. Yet getting different wild yeasts working both in succession and simultaneously often makes a much more complex and richer wine than can commercial yeasts.

Those who hold strongly to the notion of terroir are usually the ones allowing natural yeast fermentations. If the vines have been grown organically, the goal is not only healthy, balanced fruit, but a healthy, balanced microlife in the soil and all around the farm. The variety of yeasts spread about the world differs, and some believe that to give a true sense of terroir, native or wild yeasts should be harnessed with fruit from the same place. The argument rages as to whether certain terroirs naturally and consistently have better yeasts and so make better wines. Other growers counter that yeasts circle the globe in the upper atmospheres and can gradually establish themselves anywhere, even in new wine regions.

The last thing I do is make sure that, when fermentation is at its most furious, the temperature of the must is 30 to 33 degrees Celsius. For Pinot Noir, such a hot fermentation is necessary to get the riches of that special grape into the wine, although it also brings the risk of spiking above 33 degrees, killing the yeasts and having a "stuck" fermentation, or having too rapid and short a fermentation, and getting a thin, boring wine. All you can do is check on the temperature frequently when you punch the floating cap of berries and skins back down into the must.

As the first picking bubbles merrily, the raccoons and voles have plucked and rolled away about a third of the remaining Pinot Noir. I have to advance the second and third picking dates.

The second batch of Pinot Noir comes off after dinner on September 10, and the fading light means I don't see the yellow jacket under my left thumb. It stings me next to my pruning scar. Strangely, it is the first sting I've ever received in the vineyard. I'm sure it won't be the last.

I collapse in my determination to defend the remaining grapes until they hit 23 Brix. Incursions are so heavy the Friday and Saturday nights after the second picking that Lauren and I harvest the last 20 to 25 pounds Sunday morning. We bring the girls with us and allow them to snip off a cluster each. They then lose interest and excuse themselves to look for fossils. In the photos of the day, Lauren's smile as she works, peering through the canes, is as valuable to me as the wine we'll be making.

The second picking brought in just under 20 pounds, so I end up with about 80 pounds of ripe Pinot Noir, or about enough for two test cases of twelve 750-millilitre bottles. That dwarfs the four and a half bottles I emerged with last year. Next year, as more vines start to mature, I should get about 500 to 1,000 pounds, and with any luck continue to get at least double that every year.

Though I was hoping to get to at least 23 Brix for the last two pickings, to balance the lower sugar of the first harvest (though at 11 per cent natural alcohol, it wasn't too bad), what I do end up with isn't horrible. The second picking has a specific gravity reading of 1.089, or close to 12.5 per cent natural alcohol. The last lot is almost identical, coming in at 1.088. Not what I aimed for, which was about 13 per cent natural alcohol, but still a lot better than most years. The funny weather we've been having may have been for the best. The natural balancing acidities are good, and the grapes were extremely healthy. Only one or two clusters had any degeneration or rot on them, and these were easily cleaned up in the field before putting the berries into the baskets.

The first picking has nearly finished fermenting. The second batch has overtaken the first. It has ended its fermentation and started on four or five days of soaking, or maceration, to extract more colour and flavour. Then I'll press it all out to get the partially fermented juice trapped in the numerous whole berries, gently squeezing out the last 10 to 15 per cent of prime-quality must. It'll go into a glass carboy to finish, settle, and start the aging and clarifying process. The last batch is still in full bubble and foam. The cap of grape skins pushed to the top of the fermenter by carbon dioxide gets pushed back down every few hours, allowing the beautiful pink foam to rise to the surface. If you think of Breyers black cherry ice cream, you have an idea of the depth of colour. It looks delicious.

This time of year the scents of deep, rich black fruits and sweet yeasts quicken the blood and gladden the heart. It's the smell and sound of civilization, repeated for millennia around the world, happening right now in countless farms and villages and towns.

I like to reread one of Al Purdy's nearly forgotten poems, "Wine-Maker's Song," as it perfectly captures that awkward wait, as the grapes warm up, for the first tentative signs of fermentation. I've used a few lines on page 233 in Chapter Thirteen. The funny little "divulged secret" tucked in the lines – reading down from the "v" in divulge to the "in" directly below and spelling out "vin" – is a touch of brilliance.

With most of the grapes off, there is little to do but cut some weeds and tackle the powdery mildew that has taken advantage of the spray-free period leading up to harvest. My father-in-law and I folded up the bird-netting yesterday. Today it's time to take down the festive bird-scare balloons and roll up the flash-tape. Pinot Noir leaves are turning an eye-catching gold near the base of the canes. A slightly let-down feeling creeps in after spending weeks and weeks in furious work. Fall is here.

◦§

Although I've been obsessed with the grapes these past weeks, that doesn't mean that I've missed the other fruits of the season.

Tomatoes are the most coveted fruit of summer and early fall. When we first moved out here, almost everyone we spoke with would sigh at some point and say, "There's nothing like a County tomato." Unfortunately, until Lauren and I started to grow our own, we had no way of learning the truth; hardly anyone out here raises them to sell any more. Of course all tomatoes (and most vegetables and fruits), if they're eaten within a few miles of where they're grown, explode with flavour. But the limestone that gives a perfume and depth to our grapes also works its magic on tomatoes.

It was precisely this special quality that helped turn Prince Edward County into the garden of Canada for a period, from 1882, when the first canning factory opened in Wellington, until 1996, when the last factory in Ameliasburgh township closed. Across Station Road at the southern end of our farm are two large buildings that once housed the Hillier Preserving Company, and which now serve as chicken coops. Changes in the food industry pushed most County canneries to close down in the 1950s, but in 1941 this small island produced 1.5 million cases of tomatoes, or about 43 per cent of Canada's total. Peas, corn, pumpkins, raspberries, cherries, blueberries, even chickens, were just some of the products that flooded out of the County canneries. But by far the largest crop was tomatoes.

The can labels are colourful and often ornate and elegant, and those lucky enough to have them frame them like fine art. I've found a few myself, and wish I had more, especially those for damson plums such as Boulter's Lion Brand.

I discovered these great little plums taking Winona to the bus one late-September morning. There were tiny, exploded blue-black-skinned plums on the post-office parking lot where all the kids gathered to wait for the bus, projectiles the high-school boys had been whipping at each other. I followed the trail behind the post office, and found a few low trees heavy with these same fruit. The skin was thick and the pit rather large in relation to the thumb-sized plum. But the taste was a real delight, a hit of caramel, and then a mouth-filling bright plum and a good but not overly strong acidity.

Since then, when late September arrives, and after the girls are safely on the bus, I head behind the post office to grab a few handfuls, some to munch on for the walk back to the house, some for Lauren. I've also noticed a few more wild trees along the road just south of the library, and another at the start of Bay Street; if they have fruit, I'll add a few of those to my handful too. In the spring, I've learned that when they open their little white flowers it coincides with Pinot Noir bud-break.

These small, neglected plum trees are all that is left of a fruit unique to these parts. Giving evidence about plum-growing for the 1881 Royal Commission, the scribes noted:

In Prince Edward County, Mr. Dempsey has a local favourite of the same prolific qualities, and which he also calls a Damson. He says: –

"The Damson tree is thorny; is rather a slow grower and yet attains a great size. It frequently produces from four to five bushels to a tree. It is very easily cultivated. The curculio takes its share of the fruit, still the tree crops abundantly. It may almost be said to grow wild with us, and often grows in the fence corners. They are regularly harvested and marketed, and sell well in Montreal. When the tree is not overloaded it is a good dessert plum. The skin is perhaps a little thick, but not enough to make it objectionable. I don't know of these being cultivated in any other section of the country; I have noticed what were called Damsons, but they grow differently from ours. I am not able to say where it came from; it is peculiar to the county of Prince Edward."

I've managed to get permission to dig up a few of these neglected damson trees, and have planted them at our farm in the small orchard of apple, pear, and cherry trees I put in a few years ago. I'd hate to see them disappear, like the canneries.

❧

We're at the threshold of late fall in Prince Edward County. Lauren and I have for a few years now watched for our own signal of this seasonal change. It's not when all the leaves have come down, or when the first or even second killing frost hits. It's a County variation on the guessing game we use to play when we lived in Toronto near the Royal Ontario Museum. We took our cue not from the calendar but from the pair of ancient stone Chinese lions in the ROM's courtyard. Winter began whenever the lions were dutifully wrapped in plastic for protection against the weather. When that would be, we never quite knew. Spring, for us, returned only when the lions were uncovered. The date varied from year to year, subject to a more human and accurate gauge than a predetermined date on the Roman calendar.

When we fled to the County we found something similar. We now accept the inevitable approach of winter only when Mr. Palmer puts up the white storm door on the old Clapp house.

The house is the most-photographed building in Hillier. Built around 1841, this limestone building is one of the prettiest examples of the Regency cottage style: a single storey, with a hipped roof topped off with a monitor, or roofed skylight, running along the ridge. There are quite a few of these exotic farmhouses in the County; the style was very much favoured by the waves of half-pay British officers that washed into Upper Canada after the Napoleonic Wars. None of the County examples retain the bow-roofed and pillared porches that wrapped around most of the sides, which in old photos and drawings make Regency cottages look like little oriental temples or castles.

The Clapp house is unusual because, thanks to care taken by its owners, it still has its exquisitely panelled front door and delicate chinoiserie door lights with French doors on bays set symmetrically on either side. The French doors keep the house open to the porch and the scenery, and those who originally chose this style of building usually ensured they rose on sites with great views. Overlooking long narrow Consecon Lake, this one was no exception.

Doug Palmer was born in the Clapp house in 1922. His wife, Betty, joined him there in 1946 after they were married. Though their surname is an old one in the County, his people came from outside Madoc, moving in about seventy years after the house was built. Mr. Palmer farmed the small portion of arable land on the two hundred acres attached to the house, but now the land's been sold. With his close-cropped grey and black hair, Mr. Palmer looks a bit like an older Anthony Hopkins, accented with Drew Carey glasses perched on his head and a quick, almost giddy laugh. Both he and Betty were amused when I told them that my wife and I looked to the installation and removal of the storm door as the official mark of the seasons.

Mr. Palmer says the door comes or goes when he gets around to it. Same goes for the protective covers on the two French doors. No set date or time. Both he and Betty are determined to keep the French doors and the doorway as they should be, though everyone tells them to put something modern and better insulated in their place. Mrs. Palmer admits she's always much happier when the prettily latticed door lights are uncovered every spring. It removes the gloom and cold of winter.

Everything you say or do here has much more resonance than it would in a big city. Though you don't necessarily notice it, others are always aware of you and what you're up to. I've learned to adapt to that, and have adopted the same behaviour. I suspect Mr. and Mrs. Palmer will never again look at the coming and going of the storm door in quite the same utilitarian manner.

❧

In 1974 the famed British wine author Hugh Johnson wrote, "Wine is grape-juice. Every drop of liquid filling so many bottles has been drawn out of the ground by the roots of a vine. All these different drinks have at one time been sap in a stick." This time of year the term "stick" sort of echoes in my mind.

Out in the vineyard plots the vines are completely naked. Even the carpet of dead, fallen leaves has dispersed in the strong winds of the past few days. The season's vine canes are unadorned, forlorn, set amid a jagged mosaic of limestone that's been exposed by the fall rains. Though coloured a rich chocolate brown, they are, well, just sticks.

Loaded with carbohydrates but devoid of water, the canes are ready for the cold winter months. The long growing season this year has matured everything about as much as theoretically possible in Ontario. In other, gentler climates around the world, the leaves are probably still on the canes, though in their final golds and reds, hiding the brown canes in a blaze of colour. Last week I was out in Waupoos and noticed nearly full canopies on much of Ed Neuser's vines, gold and green in the morning rain. The microclimate along the Waupoos shore, combined with the heartier nature of his older rows of hybrid vines, like Vidal, Seyval Blanc, and De Chaunac, has kept the recent County frosts from killing all the leaves. I noticed that Ed's more tender vinifera vines, however, have shed their leaves like the others in the rest of Prince Edward.

While everyone wants to be out among the vines when they're green and everything is washed in the warm summer light, the late-fall and winter months are another matter. There is no romance in standing amid rows of sticks. Cold air, cold light, cold earth, it's easy to understand why. Only those who have no choice are to be found in vineyards this time of year.

I'm still cleaning up the plots, removing the larger weeds that have grown during the weeks since harvest and which threaten to go to seed and provide years of offspring if not plucked and carted away. I'm also marking out where the plots will expand next season, so that the ground can be ploughed and broken up by the winter frost before May planting. It's not joyless. Once vinegrowing has got under your skin, you seize upon any excuse to be out among the vines, no matter how stark or uninviting they are. The weak daylight gives up a treasure just before sunset: a rich diffusion of reds and golds spills over the barren ground, trees, and vines. It's strange, but a few minutes of that deeper, more sullen dusk can take the chill out of the previous hours of work – provided you get indoors before dark. Even the occasional sound of shots echoing in from hunters in the nearby bays helps give the late fall a not-unwelcome texture.

Walking up and down the rows, I find it much easier to see the health and balance of each vine this time of year. While they may appear to be just sticks, to a vinegrower they are invitations to more long hours of pruning next March or April. Some canes I have already chosen to retain and lay down to provide next year's crop; others are likely candidates for harvest in a few weeks' time, to serve as budwood for next year's new plantings; and the remainder will end up as compost or fuel.

I'm reminded why Deborah Paskus calls my vines "Picasso vines." To combat the damage of winter, I have pruned them all differently. Some are textbook examples of Guyot cane pruning, with small grey trunks eighteen inches above the ground, and symmetrical arm-bearing canes out to each side along the fruiting wire. Others show the other traditional French goblet shape. A contingent is arrayed like peacock tails. And not a few, yes, do look like a cubist painting of a vine.

Hugh Johnson also wrote three decades ago that, "the winegrower is a farmer, and a farmer learns patience by bitter experience. But one must not be too sorrowful. Can there be any more satisfying, natural way of life than tending vines and making wine?"

Even in the cold of November, I can tell you he's absolutely right.

and all I have is laughter
all I have is wine and laughter
and the spring came on forever
the spring comes on forever

• *Al Purdy, "Dark Landscape"*

Winter defines Canadians . . . or at least it does for the Americans, the people who matter most to our national self-esteem. The fringe of Americans living in the border states to the south of us, and the handful of listeners to the CBC Radio shows carried on American National Public Radio or Public Radio International, likely have a more realistic sense of Canada. But otherwise, to America – and through them the rest of the world – Canada equals winter.

It's an attitude with a history that predates the United States. In 1759, the year Quebec fell to the British, Voltaire made sure he got in an offhand dismissal of Canada, pointing out through his characters in *Candide* that Britain and France were "sont en guerre pour quelques arpents de neige vers le

Canada," at war for a few acres of snow. (Incidentally, a Québécois vineyard and winery near the town of Dunham took the name Les Arpents de Neige in the 1980s.) Voltaire's "acres of snow" is at least more poetic than the contemporary pirated Irish edition of *Candide* that renders the philosophe's dismissal as "a few acres of barren land in the neighborhood of Canada." If it's not one, it's the other. Or both.

Barren. Cold.

Those characteristics are forever displayed in our national flag, which, when it became official in 1965, gave heraldry a new term: a "Canadian pale argent," or a white square.

The fact of the Canadian winter has to be acknowledged – indeed, it could hardly be ignored – though of course the bitter Canadian winter is a cliché. Yet I'm really no different from any other Canadian, and I do take a guilty pleasure in our reputation. An example went out over the cold-climate viticultural e-mail list growwine@kawartha.com, run by the amusing and energetic Larry Patterson in Peterborough, Ontario. After a particularly bitter northern blast dropped temperatures in the northeast, one participant posted the following Official Canadian Temperature Conversion Chart.

50° Fahrenheit (10° C)
Californians shiver uncontrollably.
Canadians plant gardens.

35° Fahrenheit (1.6° C)
Italian cars won't start.
Canadians drive with the windows down.

32° Fahrenheit (0° C)
American water freezes.
Canadian water gets thicker.

0° Fahrenheit (-17.9° C)
New York City landlords finally turn on the heat.
Canadians have the last cookout of the season.

-60° Fahrenheit (-51° C)
Mt. St. Helens freezes.
Canadian Girl Guides sell cookies door-to-door.

-100° Fahrenheit (-73° C)
Santa Claus abandons the North Pole.
Canadians pull down their earflaps.

-173° Fahrenheit (-114° C)
Ethyl alcohol freezes.
Canadians get frustrated when they can't thaw the keg.

-460° Fahrenheit (-273° C)
Absolute zero; all atomic motion stops.
Canadians start saying, "cold, eh?"

-500° Fahrenheit (-295° C)
Hell freezes over.
The Toronto Maple Leafs win the Stanley Cup.

Canada's position as the world's dominant producer of icewine helps perpetuate the myth. The dependable dribble of international trophies, medals, and other gongs that icewine brings home bestows prestige and glory, but it is a wine that depends on nature to compensate for heavily over-cropped and under-flavoured grapes. Our cold winters concentrate the flavours (and sugars) by allowing most of the thin, watery grape to freeze and avoid the fermentation vat. The vast majority of our non-icewines don't enjoy the rigorous, frigid crop-thinning our winter provides, and until more of the regular Canadian wine crop is reduced and thinned and concentrated by uncompromising viticulture to produce better flavour, then the distinct qualitative difference between icewine and table wine will remain. Winter enforces the discipline most Canadian vineyards and wineries don't have.

I can't pretend, however, that the winter is anything but the defining aspect of viticulture in Prince Edward County. With the solstice, frost bites into our soil. It seems in no hurry to depart, so I've finally begun one of my defensive measures against the killing cold for the year: strawing. The vines get a covering of straw around the lower trunks for the rest of the winter. It may seem a little flimsy, but it works; on our thin, stony soil, it's about the only option I have left to keep the entire vine from dying.

In most wine regions in the northern hemisphere vine-growers plough up berms of earth over the graft unions and lower few inches of the vine trunks. Yes, even in France, though it's not very widely reported. Burgundy has been known to plummet to -27 degrees Celsius (most recently in 1985), killing thousands of precious vines on the Côte d'Or. But the temperature under just a few inches of soil rarely goes a degree or two below zero, so hilling protects the most vulnerable part of modern vines, the graft between rootstock and fruiting scion, as well as a little of the fruiting wood. If the canes and buds of the exposed vine wood get whacked by arctic temperatures, they can usually be retrained from this wood just above the graft, which safely slumbered under those few inches of soil. In the spring, when the frost is out, the berms are ploughed down again, exposing the vine to the sun.

While -27 degrees Celsius is no stranger in Burgundy, it usually comes down suddenly upon vines after temperatures have been hovering somewhere between zero and -8 degrees. This sudden, steep drop tends to be what kills vines and buds. Equally bad is a rapid dip during a stretch of warm, sunny days. In Prince Edward County, -27 is pretty much an annual occurrence, but it usually comes at the end of a gradual downward decline over a few weeks. It can be survived by vines that have been well hardened off, if they are protected to some degree. However, temperatures tumbling to -28 to -30 are much more unnerving. This is when the green tissues lurking under bark and bud scales of vitis vinifera absolutely give up the struggle. These killing temperatures seem to hit here every three to five years, and must never be ignored by County winegrowers.

Ploughing up earth against the vines is not easy in Hillier, but it can be done; some of the soils in Burgundy are as thin and stony as ours, and they do it. I worry about ploughing too deeply into the Hillier Clay Loam to raise the berms, fearing that in bad years the frost will bite deeper and kill too many vine roots. The stones in the soil can also nick or damage vine trunks, allowing disease into the wound, but as long as the hilling is done at a steady, slow speed, the rubble doesn't inflict much damage.

If the fall is long and wet, the rains can sometimes erode the soil berms before frost and snow arrive; that top dressing of straw can act as an umbrella. The straw, being light and hollow, is easy to work with, insulates with air spaces, and helps anchor falling or drifting snow for more insulation. In the spring it can be worked into the soil to provide some needed humus for the soil. Putting it on in winter is far more laborious than removing it in spring.

Straw doesn't insulate as well as soil does, and used alone it has a drawback: it can provide an alluring home for mice, which will then girdle the vines as they nibble the green cambium and bud tissue through the lean months. Laying down straw after a few good frosts usually avoids the problem, as the mice have made their winter nests elsewhere by then.

Soil berms or straw, or a combination of the two, are the primary preparations that must be made for winter. Keeping a vine low to the ground, with multiple spare parts available in case of unusually severe damage, and a modified pruning and training system are the other lessons I've learned through experience. Fortunately, the very choices I've made for the highest-quality fruit also reinforce winter hardiness.

While shallow soils and an adequate but absolutely fixed growing season dictated that I should encourage small, low-cropped vines, the same limitations and choices meant I would not only enjoy the ripest, most concentrated fruit possible, but also have vines that would ripen their wood sooner and have better stores of sugars and carbohydrates for winter survival.

Growing vinifera vines such as Pinot Noir or Chardonnay in the County means that winter absolutely has to be feared and respected; Niagara is usually warmer than the County by 8 to 10 degrees Celsius, and so growers there don't have to worry about their vines the same way. Neither region could grow grapes without the moderating effect of Lake Ontario, and the worst damage occurs in the rare years when the lake freezes over. Unfortunately, dozens of hopeful vineyard owners that have planted here in the last few years don't want to hear that, and all but a handful act like this is Australia or California and take no measures to protect against winter.

∻

On some of the more visible areas near the road in winter, neighbours sometimes see our car parked – or possibly stranded – by the road. If I'm spotted, I'm usually offered help. Lionel Weese, who runs a garage and towing service in Consecon, saw our poor vehicle abandoned on the shoulder and came back with his tow truck, thinking trouble had hit again, to find the car was gone. When I ran into him a few days later, I had to explain that I was only getting cuttings for rootstock. The week before, Carrie Taylor, Dan's wife, did a U-turn on Scoharie Road to see if I was stranded. No, I was just getting more riparia for spring grafting.

I harvest the rootstock canes first from our mothervines at the farm each year, then I start on different patches of wild riparia I've been selecting from for grafts and new mothervines. On the well-travelled highways it does tend to lead to an offer of help every few minutes; on the neglected lanes and back roads I'm left to myself to wade into snowdrifts, select, cut, and trim.

Finding riparia of a good diameter – about the thickness of a pencil – for easier and more successful grafting can be a challenge. But once I've started making cuttings at a certain spot, I find that future years provide nice sound canes due to the pruning the previous winter. Selecting the riparia that grows in drier, stonier areas has given me a good mix of rootstock. As each one is usually the product of a seed, either falling naturally from a cluster, or randomly deposited by an animal or bird, it's an advantage to use and collect as many different variants as I can, before the explosion of vineyards means the native riparia growing around the County becomes crossed with less hardy wine vines. Or before municipal workers clear it all from roadside fences and hedges.

Once a suitable quantity has been bagged and stored for grafting in March, there's no real viticultural reason to be outside, unless it's to check the snow depth in the vinerows, or inspect for damage after an unusual cold spell or temperature swing.

As winter settles upon our house in Consecon, there are the annual worries that mark the seasonal change. First, a small battle erupts with a few voles who somehow get into the house as the cold arrives and must be prevented from settling in. The ceiling over the kitchen needs watching with a practised and nervous eye, in case it unleashes a new cascade from shifting pipes in the shower, or, with dreadful fury and swiftness, the toilet. Once the frost is in, the ceiling is less of a worry, but any temperature below -23 degrees Celsius will freeze the hot- or cold-water pipes leading to the kitchen sink. The worst nights, the nights that really threaten the vines, all the pipes will freeze, though they've never burst. For a brief period around any sudden deep swing in temperature before the frost is established, the front door may shift out of alignment and make shutting and opening it difficult or, for a day or two, impossible.

From September to January, Lauren is engaged in planning and provisioning for a continuous string of birthdays and holiday celebrations. Every year in January she checks the papers for the date of the County's first baby of the year, and almost invariably it falls *after* January 5, the day Keziah was born, causing her to sulk a bit. Keziah lost the 1998 title to a preemie that spent just moments in the County before being rushed to Kingston. The winter slips by in little chunks, between birthdays, a handful of school snow days when the buses can't run, and furnace breakdowns.

❧

It just happened, swiftly and unexpectedly, on February 18. We were all staying over in Wellington with Lauren's parents for the night, and Lauren called for my help, with a sense of panic I'd never heard. Betty had collapsed at the top of the stairs into Lauren's arms. I helped Lauren move her to the floor in the doorway of Betty and Garn's bedroom, then hurried downstairs to tell Joanne and have her phone for help.

Within a few minutes there were members of the Wellington volunteer firefighters unit upstairs, and the girls were awakened by all the noise. I went in to reassure them and keep them calm. Joanne and Garn followed the ambulance; Lauren remained behind, telephoned her brothers and sisters in Toronto, and wept.

Betty had stumbled and slid down the stairs a few days before. She had hurt herself, but the doctors found nothing broken and she'd been recovering. Betty must have had a stroke after sitting in her chair for hours, an unforeseen tragedy set off by her understandable desire not to move if she didn't have to.

The girls went back to sleep very quickly, though when they awoke the next morning and learned that their grandmother had died overnight, they were inconsolable. Joanne and Garn were back from Picton in less than an hour. I then took

Lauren to the hospital, where we were shown into a small tiled room, and Lauren, the youngest of six, tried to say goodbye. A year or two before, Betty had started to attend the United Church in the village each Sunday when Lauren had agreed to go with her. The minister, Jeff de Jong, lived a few houses around the corner from Betty, Garn, and Joanne, and came by at considerate intervals over the next few days. Garn, a small, tough guy who'd seen the worst the twentieth century could do, and was appropriately skeptical about most things, approved of Jeff. One thing Garn wanted done right away was to have a thank-you letter sent to the fire department, whose members impressed him deeply that night. One of the volunteers was Simon Osborne, Ken Burford and Yvonne Millman's vineyard manager, though I didn't know that until a week or so after the service was held at the small funeral home in the village.

It is impossible to be anonymous in a small place like Wellington. Though Betty and Garn had been in the village only five years, that facet of village life made the weeks that followed easier than I would ever have expected.

✌

The four months since regular vineyard chores ended have not been idle. It's been a time to catch up on all manner of study related to winegrowing. Drinking and reading. Sometimes winegrowing in winter seems a lot like being a perpetual university undergrad. Perhaps, given the moments of quiet despair, a never-ending master's program would be a better comparison.

In the case of drinking, fall and winter are times to build up a neglected cellar and try an array of different wines from all over, dissecting them in a gentle manner, to learn more about advances, approaches, glories, and failings from other regions. It's not always easy. Yesterday I happened to reread the Ontario entry in Oz Clarke's *Encyclopedia of Wine*: "As for quality – well, individual wineries are good, but Canada's highly controlled system of selling wine means that only the most determined and cosmopolitan growers have any clear idea of what the rest of the world is up to."

The prices of my favourite Rhône wines have jumped absurdly in the last few years, so I can rarely acquire new bottles of Hermitage, Cornas, or Gigondas for tasting or cellaring any more. The price for St. Julien's from Bordeaux mock me most cruelly – often going for three or four times the price of a good, sound Rhône wine. So instead I try to focus, as a Pinot Noir grower, on all the different world takes on this grape offered by the LCBO Vintages and Classics catalogues. About half the time I fail to get even a single bottle of these. The lottery system for the Classics catalogue offerings has failed me utterly: the last few orders I made were unfilled, as the stocks were exhausted before my order form was randomly selected.

The Classics winter supplement deadline passed recently; I don't know if I was lucky enough to secure a bottle of any of the Burgundys that seemed worth trying. Maybe this time.

It is much easier to get the books needed to fill the other part of winegrower's winter. I've been reading and note-taking on a wide range of subjects. Lately it has been weeds, and plants on an esoteric level.

Identifying weeds is fairly straightforward: in a vineyard, they are the plants that aren't grapevines. Beyond that, however, it gets complicated. What to do with them? Are they all evil, and to be marked for extermination? Do they have a function? Do the different weeds growing have anything to teach us? The first question I'm still working on, though I'm definitely leaning towards regular cultivation and soil-fertility management as the solutions. These are refinements on my previous decision not to use herbicides. The other questions I'd firmly answer with "no, yes, and yes."

My ideas about plants are changing as I read more and more books like *Weeds: Control Without Poisons* by Charles Walters, and *Culture and Horticulture: A Philosophy of Gardening* by Wolf D. Storl. Since arriving here, I've gradually learned to observe and pay attention to plants. After trying an array of different vines in 1995 and 1996, I decided to concentrate on Pinot Noir when I saw how happy these vines were, and how well they were doing. The Pinot Noir seemed to be at home in our soil and climate in a way the others weren't.

Andrew Jefford had an interesting little passage in *The New France* about grapevines that I believe is appropriate:

The vine is scholar among plants. It records everything. In the middle of a windless January night, it outfaces the cold stars. The flowers that will create the following summer's fruit already lie in its tightly clenched buds at that moment of ice and silence. Something is happening; something is noted. The vine grips its stones in an equinoctial gale as the sodden, ash-grey clouds race across the sky on a dark March afternoon. This is different from an unseasonably warm bright March afternoon; the vine will inscribe both on its fruit. It is there, recording, for the dewy hour before dawn on a limpid June day, and in the fierce heat of a white August noon. The grapevine, *seule dans le règne végétal* as Colette puts it, has the ability to lend those annual records a sensual print. It does this by making grapes, which become wine.

In my studies I've been finding references to a Sir Jagadis Chunder Bose, an Indian scientist, now largely ignored, who did a lot of work with plants at the dawn of the twentieth century, and who discovered stimulus responses that are puzzling, if not astounding. Plants may not be the uncommunicative piles of cells we think. I've located a few of his old books, and intend to read more of his studies, especially since recent research by the U.S. Department of Agriculture has discovered that plants do call *specific* predatory insects by unique chemical and ultraviolet signals when under attack by other insects.

It's hard to admit that my old understanding of plants may be overly simple, if not in error. Yet I hesitate to discuss it, haunted by an old *Private Eye* cartoon published around the time when British newspapers learned that the Prince of Wales talked to plants. I think it was done by the late Willie Rushton. In the cartoon, Prince Charles leans over a row of flowers, asking one, "And how long have you been a tulip?"

a pile of moss covered stones
gathered for some ghost purpose

• *Al Purdy, "The Country North of Belleville"*

M ost days I ride my bike the five miles to our farm, and
then return home to Consecon as the sun disappears . . .
or, to Lauren's mind, a black, tense half-hour after a sensible
person travelling by bike should have returned. I've not been
able to save enough money for an old farm truck, so the bike
is necessary to get back and forth. Yet it's also a choice. If I do
squirrel away enough for a truck, it'd be hard to give up the
old routine.

I fill up a stainless-steel Thermos with cold water as well as
the plastic jug I'll drink from first, saving the cold water from
the Thermos for the last drinks of the day. Then I grab the
sandwiches and fruit I've put together and tuck them into the
blue shoulder bag I received for doing the census a few years
ago. I keep all the odds and ends I need in this bag – work

gloves, a few pairs of pruning secateurs, a box of grotty band-ages, solar radio, twine, and all the accumulated bits and tools I always forget to sort out to lighten the load.

I say goodbye to Lauren and the girls, pull my old CCM bike from the shed, and head off. A strong city model, the bike has full fenders. I learned long ago that getting mud and rainwater flung in the face and splattered up the back was a ridiculous price to pay for using a bike. In the country, though the heavy steel frame seems heavier at the end of a day's work, those fenders are great. In a steady rain there's no avoiding being soaked to the skin, but in a light rain, or heading off after a downpour, the fenders keep me dry. And less grumpy.

A few dozen yards from the house I turn onto Mill Street, and then cross the bridge over the slowing flow of the Consecon River.

As usual, the heron is standing on the rock shelf below the millpond dam, waiting for whatever frogs or minnows will pass within its reach. For the last week the great bird has been there as I cross the bridge in the morning; each evening, if I am back just as the light starts to fade, it's still there. Waiting. If a heron can put in a ten- or eleven-hour day, then I certainly can. Just before I return to the house, I'll see it, winging low, emerge from the mouth of the creek, gain a bit of height, and slowly arc towards the northeast, to one of the many heronries in Ameliasburgh. It's one of those natural timepieces out here, as telling to me now as any village bell.

(The bells of many villages like Consecon and Wellington can still be found, but they stand at ground level, preserved like stuffed animals, encased in small shrines of brick with their clappers gone. Most of these neutered examples were rescued from the last one-room stone schools closed down in the 1960s.

Now silent, all that speaks for them are the raised letters on the shell telling of the American, English, or Scottish foundry that cast them so many years ago, or those on the plaque announcing the final year of the school.)

Pedalling along the Scoharie Road south of Consecon Lake, up and down the two small vales along the road, I'm resigned to the day's work. The vines have no real need for me at the moment. They sit content, getting ready to show the signs of ripening: the yellowing, then browning of the cane, and the change of berry colour. The leaves, shoots, and fruit are still green; other than taking a quick walk through the rows to check for the first signs of colour change and note the health of the leaves and the types of insects around, I've nothing pressing to do.

And so it's time for rock moving.

I've been moving rocks since I first saw this property. Tentatively at first, here and there . . . and months later with a steady, sweaty determination.

While the farm was on the market and we wondered if we could afford it, I was picking up pieces, looking at them and smiling, enjoying the rough, angular chunks of limestone, thrilled that this was exactly what I was looking for. I started pocketing fossils of the creatures wiped out 350 million years ago in the great Ordovician extinction. Then I grabbed pieces of quartz and granite of nearly every hue abandoned by the glaciers that scoured the earth to expose this ancient rock. I still pick and pocket. And I've seen Deborah Paskus and even neighbouring bachelor farmer Ron Alexander do the same on our farm – something always catches the eye, and brings out the magpie.

Those are the fun rocks. Once Lauren and I had closed the deal, working the serious larger stones and cobbles took over.

The baseball- to softball-sized granite cobbles were collected in buckets, and in solitude I heaved countless pairs of full pails (to keep balanced while staggering over the fields) to our first plot of test vines, placing them carefully between the plants. They'd radiate heat to help the vines grow and ripen, and keep the moisture from baking out too quickly on the shallow knoll top I had planted on. They'd also aid in creating a landscape that evoked the stony vineyards around Châteauneuf-du-Pape in the Southern Rhône of France. Those driving by on Station Road who saw me gathering the cobbles would have thought nothing of it, as rock-picking is an unending part of working County fields. But no one saw me dump the contents *into* the vineyard plot, or if they did, they kept their laughter to themselves.

As well as the colourful cobbles, dog-sized granite boulders here and there would ride like icebergs, with just a tip above soil level. After vainly trying to coax out what appeared to be a cobble, I'd have to fetch a spade and pry bar and excavate what the locals call hardheads. They couldn't be left there, where one day they'd cease lurking and shatter or shear farm machinery. If you find them, you have to move them. All through Hillier the snake-rail fencerows, now mostly over-grown by trees and brush, are studded with hardheads, moved with tremendous efforts of animal, man, and machine. Some farms have nearly two hundred years of accumulated boulders. The oldest ones are now half buried again in moss and earth, stained dark by decades of leaf mould and chokecherry bird droppings, while the youngest – deposited by a front-end loader – sit in packs, gleaming with the light of a bleached-bone grey.

I had noticed long ago that most of the big hunks of lime-stone that had lain, or still lay, all over the fields usually had two or more flat, level sides, and were good candidates for building. These large field stones, thrown up to the surface every year, migrated from the bedrock through only a foot or two of soil, and were strong pieces. They had acquired their shape and held it through uncountable frosts and collisions with ploughs and other agricultural equipment, and so showed character and integrity. Another, rarer type of limestone chunk found here and there was like puff pastry, with lots of thin layers. This kind was useless for building. Often it could be shattered into smaller rubble; most of the powerful farm tractors pulverize this type of limestone, and only the most inconvenient sizes have to be removed to the fenceline piles.

In Ontario's geography and geology books of the 1940s and 1950s it's called Black River or Trenton limestone. Now it's been reclassified as the Lindsay formation of the Ordovician period, and has lost those local earlier names. It's not a majestic limestone, like the bright whitish grey of Kingston rock, nor does it have the creamier tones and even textures of Indiana limestone, often used in architectural carving. The Lindsay stone is rather thin, a few inches thick, maybe as much as six or seven in the really good courses. The weathered fieldstones can be off-white and stained with a bit of tan from the soil, but fresh stones, or those recently split, are a persistent blue-grey.

The limestone is referred to by geologists as bioclastic, meaning that it has fossils in it rather than being a uniform chemical form precipitated and created from the drippings of other, older limestones.

The other night, at dinner with Mary Jane Mcdowell and Kevin Howlan on Huyck's Point Road, something caught my eye. It wasn't the display of antique iron trivets on the wall above the couch (though I did notice that too). In their living room was a table arrayed with fossils collected on their walks along the water. There were some amazing examples of arthropods – trilobites the size of my fist, perfectly frozen in rock. I've seen fragments of these creatures on our farm, but these were some of the best examples I'd ever seen. Some of the molluscs may have looked a bit naughty, and a few of the whelks looked like, well, grey stone turds, but it's a nice collection. Lauren said no one other than I would have gravitated to it. She's probably right.

But the limestone rubble and the layers below that are so quick to breach the thin soil are vital to defining what this place is. They matter to me. They are invaluable to the vines. Rereading sections of Matt Kramer's book *Making Sense of Burgundy*, I noted a page I had dog-eared a few years ago:

> In the same way that Eskimos distinguish various types of snow, the Burgundians are connoisseurs of rocks. They've got names for all sizes, shapes, and types of rocks that they have laboriously hauled out of their vineyards. Les Lavières is named after one of these species of rocks, a flat, broad piece of stone called a lave. The larger sizes became tombstones; the smaller ones were used as roofing tiles. (The largest roof still using laves in France is the forbidding fourteenth-century Château de Rully in the Côte Chalonnaise, which was reroofed not long ago.) Anyway, Les Lavières had plenty of these rocks.

Burgundians do have quite an array of names for their rocks. There are other stone-specific vineyards such as Perrières in Meursault, and Les Cailles, in Nuits-St-Georges. *Perrières* comes from *Pierre*, or Peter, meaning, "rock." *Cailles* is yet another variation on *caillou rond*, or pebble.

In *Terroir*, one of the few English-language books about the vines, soils, and rocks of France, James E. Wilson writes: "Several of the hyphenated names of Grand Crus reflect soil conditions as they were observed in the early days: 'Latricières' means shallow soil covering a very hard substratum; 'Griotte' may have meant pebbly terrains, but some think it refers to the wild cherry; 'Charmes' may stem from *chaume*, meaning fallow land, or it may be just what it sounds like; 'Ruchottes' may be derived from *roichot*, an area where there are rocks. Even today, the topsoil of Ruchottes is thin and the subsoil shallow and pebbly. For those who hold that thin, stony soils make good vineyards, Chambertin is your perfect model."

Our plain-spoken Upper Canadian tradition has no flair for naming rocks. Yes, there are the hardheads, as I've mentioned. But for the different types of limestone, we've got nothing. Hillier Clay Loam was long known locally as either clay gravel or gravel clay, depending on how thick the mix of stone was. Practical. Simple.

In buildings, our limestone never has the size and perfect dressed squareness of the quarried Kingston "prisoner marble." But there are buildings such as St. George's Anglican Church in Trenton, or on the exposed interior walls of the Urban Herb restaurant in Belleville, where the masons have elegantly pieced together strong and beautiful walls that appeal to me just as deeply as the huge squared blocks of Kingston's old downtown buildings, or those of Queen's University, or the city's large Martello towers, or the walls of Fort Henry.

I'm sure the masons would rather have worked with limestone from Kingston than the thin stones with which they coursed and raised their rubble walls. In some of the better stone houses, you see that they did get hold of some Kingston limestone, reserving their use for cornerstones and lintels. In some walls, the impatience or incompetence shows. But as I've said, with others the deft mix of lightness and security makes for a pleasant change from the massive, blocky power of the buildings to be found in that wealthier part of Upper Canada to the east of us.

The village of Hillier, at the base of Station Road, once had four substantial limestone buildings. Of these, only the large but plain Hillier Hall remains. The limestone school was eventually pulled down in 1912; the two-floor blacksmith shop by the bridge burned down in the nineteenth century, and was replaced by the wooden shop still standing; the Orange Hall and shop across the road from Hillier Hall and the blacksmith's was destroyed about thirty years ago. Edith Taylor Ashton, who wrote the history of the village, lamented when I asked after its fate that the stone was crushed and was used as surface gravel on Station Road, a waste that still gets her mad.

While there are maybe a dozen stone buildings still in use around the old township of Hillier, in the hamlet centre, apart from the town hall, the only other limestone structure is a small smokehouse that sits next to a tiny Quaker house we bought above the creek. John Cardinell, the stonemason for the village, lived in the house in the middle of the nineteenth century. So, with the demise of the blacksmith shop, the Orange Hall, and the oldest of the schools (there were a few built on the same site over time), only the smokehouse remains to show Cardinell's professional hand. Two Irish brothers named McComb took over as stonemasons, and got the contract for the town hall.

I do like owning the small house that was home to Cardinell and his family, along with his old smokehouse, all sited nicely on the height where the old sawmill dam used to cut across the creek. It creates a connection to my own stone gathering and plans for building. Lately I found out that one of my great-grandfathers was a stonemason; that's not much either, but I like that connection too.

I began piles of good, strong limestone for building at certain areas of the farm, ready for the structures I planned to raise. The piles have grown large, and are all that exist so far of the intended house and outbuildings.

Today the piles will get a little bigger.

When I start to work, piling rock in loose cairns in the fields so I can load them later into the wheelbarrow, I inevitably think about related conversations and stories. Whenever I have to dig and pry a piece out of the ground, one comes to mind right away.

Don Akenson, gentleman farmer, Queen's history professor, and friend to the east in Gananoque, was quite worried when I first told him of my plans to build a stone house – by myself, if need be – out of fieldstone from our land.

"Sounds like *The Emigrants*. You ever see that?" Don asked after dinner not long after we purchased our farm. "Von Sydow was appropriately moody in it. You might want to have a look. I don't think you should work alone."

I told him I hadn't seen the film. He fetched an old paperback edition of the original Vilhelm Moberg book off one of his many laden shelves in his farmhouse.

After a few pages, I hit what he was alluding to.

Then, one day in the early spring of 1844, Nils Jakob's son was alone in an outlying glade, breaking new land. Here he encountered a stone which caused him much trouble. It was smaller than many a one he had removed alone, but it lay deep in the earth and was round as a globe so that neither bar nor lever got hold of it. Nils used all his tricks and soon the stone was halfway up. He now wedged it with the iron bar, intending to roll it away with his hands, but as he bent down to get a good hold for the final battle the earth slid away from under his foot and he fell on his face. In the fall he moved the iron bar that held the stone, which rolled back into its hole – over one of his thighs.

The happiness quotient stays about the same for the rest of the novel. I haven't got around to reading the others in the series. Don, whose people are Minnesota Swedes, enjoys, or at least can quietly coexist with, these kinds of truths about human life. They scare the hell out of Lauren though.

Moberg's vignette was added to the Gallic example of *Jean de Florette*, the Gérard Depardieu film based on Marcel Pagnol's novel. This one really bothered Lauren, or so she eventually told me.

Depardieu plays a city-bred hunchback whose idealism and theoretically perfect farming plans – based on great research and reading – are defeated by jealous and unfriendly neighbours who covet his land and his natural water source. For a long time I thought that the rocky, parched landscape and the poverty in the film sat uneasily with Lauren, reminding her of our farm. Or that she feared my repeating the hunchback's terrible end, struck down by stone falling from a dynamite blast he sets off in a desperate attempt to find the missing spring that the maps told him was on his land (and, unknown to him, was plugged with cement by his neighbours). I promised I would never play with dynamite. But it wasn't the stone, or the drought, or the idealism and stacks of technical books that worried Lauren. It was the reaction of the neighbours to outsiders. Or so I thought. Now, years later, she corrects me. It wasn't Jean de Florette's conspiring neighbours that bothered her. It was that fate could mock and destroy him, even though he did everything right and deserved to succeed. That he didn't know when to give up didn't encourage her either.

Any fears about our neighbours have been groundless. We were cautiously left alone for the first year or two, but now every few days someone stops by to visit and have a look at the vines. Starting a new stone pile of last winter's frost heaves, I look up whenever I hear a car or truck going up or down Station Road. It's too early to hope for the distraction of a visitor, but one likes to track who's coming or going – Mike Heuving, who owns the vast chicken barns across the road; a County public-works truck headed to the yard in the hamlet; an unknown pickup truck slowing down to have a look. I haven't yet resorted to the tactic of Jacques Reynaud, a legendary wine grower in Châteauneuf-du-Pape: when he saw or heard someone coming, he was known to throw himself flat in a ditch until the person gave up the search and went away. Sometimes, when there's a lot of work to do and I feel hopelessly behind, I've been tempted to lie down in the vinerows until the visitors gave up. Just tempted, though.

Musing over this, I find I've assembled three or four small piles of decent building stones. I go off to fetch the ancient, rusting, but solid construction-grade wheelbarrow I got from

Lauren's father. Piling and loading the stone into the barrow mainly tires the shoulders and upper arms, and not heavily. Propelling the fully loaded barrow up the mild slope, aiming for one of the larger piles of stone a few hundred yards away, is actually the wearing part of the day. Around the fourth or fifth load, I bark my shins trying to get the load up to a comfortable cruising speed. The undercarriage of the heavy steel barrow is all too solid in its cross-bracing. A few inches too far forward in transferring the momentum of my legs into the barrow inevitably slams my tibia into the cross-brace, and the intense shock of taking a metal blow to the sharp edge of the shin is sobering. Being broken on the rack in New France meant that the *borreau*, or executioner, would take a metal bar and smash it into the long bones of the party being tortured. The first time I mangled my shin this way, I had an entirely new understanding of why this was a feared punishment, and that victims who were pitied or admired by the *borreau* were first strangled before the rod was brought down.

Working with rock certainly increases one's awareness of history.

⁓

Out of water, and nearly out of light, I turn the wheelbarrow upside down over the last pile of stones I've unloaded. I walk back to pick up my shoulder bag, put my sweaty work gloves back in, check the Thermos for a final drop or two of water, and then put it away too. I walk back to the fenceline where I've left my bike.

It's only on foot or on bike that one really notices the smells of the countryside. Entombed in a car, whipping by at

110 kilometres per hour, one gets whiffs of the area if the windows are open a crack, but at that speed only the most aggressive odours register: dead skunk, manure piles, a recently harvested pea field with the sour, sick aroma of the rotting shells and vines disgorged by mechanical pea-viners. Very occasionally beautiful smells will penetrate the confines of an enclosed vehicle: the faint, wafting perfume of lilacs in late May or early June, or new-mown hay some weeks later, but usually just hints, and only at speeds closer to 60 kilometres an hour, a speed most people find maddingly slow.

Riding my bike up the slow series of rises on Station Road, north from our farm to the paved Scoharie Road, I start thinking on all of this when I am hit by the smell of fermenting clover in the round bales of hay sitting on our fields. They were baled wet, I guess, our tenant unsuccessfully trying to beat one of the rains. All day I could smell the fresh, newly cut hay drying on the fields across from ours. The failing light in our woods sets off the dazzling flicker of fireflies, more this year than I've ever seen. In the dusk, the hayfields awaiting harvest are spectacular, the grass heads gently rolling in the breeze, with thousands of little lights as far as one can see.

The narrow old back roads in most of Hillier have trees reaching over them like soaring cathedral ceilings. Bats flitter drunkenly, scooping up mosquitos. I can smell the damp of the swamp woods, and feel the temperature dip a few degrees passing along one of the odd ninety-degree turns on Station Road. As I climb the hill to the Goodmurphys' farms, I get hit with the stench of death: a farm cat is rotting on the roadside, and I gasp and hold my breath for a few yards.

Near the Goodmurphys – father on the west side of Station Road, the son on the east – there's a wild apple tree that broadcasts smells of the changing seasons. In spring this section of the road gently gives off apple blossom. I don't notice it again until fall, when gradually, with increasing strength, the smell of fresh, ripe apples fills the air. As the windfalls accumulate, the fruit smell harshens, and then suddenly the rotting fruit unleashes the not-unpleasant pungency of apple vinegar.

At Station and Scoharie Roads I leave the gravel surface, which sits somewhat uneasily in places atop the logs of the old corduroy road, and turn onto the paved County highway. It is Friday, and that has a special danger, as tourists and weekenders are thick on the road, whipping by at insane speeds, passing two and three vehicles at a time to get to their destinations. On a bike, I'm treated as irrelevant, an oddity with my wavering dynamo lights, with no right to be on a modern highway.

Sometimes an old house
holds me watching, still,
with no idea of time,
waiting for the grey shape
to reassemble in my mind,
and I carry it away

• *Al Purdy, "Winter Walking"*

J ay Stuller wrote almost fifteen years ago in *The Journal of Gastronomy* that "no corn cannery ever used its plant in promotions, but winery architecture has become a marketing tool, luring visitors and projecting the image of European châteaus. In recent years, it has been suggested that several upstart Napa Valley wineries are more façade than true wine-making businesses – even that architecture comes first and enology later. According to Nathan Good, a Napa Valley architect who is researching a doctoral thesis on winery archi-tecture and its role in marketing, many vintners consider a winery's look one of its strongest selling points. 'Robert Mondavi's bell tower is his winery's signature,' says Good. 'He told me it was important, in that it showed a commitment to making great wine.' It's also clearly great for business. Since opening in August 1989, Tattinger's Domaine Carneros, a château overlooking the Napa Valley, has drawn visitors perhaps as compellingly as its wine."

In the 1990s a reaction seemed to set in. And it arose in, of all places, France. Garage wines arrived. The *garagistes* produced minuscule amounts of wine that turned the heads of critics, and caused a stampede of wealthy consumers wanting the praise of their neighbours and acquaintances for being clever enough to secure a rare bottle or two. For every Clos Pegasse that emerged from the collective egos of architect and owner in California, there seemed to be a counterweight, people who literally made their wine in a garage or basement, putting the money into fruit quality and careful husbandry rather than glass and stone.

But for the most part, North America still envies the moneyed wine estates of the Old World. We burn to emulate the monuments left by successive waves of France's nouveau riche ranks – the claret-growing legalists of the Bordeaux *parlement*; Bourbon court officials who made a killing cooking the books; Bonapartist flunkies; the later corrupt generation of Parisian bankers and businessmen.

The châteaux of Bordeaux, especially those who made the Classement of 1855, are hard not to covet. Nor are the great nineteenth-century Champagne palaces of Epernay and Reims. To a lesser extent the grand church residences and building complexes of Burgundy help fuel the burn to compete, but more likely it's the rural palazzos of Italy and the castles of Germany. Apart from some remarkable buildings here and there, however, most winegrowers and wineries lurk in small, sometimes storied, sometimes charmless buildings no different from what is considered the norm for their area. Even in Burgundy, it's the actual vineyard holdings and the very limited quantities of wine they produce – and the insatiable market willing to pay for that exclusiveness – that perpetuates the fantasy more than the buildings themselves, which are modest and honest and made to fit the landscape.

You'd think that those who make such a marketing point of the particular place on earth their product came from would have a better appreciation of their surroundings.

The bigger wineries, or those with ambitions of making it big, the ones that market and position and price their wine as luxury products rather than as foods and joys and necessities of a good human life, really are the worst offenders. They gleefully throw up "signature" premises of alien materials and scale that violate the very qualities – the natural setting and compact with the land – they tout in their literature. Wine is often *the* prime agricultural product of an area, and once appreciated and noted, can greatly raise the value and variety and reputation of other foods grown in the region, as people naturally expect winemakers also to value and celebrate the table. But this benefit often comes at a great cost, as wine operations feel they must make a celebratory marketing statement about the quality and price point of the wine, rather than about the land that gives birth to it.

A step down in the pecking order, massive beverage operations that depend more on volume than on quality or perceived quality become industrial wine factories and theme parks. They must have the restaurants and other facilities of one-stop lifestyle destinations rather than places that merely make good, unique wine. The Niagara region of Ontario, for example, has taken this to dangerous extremes. Every winery in Niagara feels it must offer a spa, restaurant, helicopter landing pad, banqueting space, special-events schedule, and endless jazz concerts to compete with its neighbours. Agricultural land is being devoured by the very industry that may have saved depressed, declining agricultural regions. In California, they have the sense to keep restaurants and other services in the towns and small cities, where water and sewage systems are available; in Niagara, the industrial and entertainment complexes arise on unserviced agricultural land, eat up the acres, and require large septic systems and copious amounts of well water, sowing dissent through the local communities.

I fear that the disease will spread to Prince Edward County. So far it hasn't happened. Most of the first wineries here, small in scale and family-run, have refitted older farm buildings or have tried to build in a manner that works with the existing scale and composition of the County. I don't believe it's just parsimony and a desire to keep loans to a manageable level; I see growers who recognize the gifts they have here.

One of the priceless (and so, to the modern mind, uneconomic) components of this County's great beauty and profound, easy "somewhereness" is the store of buildings that can be found here.

Prince Edward County is a treasure chest often barely visible under the sands of cheap siding, sad vinyl window frames, and cold aluminum screen doors. If you can undress a house whose proportions and location whisper of great age, you may be looking at one of countless examples of tarnished and forgotten gems. Some do recognize their value, and restore and revive them to what they should be. But many do not. It's often too much of an imaginative, aesthetic leap for this tasteless age.

Just west of Wellington, along the only stretch of the Loyalist Parkway with a view of Lake Ontario, and the glorious vista of Sandbanks in the distance, two signs went up not long ago. With their grape cluster and clinking wine glassware motif, they read: "Vintage Shores. An enclave of 12 architecturally controlled estate residential waterfront lots. Size 2 to 5.5 acres, $120,000 to $160,000." One of the signs had been set up right across from the driveway to Richard Johnston and Vida Zalnieriunas's lovely farm, vineyard, and new By Chadsey's Cairn Winery on the north side of the Parkway.

It's brazen and delightfully presumptuous. The first wines have barely been released, but the developers are well out of the starting blocks and taking the first curve. It's not yet as bleak as the Niagara Peninsula, where new housing developments for urban empty-nesters who want to live in "wine country" devour fruit-growing land at a depressing rate. Celebrated Inniskillin co-founder Don Ziraldo is now calling for a Niagara agricultural-reserve act (as found in California) to preserve what does remain of the fruit land. Yet I wonder about the conflict wineries face. I've seen one recent development advertised in some Canadian wine publications and in the *Globe and Mail*: new houses, with the models named after different Niagara wineries, like the Reif house, or the Konzelmann.

The pressure for development is not quite the same in Prince Edward, given the stagnant economies of Trenton and Belleville, our remoteness, and the lack of water, sewage, gas, and cable across most of the County. However, it is slowly coming upon us, as wealthy retirees want their piece of rural paradise, which means more Tudor manors with rolling acres of lawn, or, in the silliest case so far, a gulag of cheaply built condominium houses making up a gated community. I still boggle at that one. I fear the future, given that almost no municipal government these days will turn down a development if it means denying themselves a source of tax revenue to survive the provincial downloading of services and costs.

There still remains a strong stock of heritage buildings in the County, and they provide great delight to visitors who have long since squandered their own inheritances. A hamlet as sad and forgotten as Consecon has six to a dozen houses patiently awaiting gentrification, or further defilement, or demolition. I'm a bit torn about the choices. The houses survive, forgotten and decaying, homes to people who may not have much money but who have been good neighbours. If a place like Consecon is gradually bought up and renovated, the buildings may be saved, but the poor residents will be quietly shuffled out. People or historic and charming buildings? I don't have to make the decision, and I'm glad.

❧

Driving one day down into the depression of the pleasant valley where Hillier Village sits caused me to comment to Lauren, "Someone's going to recognize those buildings for what they are and do something with them."

"Which ones?"

"The mill there, with the corner house and blacksmith shop."

"Probably."

Through the leafless trees it was easy to see all the buildings that made up the Taylor property. A board-and-batten two-storey blacksmith shop stood nearly at the road's edge. Dorland's Creek flowed strongly in the late-fall swell. No longer swathed in its usual cloak of greenery and dark shadow, the old cider mill, clad in pewter-grey warped clapboard, nudged a toe of its limestone foundation into the edge of the running creek. A 150-year-old house stood right on the corner – Mary Taylor's house. Another house crowned a small hill on the opposite side of the creek, behind the blacksmith shop and cider mill. Off to the west stood a fair-sized barn, blocking the view of a large drive shed. Between the houses and the road were a few different workshops and sheds. It was really a small village inside a village.

Countless times, when we passed along that route during the leafless seasons, that snippet of conversation repeated itself. One day I asked, "Does it *have* to be someone else? Why not us?"

Lauren was too smart to answer.

Well, why not? It'd be a shame to see the village gutted, and it would be if the buildings, outbuildings, and houses on the Taylor property were allowed to decline and disappear, or, more likely, bulldozed as soon as Mary died, to make way for a sensible, sterile modern bungalow. Our farm was going to be paid off in a month or two – a five-year loan the credit union had pieced together. We'd be able to take on a house.

I had asked Frank Westerhof about the land that shared the west fenceline with ours sometime in the first year, when we were both out in the field – I to weed, he to check over the crop that we let him grow around our test plots.

"Oh, no. They'll never sell that. No . . . no."

So I was surprised when Mary's sons put three other houses they owned up for sale: a tiny cottage behind the stone town hall; the "new" old schoolhouse close to the fire hall; and a little tin-sided frame house that bordered both the creek and the Taylors.

I watched that little tin-sided house sit there, and noted its photograph in the weekly real-estate pages of the local papers. The houses were Sharon Armitage's listings. Lauren and I were slowly (very slowly) working on ideas for building at the farm; I surprised her – and probably ticked her off – when I suggested we have a look at the little frame house next to Mary Taylor's place. But she agreed to it, to break the routine if nothing else.

We pulled up past Mary's house and the gaggle of cats and kittens that always hung around her door. Sharon met us, and already had the door unlocked and open. She said that Mary was somewhere in her nineties and blind, but wouldn't leave the house. She didn't have cats; where they came from was a mystery.

Sharon seemed embarrassed to be showing the house to us, and leaned with her arms folded across her chest in the kitchen, waiting for us to reject it out of hand, or maybe even run screaming. I purposely kept between Lauren and the exit as much as I could.

Under the siding was an 1847 Quaker workman's house, a storey and a half high, in a classic, eye-pleasing proportion of sixteen by twenty feet. It still had the original window and door bays, which was rare, as most of these older buildings at some point had holes brutally knocked in them to accommodate larger, uglier, cheap modern windows. The original framing was intact in this house. A very narrow, rough staircase led upstairs to a pair of rooms separated by the original plain, beaded wood door. Some of the same beaded wainscotting in the small kitchen wing to the rear of the house could be detected behind the rude chipboard cabinets and Formica counter, and beneath countless coats of paint.

On the outside, the western wall, which intersected with the kitchen, had never been sided in metal; it showed the original clapping (a faded oxblood red) and plain cornice. The eaves returns retained their mouldings, though they were worn and weathered, offering a bit of grace and more trim detail than I would have expected on a Quaker cottage.

That's what I saw. It's not that I was blind to what Lauren saw. Where she observed a kitchen in shambles, a bathroom that was toxic and likely illegal, and just four tiny, charmless rooms in the main "wing," I did too. But I could pretend it didn't matter all that much, because the fundamentals were right. Call it a gift we men have. (Lauren calls it treatable.)

Outside, it was an easier sell. The house sat on a sudden rise about twelve feet above the creek, which trilled and burbled a melody over some stones at the base of the drop. The house sat on the east side of the old sawmill dam. Across the creek the remains of the dam's west side rose less suddenly from the water. It was nice. On our right a board-and-batten workshop somehow managed to maintain a perch on the hill. (In a photo dated 1913, it holds its ground in exactly the same precarious manner and condition.) Next to that stood a solid, pleasant limestone smokehouse. Off behind the smokehouse, the rest of the lot continued for quite a distance between the creek and Station Road, to within a few dozen feet of the schoolhouse.

We thanked Sharon, she apologized again, and we headed home.

The next day, while I was getting my bike out of the shed in Consecon, our neighbour Bob Moran waved hello from his yard. "So you're moving, eh?"

"No."

"You're sure? If you've bought a place in Hillier near the farm, it'd make more sense to be there. At least it would to me anyway, if I owned it."

"But we don't. We don't have a house."

"Well, at Joe's they said you got one just the other day."

So Joanne and some, or all, of the crowd nursing their coffees at her snack bar in Hillier saw Sharon meet with us. I pedalled off to the farm for the day. I'd tell Lauren at dinner.

While Lauren was getting dinner ready, a woman came to the door. After they had finished talking, Lauren came and told me, "She wants to know if they could rent this place now that we're moving."

"Did you tell her that you don't recommend it?"

"No. But I did tell her we weren't planning on moving. And she was confused, since her friend told her we had a new house."

I went over a plan with Lauren: as the Taylor boys (both maybe a decade older than my father) were selling off the houses, they might be willing to sell the farm too, when the time came. If we could get the small house next to them – provided it was realistically priced – and the right of first refusal on the farm, then *that* might not be a bad idea. If we were ever to buy the farm, our own farm on Station Road would be linked right down to the Loyalist Parkway.

We'd have a selection of old buildings to repair gradually, 130 acres next to our 40, and a forest that is much more mature than ours. And we'd have use of the nice south bluff stretching from the village to the railbed, overlooking the creek. Ever since I had seen it in 1994, I knew it would be perfect for a vineyard . . . maybe one of the best in Hillier and the County.

The steep but short slope was covered in small trees and brush, but it could be cleared and planted.

I stopped in at Sharon's office in Wellington to go over my idea, and she said she'd try it on Mary's sons.

Somehow, with Sharon working hard and fairly for both parties as always, the deal was done. Our credit union, after a frustrating few weeks, came through with a mortgage. We owned about as much of a venerable County house as we could afford. And had a beachhead position on the farm on our western border.

I started to learn more about our house in the village. Before we made our offer, I had asked local engineer and heritage buff Ernie Margetson if he'd be willing to come over and have a look at it with me, to spot any problems.

The structure was fine. The main timber frame was still square and true, as was the roof. Looking into the crawl space under the floor, Ernie found one rotten floor joist, next to where some amateur plumbing for the bathroom had been installed. It'd have to be replaced. The others, still covered in bark, were in good shape.

"Here," Ernie said, handing me the hatch for the crawl space inside the cellar. "I think we should leave this open. These places were built as living houses. They need airflow around the beams to keep from rotting. Most people make the mistake of sealing their renovations up too tight, and the building starts to fail."

Ernie somehow managed to keep his large frame from going through the kitchen floor as we looked over the small cellar. The stone walls were in good shape.

"Look at this," he pointed out. "See those marks on the boards? They're from an old vertical mill saw. Not a circular blade. The wood was probably cut right here." Ernie knew that the old sawmill once sat a few feet away from the house.

We took a quick look over the smokehouse, which was also in good shape, and then wandered near the creek to check out the old cider mill.

Ernie didn't bother to comment on the limestone foundation, part of which sat in the creek; it was obviously fracturing in spots. He found a few of the beams that were rotting and would need to be replaced. The weathered grey of the clapping and the gentle curve along their length gave a refined decrepitude to the place – the building equivalent of Peter O'Toole. I told Ernie that the building had been moved maybe a century ago from a spot a few miles to the west, and placed on the high stone foundation. Whether it was originally a home or a meeting house was hard to tell – there were details that could make a case for either. The Taylors had last used it as a chicken cannery in the 1950s and 1960s; connecting the blacksmith shop to the mill was a string of old cold rooms and galvanized-steel hanging rooms for the birds awaiting processing. Prior to the chicken cannery, the building served as a cider mill. It was the last mill on the creek; the old sawmill and then the gristmill downstream had long ago disappeared.

I thanked Ernie for his help, and walked for a while over the house lot when he left. Edith Taylor Ashton called the place Mrs. Jones's house, after the last owner before it was willed to the Taylor family. In Edith's local history, there's a photo of the stone smokehouse with a caption. In another chapter she writes briefly, "An architectural gem is the tiny stone smokehouse on the lot once owned by stonemason John Cardinell." The building is coursed in large pieces of limestone, worn smooth by the weather, or possibly by the creek from which they were gathered. The soft, gritty old-fashioned mortar still holds them together, though a century and a half on, it might stand a bit of pointing. The nails, hinges, and latches on the door, and the meathooks dangling from the roof, all would have been hammered for their purpose either by Robert Pye or a young John Crippen, two blacksmiths in the village at the time. I find that stunning, to look at something of stone and metal, and know whose labour created it, all this time later.

I hit the archives and registry office, and dug out the old Hillier land registry, various deeds and other documents, and censuses.

The house appears to have been built in 1847, the year a quarter of an acre was severed from the farm now owned by the Taylors.

Thomas Flagler, Esq., was the first owner. The Flagler family owned the sawmill, and so they likely built the house from the wood they gained in payment from customers. The small, plain house was painted yellow and quite quickly over the years changed hands among others in the village: a rural gentlemen, a wagonmaker, a shoemaker, a mason, a pair of blacksmiths, a few yeomen.

I've collected copies of their signatures, some childlike, others confident and clear.

Except Leer's.

John Leer, yeoman, was illiterate. On his documents one finds:

his
John X Leer
mark

All but the "X" is in the hand of the clerk. Yet Leer owned most of Hillier, off and on, through his life, and brokered, arranged, and financed dozens of deals around the hamlet. A French Canadian born Jean de L'Eveille in 1819, his father's family had arrived in New France over a century before. In 1822 Jean's father died, and Jean did not get on with his step-father. It's not exactly clear how the young Jean and his younger brother, Joseph, came to the County, but they did. Being illiterate and French, his name was anglicized in the County: he became John Leer, then Lear.

John Lear called our house his a few times over his life, and for a long time owned and farmed our property on Lot 20, Concession III in Hillier. It's nice to know there is a real French heritage to our vineyard . . . however tenuous.

CHAPTER

THIRTEEN

And I got interested in the place
I mean what the hell else could I do
being a little too stupid to ever admit
I was a lousy carpenter and a worse writer?

   •   *Al Purdy, "In Search of Owen Roblin"*

Literature and wine have danced together as far back as humans can remember, possibly well before the days we developed cheat sheets – or rather clay slabs – of pictograms and cuneiform. Gilgamesh's pal Enkidu was first ensnared by a singing, dancing woman armed with wine. The Hebrews proclaimed Noah the first winegrower. Homer's Laertes happily grew grapes. The Greeks had their symposia, which were really drinking sessions, where the dregs were flung from their cups at a target. Euripides thought he'd help explain it all in a terrifying play called *The Bacchae*, musing on how the eastern god Dionysus came to party in Greece.

At university I was in no way suspected of being an enthusiastic consumer of poetry. A number of friends and acquaintances wrote what I was assured was decent stuff. Then there was Peter Ormshaw – in the intervening years since school reforged as the poet Mountie. Actually, his poems I've always liked and recognized as seriously good things. And yet it never stopped me from appropriating his voice and reciting,

I think that I
shall never see
a rhyming poem
that's done by me.

To my sensibilities, a lot of what was passed off as poetry reeked of do-it-yourself therapy, though I appreciated that Peter (and a handful of other poets with whom he'd show up at bars in Kingston or Toronto) had something to say, and said it well.

It could have been the instinctual defensive impulse that came of being a high-school kid force-fed the first hothouse growths of CanLit back in the early 1970s. Much of it was of very poor nutritional worth, more the product of novelty and nationalism. Yet I can't gripe. A few things stayed with me.

In grade nine I remember seeing the old NFB film by Donald Brittain about Leonard Cohen, and being impressed – impressed enough to hang out at Ben's in Montreal every chance I got. In high school a few other snippets of the compulsory Canadian content in English classes lodged themselves in my mind too. Margaret Atwood's disturbing "You fit into me / like a hook into an eye / a fish hook / an open eye" more than made up for spending weeks reading and analyzing *An Edible Woman*. A few other writers also dug themselves into my grey matter. There was something about Hugh Hood's short story "Getting to Williamstown" that has stayed with me since grade ten or eleven or whenever it was I read it. Haunted me, actually, though I've never really figured out why. Same as that bite of Atwood.

Al Purdy made more of an impression, but one that lurked below the surface for many years. I'm sure it was discussed in class that Purdy lived in Ameliasburgh, Ontario, an old part of the country, and that it showed in his poems. I can't recall what poems of his we messed with. But I do remember he was one of the editors credited on the cover of the poetry anthology we used at the time.

During a phone conversation with David Carpenter, in the days when there was only the Wicked Point boys, Ed Neuser, Phil Mathewson, and myself, growing grapes out here, he pointed out that the County had a long-forgotten grape history . . . the same thing Mathewson had mentioned before. And as part of it, surely I had read Purdy's 1968 book of poems, *Wild Grape Wine*?

I hadn't. But I had already begun reading and rereading Purdy poems – the ones in the thick 1986 *Collected Poems* I unearthed one day in one of Toronto's Harbord Avenue bookshops.

Poetry is wasted on people south of their thirties and forties, unless they are poets themselves, writing for other poets, reading, and warring with each other. I've come to believe this. Either it's a maturity milestone, or it may come from my own pulling back a bit from the modern world . . . or at least getting my head out of television.

I couldn't find a copy of *Wild Grape Wine* in any of my sweeps through Toronto's used bookstores, so I figured I'd go to the source. Ameliasburgh was just up the road. I knew Purdy collected books, and that authors often accumulated spare copies of their own (especially when allowed to slip out of print) for readings or special sales. Purdy had done just that with *In Search of Owen Roblin*, dropping off a box for sale at the Ameliasburgh Museum. So I wrote the poet and asked if he had a copy he might be willing to sell a County winegrower.

A December morning many weeks later, I pulled out of our post-office box a small envelope speckled in an old, jumpy typewriter face. My name and address were riding high and to the left. The return address ran in a single line across the top: "Purdy, 9310 Lochside Dr., Sidney B.C. V8L 1N6."

I had almost forgotten about the query I had sent to him, addressed simply to "Al Purdy, General Delivery, Ameliasburgh." It had eventually reached him . . . on the other side of the country.

Dear Geoff

sorry, I don't have a copy (extra) of Wild Grape Wine. I wish I did have a few copies. Price is up to about $40. these days.

And thanks for the good words re my stuff.

I'm in bad shape right now – pain from arthritis. Taking anti-inflammatory pills et. Tylenol no good at all. I mention this to explain my short letter. It's like a sword, in at the mouth and out at the ass. Along the way, it hurts. . . .

A vineyard in Hillier!!! How about all your Presbyterian neighbours? – don't they think wine is wicked? Quakers don't apparently. . . .

Best Wishes,
Al Purdy

I got in touch with him again and asked whether he'd agree to an interview for a piece I wanted to write for *Saturday Night* magazine about his poems on wine and beer and his experiences as a brewer and winemaker. He left an answering-machine message saying it'd be fine to come by, now that he and his wife were back in Ameliasburgh. I called and made arrangements to visit.

To help identify the house, on the south shore of Roblin's Lake, about half a dozen miles from our place in Consecon, Al said there was a burnt-out hulk of a garage in front, the result of relatives stowing a still-smouldering blanket they had used to smother a blazing lawn mower. As I walked down the gravel, past the cement-block foundation of the garage, I looked across the complex of board-and-batten buildings, grown from the original A-frame house for which Al and Eurithe used "our last hard-earned buck to buy second-hand lumber / to build a second-hand house / . . . so far from anywhere / even homing pigeons lost their way."

The tall poet shambled to the door, rumbled a greeting in his unchanging benevolent growl, and apologized for his slightly awkward gait. We settled down at a table in front of a large window overlooking the lake, on a wooden floor salvaged from the gym of an old Belleville high school.

I brought out a nice nine-year-old Riesling from the Mosel, and learned something I hadn't expected. The Canadian poet who had written more on creating and consuming wine and beer than probably all the others combined no longer drank.

After some pleasant small talk, he started to speak of his own wines. "I remember taking some to Montreal to Irving Layton's party, and Jack McClelland was there. Jack McClelland claimed it was bad wine. But everybody else drank it. And

Jack McClelland, considering his record, would drink almost anything."

I thought that was a good point at which to open up the Riesling, a pleasant afternoon wine with just 7.5 per cent alcohol. Mr. Purdy looked at the label, and grabbed an empty glass for himself.

"Oh, yeah. A little bit. . . . That's pretty good. Yeah, that's . . . I've pretty well sworn off drinking."

"That must be hard for you."

"Yes, as a matter of fact it is. This is a lapse that I hope my wife doesn't see. She went out anyway to do some work in the yard."

"So when did they tell you to stop drinking?"

"Oh, I went pretty near ten years ago to a . . . specialist – a urologist. He claimed that all the beer I'd drunk in my misspent youth had drowned the nerves. Nerve damage right up to my knees. My legs are clumsy now because of the dead nerves."

From 1957, when Al and Eurithe moved across the lake from the village of Ameliasburgh, until 1964, when a young lawyer finally pried Al's inheritance out of the trust company holding on to it, the Purdys lived in dire poverty.

"But hell . . . when you go through all this, when you're as broke as all that, it's pretty hard to dramatize," he said, turning to Eurithe, who had returned inside. "I was telling him about the time that we were so broke we went over to Mountainview dump and the air force had thrown out all these envelopes of dried –"

"Dehydrated," Eurithe said.

"– dehydrated foods. Potatoes, apples, every damned thing. We used them. And we used the paint and the plywood boxes in the house."

"Them were the days," teased Eurithe.

"I wouldn't want to go through them again," continued Al. "On the other hand I'm not sorry for having gone through them, because it's all in my own writing and the poems and everywhere else."

"The only thing is, it doesn't do anything for me," added Eurithe. "I don't write. So there's no saving element to it at all." She laughed gently.

Al looked at her and said, "In other words, you look back on it in a lot of –"

"Horror," she said, without missing a beat.

"Horror," Al echoed.

This time everyone laughed. Eurithe got up and returned to her own tasks.

Al immediately continued. "I don't. I don't, matter of fact. It was a hard time. I didn't enjoy it at the time. I was depressed because of it. You can imagine building . . . we built this house in used lumber. Not all of it. Most of it. Not all of it. This room was built long after.

"I used to chop a hole in the ice. In March it was three feet thick. I'd get out there and I'd sweat so much I'd take off my shirt.

"You go through all this, and you don't enjoy it. But at the same time, it puts you through something, and you get through it and look back on it. I don't regret it a damned bit."

Al paused just for a second, and said, "I've worked when I've had to. And when I got away with not working, why, I did."

Honest words, I thought.

We got back to talking about wine. During the early Ameliasburgh days, Al realized the only way he was going to drink wine was if he made it himself. "I've forgotten who told me how to make it, but I picked wild grapes. And I picked them in quantity. Real quantity. We had about five garbage pails – seven- or eight-gallon garbage pails – bubbling all at once. And I cleaned them. It was a helluva job!"

The most common wild grape growing in Canada, from the east coast to Riding Mountain in Manitoba, is *vitis riparia*. Broad, deep-green leaves ripen straggly, loose clusters of a few small berries. Though it makes a good rootstock for European vines, riparia fruit is highly acid, and has deeply coloured juice and skins. In Prince Edward County they're everywhere, even growing in the huge dunes at Sandbanks Provincial Park. Al would pick about three bushels of grapes for each garbage can. Unless you've tried it, you can't really imagine the determination and effort needed to harvest ten to fifteen bushels of wild grapes.

"Yes," Al admitted, "I was picking for weeks."

He started thinking back to the fermentations he had gently guided along, bottling the product in old wine and rye bottles he picked up for free from a friendly bar owner. "They make a beautiful music, don't they?"

In his collection *The Cariboo Horses* (1965), Al published "Wine-Maker's Song," which begins:

After a while the grapes confer
among themselves
                    begin to whisper
marvellous bubbling secrets together
which they may divulge
                    in a few weeks

Three years later, in a beautifully published collection called *Wild Grape Wine* (the dust cover of which is an amazing, simple typographic construction of single quotation marks arranged to look like a cluster of grapes), came the opening poem titled "The Winemaker's Beat-Étude." It begins:

I am picking wild grapes last year
in a field
      dragging down great lianas of vine
tearing at 20 feet of heavy infinite purple
having a veritable tug-o-war with Bacchus
who grins at me delightedly in the high branches
on one of those stepchild appletrees
unloved by anything but tent caterpillars
and ghosts of old settlers
become such strangers here

Besides the many poems Al has offered up as proof of his understanding of beer and wine production and consumption, back in the 1960s he wrote an article on wine for the old *Canadian* magazine, which used to be tucked in weekend newspapers. I never located the published version, but I found a typescript draft in the Queen's University archives, hammered out onto the backsides of old Canadian Pacific Railway schedules. In it was a slightly more detailed version of the wild-grape wine recipe he gave me.

For two years we were flat broke, or so close to it that large cracks were apparent in both economic and matrimonial relationships. I kept on writing, while the neighbours audibly pitied my wife for sticking with that nogoodnik who refused to work for a living. And I used the local wild grapes to make wine. My recipe was simple. You strip off about three bushels of the very dry, pea-sized grapes, filling a ten-gallon plastic garbage can to the mid-point, add twelve pounds of sugar and fill with water to about four inches from the top of the can. Then cover to keep out fruit flies and too much air. Before you're finished cleaning grapes the alcoholic midwives are chuckling merrily. Three or four months later you strain and bottle, while the fruit flies form a dionysian halo around the house.

At the end of the piece, he took a stab at trying to analyze why humans had taken to alcohol.

Reasons for drinking might seem very simple, but when you attempt to explain them they become idiotic simplicities. People have always tried to change the tempo of their lives, speed them up or slow them down, with alcohol or drugs. The human animal, aware of his own inevitable death, is continually afflicted with discontent. Intangible things and sometimes material things recede beyond grasp, or else seem not worth the effort to keep them. Greek tragedy, in which humanity faces heroic but inevitable defeat, is involved in many of our activities.

There is a madness comes upon some of us when we realize all this. I'd prefer to call it divine madness, a Dionysian passion for the unreachable perhaps.

At a time when most Canadians drank heavy brown liquids out of heavy brown bottles – ryes, whiskies, and dubious, doctored Concord sherries – writing about wine was pretty avant-garde. Canadian publisher Mel Hurtig offered Al the chance to do a book on the subject, when very little on it was in print in English, or at least in North American English.

"I don't know why I didn't," Al told me. "I probably should have, because it probably would have made money."

It might have helped start Canada down the road to table wines a decade or two earlier. And it wouldn't have been all that mercenary either; Al knew the importance of wine and beer in civilization.

⁊

Al asked me to stop by a few days later, saying he had something for me. When I arrived, he gave me a poster that had been made of a recent poem he'd done in memory of his friend Charles Bukowski. The last lines read,

– Bukowski in his coffin
dead as hell
but reaching hard for a last beer
and just about making it

He had also typed out (rather than photocopied) the text of something he had half remembered the last time we were going over all the different things he'd written about wine and beer. It was simply called "Beer Poem." "Wasn't a very good poem," Al said as he handed it to me. "But it was a poem about beer."

I made one more trip back, a few months later, to check some facts in the piece I was working on and to give Al and Eurithe a few clusters of Hillier grapes. I couldn't feel as guilty giving him unfermented wine grapes as I did surreptitiously serving him a glass of Mosel.

"So that's it, is it?" he stated more than asked, holding a Pinot cluster of midnight black.

"Different grapes than you had to make wine with," I said.

"Yeah, very different." He looked more closely at the very small berries, and it changed his first impression. "As a matter of fact no. Not so much different . . ."

"In the rough draft I'm working on," I said, "I mention the fact that the same time you were making wild-grape wine, a lot of the people in France – including Burgundy – were still making wine from two varieties named Baco Noir and Oberlin Noir. One of their parents is the same wild grape, so they were making wine pretty similar to you in the '60s."

Al had a chuckle at that.

"Did I tell you that Jack McClelland said that my wine was terrible?" he asked. I ignored the fact that he had. "At the time I took some bottles down to Montreal. There was sort of a do at Irving Layton's, and he was there. As a matter of fact, he was quite wrong, because a lot of people liked it." Al thought he knew the real reason his former publisher didn't enjoy the wine. "There was also an element of anti-Purdy." He continued, admitting, "It was strong. You were liable to piss purple. No, no, I'm exaggerating. I exaggerate sometimes, as you've noticed."

Eurithe sat down with us, and Al recounted some of the less cultured aspects of alcohol decades ago.

"Well," he said, nodding to Eurithe, "she has stories to tell about me going down the road, driving by the white line in the middle, drunk as hell. She was nervous about it. I don't blame her. I was nervous about it at the time too."

Eurithe simply said, "In retrospect, one wonders why one put up with it. Most of the women I knew our own ages did. Men were much more jealous of the wheel."

"That's them, the grapes?" Al asked once again, more to bring them to Eurithe's attention.

"Yep. I brought the poet's portion from the vineyard this year. The black ones are European wine grapes. The white cluster is Vidal, a white-wine grape they often make icewine from. The white isn't ripe yet; it's about 16- or 17-per-cent sugar. It's about two weeks away from harvest. The black ones I think we have to pick tomorrow to make a little wine from, because the mice are getting at them."

"This is a solid grape," said Eurithe, holding the cluster in her hand.

"Yeah, it's Pinot Noir, the grape they grow in Burgundy."

Al picked up another black cluster. "Are they always that size?"

"Yeah, that's why they call it Pinot Noir – pine cone – because it's about that size, about the size of a pack of Gitanes, and a solid cluster. That's why when the weather gets bad in the fall, the French in Burgundy start to cry, because they're so close together there's no give, and if they split because of the rain coming up through the roots, then they rot, because the sugar gets over the other grapes. So rain during harvest is especially bad in Burgundy. Or eventually in Hillier."

Once I had confirmed a few of the facts he'd told me before, we drifted off the subject of wine. Al spoke of Trudeau, other writers, various publications, editors . . . the different things writers usually gossip about.

Somehow his amusing "At the Quinte Hotel" came up. "It gets around, that poem," Al noted with pleasure.

"If you have two or three poems that more than a handful of people know," I said, "then you've done –"

"Then you've done something," he finished. "Yes, you

really have. As a matter of fact, I think if any of the really great poets, if they've done more than five or six – and five or six is a great many – call them the best. Even Yeats, whom I admire a great deal, or even Lawrence, although a friend of mine and I have picked out twelve.

"The line that always sticks in my mind about Lawrence," Al continued, "was about a goat that was up one of the low-lying trees – I forget, was it an almond tree? – in Italy: 'like some horrid hairy god the father in William Blake's imagination.' Can you imagine anyone saying a line like that . . . ? That is absolutely . . . that's genius."

"Same thing as lines like 'having a veritable tug-o-war with Bacchus,'" I offered.

Purdy countered: "How about: 'License my roving hands, and let them go / Before, behind, between, above, below.' That is four hundred years old. That's John Donne. Well, you ought to look it up, because he's a great modern poet, four hundred years old. After he died, his reputation died completely. It was revived around the turn of this century. I'm not sure exactly how . . . there are poems of his that are just so modern it's hard to believe, until you come to an archaic word here or there as you do."

He recalled titles of Donne's poems, and shot out bits from what he referred to as "all these great love poems."

"Well, as I say," he went on, "if you read his poems, you've got to read the right one, because the early love poems appeal to me more than the religious stuff."

"I'm shocked."

"Yeah, right. Let's see, have I got any here? I have a couple of books as a matter of fact. I'm starting to read them because we'll probably do the same thing with Donne as we did with

Lawrence. We want people to like him. They're missing something great. Let's see. Does he have anything in here . . . ?"
Purdy peered hard at the pages. "I'm not going to read this because it's too fucking fine print."

And yet he went right into it, fine print or not. I listened, enjoying his enjoyment of words forgotten and remembered. When he finished reading a few of Donne's poems, Al mentioned a new poem that would be going into the book he was at work on.

"A little coaxing and I'll get it out and read it to you. I read that much better than I do John Donne's stuff."

And he did, standing there on unsteady legs, reading a version of "Say the Names" for an appreciative audience of one.

❧

After spending a few days in the County, anyone familiar with Purdy's Ameliasburgh poems comes to understand them in a way not possible anywhere else. Live here for a few years, and the landscape rings with his words, not because they impose themselves, but because he's distilled the truths of this place in strings of simple lines.

Even though the poem may be called "The Country North of Belleville," I can barely look out the car window in the County without hearing:

A country of quiescence and still distance
a lean land
            not like the fat south
with inches of black soil on
            earth's round belly –

And where the farms are
        it's as if a man stuck
both thumbs in the stony earth and pulled

           it apart
           to make room
enough between the trees
for a wife
        and maybe some cows and
        room for some
of the more easily kept illusions –

Critics say this may be Purdy's single best poem; read all of it, and I don't believe you'll find a misplaced syllable. Purdy's "Prince Edward County" is not at the same level, though it has some good lines. His numerous others about different pieces of the County shine much brighter.

A prophet is without honour in his own country, proclaim the gospels, and the County is no different from Galilee almost two millennia ago. Purdy is neglected here. The village of Ameliasburgh did name a small lane after him a few years back, but when asked about that Al usually quoted Thomas Gray's "Elegy Written in a Country Churchyard" – "the paths of glory lead but to the grave" – and then laughed. Purdy Lane is the steep gravel road that ends down at the village cemetery.

Al Purdy's death caught me a bit by surprise. We had drafted him as the Honorary Founding Chairman of the Prince Edward County Winegrowers Association. Eurithe wrote back, accepting on his behalf.

His ashes were to come to the cemetery at the end of Purdy Lane in Ameliasburgh.

Filling a rain-soaked day that kept me out of our vineyard, I drove to the Ameliasburgh Museum to buy the last two copies of Purdy's long poem *In Search of Owen Roblin*. I'd meant to purchase one, but never had the money while I had the thought, and mislaid the thought when my pockets were full; the other was destined for Alberta as a gift to Peter Ormshaw and his wife, Marina Endicott. The books were signed by the author.

Purdy Lane is quite near the museum. Now for some silly reason it is officially called Purdy Street, though a small and weather-beaten hand-routed sign calls it by its earlier name. I walked down its steep drop. A few yards along I could see a wall of wild grapevines. Many had begun to flower. It was a cheering sight, though I couldn't smell any of that musky, citrusy perfume no matter how close I pressed my nose – it had been washed out of the air.

It was the first time I'd ever explored the lane leading to the millpond and graveyard. At the base of the escarpment, I wandered into the cemetery and looked over the tombstones, noting many familiar County names on them. There was a fresh foundation for a marker, poured in the last few days. I wondered if this was going to be for Purdy. If so, it was nicely sited next to the pond bank. (On a later visit I found that it was indeed his spot.) I wandered back to the gate, and noticed the Roblin family marker. I don't know how I overlooked it coming in. I dropped my gaze and saw I was standing on a small stone nameplate. It said "Owen." I had found him without looking.

❧

Al and Eurithe Purdy moved to Roblin's Lake at around the same age Lauren and I were when we moved to the

County, and they had a much harder life than we. As a poet, he didn't really get things going until he was forty. Though our culture only seems to celebrate newness and youth, Al and Eurithe offer a bracing example to everyone who hates their life, finds it wasted, fears they are failures (as Al said he had felt about his earlier writing efforts).

So many people in their forties rage quietly, internally, against their lives in Toronto or Ottawa or any other city. Most of the people who are planting vines in Prince Edward, or who are looking seriously at land, fall into this demographic slice. The obstacle is always the question of how one survives in the country without two salaries – actually, without any salary. With telecommuting, or the explosion of work to be had in consulting, it is less of a problem than it was in 1957 when Al and Eurithe took off to Ameliasburgh. It can be done, if the passion is there. Al Purdy had the passion to be a better writer. Winegrowing, at least in parts of Europe, is seen as an art form similar to poetry, and it can become a calling many seem to hear but are frightened to acknowledge.

Al Purdy's last poem in his final collection had a few lines that I have taken to heart:

On a green island in Ontario
I learned about being human
built a house and found the woman
and we shall be there forever
building a house that is never finished . . .

But reality is an overdrawn bank account
my myths and cheques both bounce,
the creditors close in,
and all the dead men,
chanting hymns,
tunnel toward me underground.

•   *Al Purdy, "Joint Account"*

I t's the little things in life that trip us up. The want of a nail, or so we were told in the nursery rhyme. I recall being told in school that countless lives in Europe were extinguished because a bacteria, a flea, and a rat got together. After man did his best to wipe out civilization in the First World War, a strain of flu virus improved on his efforts.

Sometimes it's plain bad luck. Other times it is a technological oversight: that loose horseshoe nail, maybe the unexpected quirk of a genetically modified organism. I don't discount that occasionally it may be a deliberate evil. We've been pulled down so many times when at the top of our game, our victory-party preparations revealed for what they were: vainglorious.

One little louse changed the course of history in modern Europe, starting about the time our house in Hillier was being hammered together. It never made the list of things for school-children to learn about the nineteenth century; it wasn't as sexy as the limited-liability company, the steam engine, or the theory of evolution. It didn't even rate a footnote. But this aphid ate through villages and provinces and nations. If you hold very, very still and listen closely, you may hear it chomping yet. It also helped confirm the Anglo-Saxon taste for doctored, alcoholic wines as well as Scotch and whiskies with steak or roast, something that didn't start to die out until the mid-1970s in Canada.

Wine began to dry up in the 1860s. Literally. Right in the ground. The roots were set upon by a nearly invisible creature the French first called *Phylloxera vastatrix* – the devastator.

Very little of its horrors are remembered now, except among wine geeks and winegrowers and their suppliers. That seems odd, given how it really changed much of the world, and helped bring rural populations to near extinction.

I raise the subject with some trepidation. Having only just managed to wade through Melville's great *Moby-Dick* and its internal how-to companion manual on the carving and rendering of whales, it's not lightly that I cast the reader into the world of phylloxera. But as Melville shows, any tale of one man's obsession is hardly worth printing without the gory technical bits to heighten the tension and sense of doom.

❧

Phylloxera was first identified by an American, Dr. Asa Fitch, in 1856. He called it *Pemphigus vitifolii*, though it was placed into another family shortly after. It has been renamed again, becoming *Dactylasphaera vitifoliae*, though most everyone still refers to it as just plain phylloxera. It is native primarily to northeastern North America, and the vines of this continent have developed the ability to coexist with the creature. Unfortunately, like North America's Native population and its unfamiliarity with smallpox, the European family of wine-grape – *Vitis vinifera* – had no biological concord with the aphid. Somehow phylloxera was introduced into Europe, and the thick fleshy roots of the European vines offered it an unending banquet of sap. Vines in some areas of the south of France started to appear stunted in their growth. Leaves gradually reddened or yellowed ahead of their seasonal time, and fluttered dead to the ground. Within a few seasons the vines themselves were dead, whereupon the symptoms dispersed from the original dead or dying patches like oil spots spreading on water.

The French, reeling from the unstoppable destruction, finally agreed with the scientific assessment from M. J.-E. Planchon of Montpellier University that it was a form of aphid; it was Planchon who named it *vastatrix*.

It was a very difficult puzzle to put together. Dead vines didn't have the phylloxera louse on their roots. They had moved on to other vines as soon as the flow of sap weakened in a dying vine. And the leaf-galling habit identified by Fitch seemed unconnected with the root louse. It appeared unconnected because the phylloxera has a fiendishly complicated life cycle. There are nineteen different stages, and a diagram of its numerous disguises from winter egg to winter egg looks like the proof of a mathematical theorem.

George Ordish's amazing work *The Great Wine Blight* is pretty much the only book available in English about the disaster. In it he writes about the difficulty in identifying the aphid as the problem:

> The complicated story was difficult to unravel for two reasons. Firstly, the idea that the life history could be different on the vinifera and the American vines had to be discovered and accepted, and secondly the much more difficult concept had to be swallowed, in that age of Victorian male superiority, that here was a species that throve without any sexual stage at all, that got on very well without the use of males; not the sort of news one would want to get into the hands of George Sand, Louise Michel and the pioneers of women's rights in France at that time. Possibly the basic secret fear of men to this day is that, biologically, the male is the less important sex.

Phylloxera, though but a tiny yellowish pinprick of a creature, more than made up for its size through numbers. Ordish points out the conceptive horrors:

> The reproductive power of insects is enormous and only very few have to survive from each generation for the species to continue; with an insect feeding on a crop the survival rate has to be only slightly above normal for the insect to become a severe pest. This can be seen with phylloxera reproduction. One fundatrix has a potential progeny of 4,800 million above-ground insects in the season; as the insect weighs about 1mg. this means that, if all survived, some 5 tons of insects

would be produced from one stem mother. About five of them per hectare growing and surviving at this rate would give a bigger weight of insects than grapes! Of course they do not grow and survive at this rate; the wastage is enormous. Millions fall by the wayside and fail to find a vine leaf; birds and predacious insects eat millions more but, in spite of all, enough survive to spread the pest and maintain the species to this day. It is a wasteful process, but it succeeds.

The roots of vinifera fed and maintained the aphid. In turn, as best we know, the insect injected a venom into the root tissue, which caused it to form a tumorous gall. North American vines had managed to develop a resistance to this venom, or were better adapted to forming a barrier against its penetration to any damaging degree. The tender European root would soon allow other deadly fungi into the wound site, and gradually the root tissues rotted away. The little phylloxera bug didn't mean to kill off the vines; that was a secondary effect of a wound that its usual hosts had been able to survive.

The check to this plague was torturously slow in coming. The French offered a pair of prizes for the solution: 20,000 francs from the ministry of agriculture; 300,000 francs from the national assembly. Nearly every crank in Europe responded.

M. J.-E. Planchon referred to the legions who offered cures as "those bright spirits who ride a hobby-horse to the borders of madness." The scientist Valéry Mayet wrote in 1890 with less charity, "What floods of ink and ineptitudes, what madnesses were put forward for the attainment of the 300,000 fr. prize!" The Commission supérieure de phylloxera itself wrote in 1897 that "the names of the inventors change each year but the remedies they suggest are always of the same kind. As usual a few facetious suggestions slip in among a number of eccentric proposals put forward in good faith."

One of the many deliciously recounted by Ordish almost literally fits the description of snake oil. In 1877 "a 'Mozambique Oil' was patented. It was said to be fish oil in which anti-helminthic plants (intestinal worm remedies) had been steeped. Obviously it had but little effect on the pest, but it achieved great fame in the Bouches du Rhône whose horticultural society gave it a silver medal. A litre cost but 2 fr. and treated 100 to 200 vines. Cheapness must have been one of its attractions, for it came out at 50 to 100 fr. per hectare compared to 600 fr. for sulphocarbonates. One wonders what it had to do with Mozambique. Perhaps the name brought in a suggestion of African magic."

Two bitter, hostile camps developed as the years dragged on – the chemists versus the Americanists. The chemists (this was the first golden age of "better living through chemistry") plumped for the application of carbon bisulphide. This was a very dangerous and expensive solution that was injected into the vineyard ground every few feet. It killed the louse, but eventually the interloper would recover and reinfest a vineyard. Carbon bisulphide required regular applications, each one tempting fate, as more than a few users were blown up by the unstable chemical. The Americanists, noting the resistance of various North American species to phylloxera, advocated grafting the tender European vine as a scion on rootstock of either pure North American vine (such as riparia, berlandieri, rupestris, cordifolia, champini) or a hybrid of two or more of these.

Years and decades dragged on, but eventually the safety and effectiveness of grafting won out. The worries that American roots would give horrid American wine flavours proved groundless. (This is, however, a topic that wine geeks debate endlessly even today.)

And the contest? The French, leaning on a technicality, never awarded the prize. Two men had just claim to it: Léo Laliman and Gaston Bazille, who both suggested grafting and the use of American vines. In Ordish's opinion they probably should have shared the gold and glory, but neither saw a sou of it.

The Commission supérieure de phylloxera wrote in its report of May 31, 1897: "M. Laliman's claim is rejected because all M. Laliman's work, important though it is, had as its object the substitution of American vines or American roots for our French varieties on their own roots. At no time did M. Laliman try to destroy the insect; nor did he try to any greater extent to stop it doing damage; the claims he has made several times to the Ministry or the Agricultural Society are rejected on the grounds that the petitioner has not carried out any of the obligations imposed on him, by the law [i.e., the law establishing the prize]. Consequently I consider the matter need be taken no further."

This cynical, legalistic decision saved a few hundred thousand francs, while Laliman and Bazille gave to the nation billions in the salvation and continuation of the French industry. *Vitis vinifera* are now nearly always grafted wherever they grow. There are a few areas, such as Chile, that have avoided the pest up until now, though it always seems to show up. Just ask the Australians or Oregonians. Grafted vines have not always helped though. The rootstocks have to be resistant to the aphid's venom and the horrors of infection a wound can set loose. In California, the use of a rootstock the French warned them to avoid because of its lack of phylloxera tolerance led to the recent destruction and replanting of millions of vines costing billions of dollars.

Now I *knew* all this before I planted vines.

❧

Phil Mathewson had steered me away from SO4 as a rootstock during a few of his generous viticultural discussions. He favoured 3309 Couderc, and had done a lot of his own rootstock experiments on other hard-to-find options. I'd keep planting mothervines of rare European and selected native County rootstocks for my own grafts, and I had my original 41 B vines too.

I ordered and planted a mix of rootstocks for my first experimental planting – 5 C Teleki, 3309 Couderc, and a faint hope called 1103 Paulsen (don't these names twang the heartstrings and kindle the romance of vinegrowing?). This last had excellent lime and drought tolerance, but I expected its vigour and longer growing season to cause me problems. And it did.

As for the majority of carefully acquired, exotic, and relatively rare Pinot Noir clones, well, these would have to go into the ground on their own roots, to serve as mothervines for grafting. They'd probably die at some point, I told myself in a cold, rational, intellectual manner. But the gambler that seems to be at the core of every farmer whispered a seductive question: "What if phylloxera *didn't* latch on to your vines and turn your efforts to dust? What if it could be managed?"

Knowing in theory that the vines could be infested failed to stiffen my spine one summer day while answering nature's call at the fencerow closest to my planting of own-rooted Pinot Noir. If I didn't exactly shriek in terror at that moment, I don't know why; I still wince whenever I think about it. I was looking at the wild grapevines above where I stood. On one leaf were phylloxera galls. This is one of those nineteen stages of the phylloxera life cycle, and the one that usually affects North American vines. When my hands were free, I plucked the leaf, and one or two others with the same tiny lumps, and ground them into the dust with my boot. I may have destroyed hundreds of thousands of the feared aphid at a stroke, but obviously there were millions more massed just a dozen yards from my vines.

That evening I reread a few old dog-eared sections on phylloxera in my library. Ontario was enjoying a string of mild winters and very dry summers, and in Ordish I found a note that even in France at the time of the outbreak there were worries about how the weather was speeding the ravages of phylloxera. It had been pointed out "that bad weather, poor soil and bad management were contributory causes, though not the main cause. For instance, there was some reason for thinking that bad weather was the culprit. The winter of 1868 was very cold and dry; the summer was yet drier. The Rhone fell so low that it was blocked with sandbanks, and some areas, it is said, had had no rain for eighteen months."

Tim Unwin, in his scholarly and entertaining book *Wine and the Vine*, describes how a collection of factors helped spread the plague: "Some combination of a new source of vine supply and the introduction of a particular strain of phylloxera may therefore have been the explanation. Given that the arrival of phylloxera came close on the heels of the outbreak of oidium [powdery mildew], it is also possible that the European Vitis vinifera vines had been in some way weakened, either by oidium or by treatments to control it, making them more susceptible to destruction by the particular strain of phylloxera that had been introduced. Furthermore, the coincidence of the spread of phylloxera with a series of warmer than average years between 1857 and 1875 may also be of some significance."

Weather is by nature unpredictable. Maybe even by design it confounds our plans and conceits and keeps the game honest. In Prince Edward County, as one mild year – an unusually warm winter followed by a hot and dry summer – gave way to another, and then yet still another, I finally saw what caused the broken hearts of nineteenth-century Europeans (and twentieth-century Californians), four years after my first sighting of phylloxera galls on the wild vines. Healthy vines shot out of their buds in the spring, producing beautiful shoots, leaves, and nascent flower clusters. The vines flowered, and enticing small Pinot fruit set, as it always had. And then, slowly, the tendrils that normally gripped the wires or nearby shoots and supported the climbing vine began to dry up. Leaves started to yellow from the base of the shoot. First two, then four, five. They'd fall off as if it were autumn, not the late July or early August it was. Phylloxera damage at the roots, combined with the severe summer dryness, were robbing the vines of life-giving moisture. Normally, a little drought stress in the late summer weeks before the grapes turn colour and soften is a good thing: it slows growth, and forces the vine to turn its attention to the fruit. The County is one of the driest places in Ontario during those weeks, which is one of its great attractions for growing top-quality fruit. This extra measure of drought put the vines into that well-known phylloxera death spiral.

The rows that in previous years were green and balanced in growth, with ripening wood and textbook clusters of Pinot Noir, were now ratty, nearly leafless. Here and there islands of healthy green showed where a few hand-grafted vines were put among the own-rooted for comparison. No comparison was needed now.

Where being among the vinerows before was a constant joy, the deep gloom and injustice that cloak the world around a gravely ill child hung off those bare wires and naked shoots.

For visitors who were curious, I'd dig up a dead or dying vine and show them the lice, their feeding sites, and their legacy. I would have a season or two, maybe three, to fall to my original plan: I'd collect what good wood I could from the dozens of Pinot clones I had collected, and graft them over on those rootstocks I had first planted at the farm. I'd have to dig up the dead instead of burying them. In their place I'd be putting the vines I'd be grafting each spring. A gamble lost . . . part of a farmer's life. Replant; reseed; the next season would be better.

Words do have smell and taste
these have the taste of apples
brown earth and red tomatoes
as if a juggler had juggled
too many balls of fire
and dropped some of them

• *Al Purdy, "Prince Edward County"*

The work of planting and tending the vines at first allowed me to joke with friends that I'd given up Toronto to be a peasant. As I filled winters reading books and essays by various agrarian writers, I realized that I wasn't a peasant, and to pretend was rather an insulting pantomime to the real ones. A small landowner, working on my own land, I can now see I'm just a garden-variety Anglo-Saxon yeoman.

Like John Lear, who owned both our house in Hillier and our farm, I am a Hillier yeoman. Sometime after the 1860s the term disappeared from Hillier and Prince Edward County, replaced by "farmer." The term has been defined at one end as "a class of independent peasants" or at the other as "a gentleman in Ore whom the next age may see refined," and rarely attached to a man until he was out of his twenties. It seems, from the size of holdings and their numbers, they were the original agricultural middle class, between gentlemen landowners and day labourers. By the mid-1700s they had disappeared in England, and one anonymous writer in 1773 noted that "I most lament the loss of our yeomanry, that set of men who really kept up the independence of this nation; and sorry I am to see their lands now in the hands of monopolising lords, tenanted out to small farmers, who hold their leases on such conditions as to be little better than vassals ready to attend a summons on every mischievous occasion." (He reads almost like a modern-day critic of corporate farms.)

I smile that the term, though extinct in England, was still used in Hillier up until Confederation; it's just one of those little quirks of this place, such as calling the seat of government in Picton Shire Hall.

Until small farmers return to the land, there is one working model that should inspire anyone willing to attempt the challenges of a modest vineyard. Andrew Jefford writes in his book *The New France*:

> Small, family domains across France's vineyard areas are thriving, while it is cooperatives and *négociants* who have found life hard over the last decade. . . . Families mean children, children mean succession and continuity; succession and continuity mean sustainability and sane stewardship of the land. Families mean aesthetic freedom, too; since the economic unit is a small one, it need find only a small market. Families mean a healthy and vibrant countryside, which can only deepen what is already a rich cultural relationship to the land. And yes, family domains mean a hugely diverse offering of

French wine to the world. This may, for the time being, be perceived as a disadvantage, since fashion and the economic power of capitalism have succeeded in gulling individual human beings (who may not have given much thought to the matter) into putting a high value on hollow mass-marketed products which leave them both physically and spiritually unsatisfied. When it comes to good wine, however, human beings are more swiftly ready to step off the treadmill of monotony than they are for soft drinks, electronic equipment, or hamburgers. . . . Complexity is not a problem; it is a badge of virtue. The worthwhile is never easy; only the worthwhile endures.

When we arrived, a small and unbloodied family, and I smashed and shattered my way into the limestone with our first bundle of vines in 1995, the only other small plots of vines to be found in the County belonged to Ed Neuser in Waupoos, Phil Mathewson in South Bay, and a collection of writers, teachers, and poets in Athol who flew the banner of something called Wicked Point Winery. In the past few years about fifty or sixty vineyards have gone in, most mechanically, and with each new planting season in May and June, thousands of vines are introduced into the earth in a day, appearing as if by magic. Speed and size. Money can invoke a vineyard in an afternoon.

It costs about $15,000 to $20,000 an acre to plant, trellis, and maintain vines until they begin bearing in three or four years. There are savings if you can take on much of the work, or convince your family to assist, and if you limit your vineyard to a manageable size. But if you want to go from zero to ten, twenty, or thirty acres at a jump, then winegrowing to you means a good pen and a supply of cheques.

As Lauren says, I've chosen to play in a rich man's game without being rich. Seeing just what those who are rich, or who have rich backers, have accomplished is, well, depressing. Actually, it's bittersweet, because I'm also amazed at and proud of how seriously and rapidly viticulture has progressed in Prince Edward since the early days when I was laughed at for even entertaining the idea, even if it means that now, in comparison, I've fallen off the radar screen.

There is no middle class in wine — you're either a huge wine operation, or minuscule. There are few if any economies of scale once a winegrower jumps from the one or two thousand cases he and a family can produce well, to ten, twenty, thirty thousand cases. As a winegrower rises to that moderate level (by international standards), the extra expense of employees, marketing, and equipment are pretty well fixed, and the numbers won't start to make sense until annual production rises to about ninety or a hundred thousand cases. So it's either lairds or peasants (or yeomen). And with that comes the mutual unease and dislike that has historically existed between such great class divides.

The big owners hire winemakers and field labour. Corby Kummer, columnist for *Atlantic Monthly*, wrote an amusing article about the differences, commenting that in Napa "vineyard owners are likely to talk about a love of wine, nurtured during restorative trips to Europe, and a dream of life lived according to the rhythms of nature that kept them going through the darkest days of stockbroking and orthodontia," while the small Pinot Noir growers of Oregon were "full of the passion and near fanaticism that draws me to artisan cheesemakers and bakers and to farmers who raise heirloom breeds. I saw in them and their wine the same link to land and learning that guides great chefs and food makers. Oregon is still a haven for radical idealists who, like those other artisans, are fueled by stubborn eccentricity and a need to make the most of limited resources."

The worlds are as different as chalk and cheese. Or Kraft and Saint-Basile de Portneuf.

❦

I didn't think much of it at the time.

Deborah Paskus hired me to help pour wine with her at a booth at Feast of Fields, the annual gourmet food-athon held in the countryside north of Toronto in support of organic farming. It was about as far from "work" as work should always be, but for most never will become.

We set up the booth amid what seemed like a Napoleonic military bivouac of some of southern Ontario's finest chefs and kitchen staffs. Amid the colourful jostle of other wine companies, organic farmers, and culinary artisans, the day blazed by. The wafting smells of brilliant food cooked, in many cases, over wood fires, and the faces of happy strolling people, with barely one reaching for a cellphone, made me think that the question we should ask ourselves is not "Do we live to work?" or "Do we work to live?" but "Is it possible that life and work can be the same thing?"

Just before the afternoon ended, Deborah asked me to take a few bottles to Jamie Kennedy's booth, as she had promised some wine to the staff there. When I padded over, there was no one around except for a tall fellow about my age. I handed over the bottles with Deborah's compliments, saying, "These are for Jamie's staff, uh . . . Jamie," reading too late the name off his whites.

"Thanks. Thank you very much. Tell Deborah we really appreciate it."

I had attempted to buck up Lauren once in a while, whenever her spirits fell, by telling her it wouldn't take long for daydreaming artisanal foodies and talented chefs to recognize what the land in the County offered. The County was fortunate that the owners of Angeline's in Bloomfield had managed to keep their doors open all these years; soon they'd be joined by others. Good, authentic wine has a way of kickstarting moribund land, through its prestige and appeal, allowing other small farmers and producers to abandon commodity agriculture to call from the soil brilliant local tastes. "One day," I'd assure Lauren, "someone like Jamie Kennedy will find this place."

I had always thought it'd be a sous-chef with wanderlust, so I looked up at Jamie and said, "If you ever have a sous-chef or someone ready to strike out on their own, why don't you suggest they take a look at Prince Edward County?"

Jamie contemplated the clouds a moment and countered: "And why would I do that?"

I sketched out things in the County. Jamie knew Phil Mathewson fairly well, and regularly bought from Phil for his famous restaurant, JKROM, and for his catering business, so he had heard a bit about the place. A sudden hard cloudburst sent us both under a canvas shelter nearby with other event participants waiting to finish striking their camp kitchens and booths. I continued to jabber on about the County as Jamie poured out Deborah's wine for his staff. Very soft-spoken, he would offer a pointed question, or make an observation that flashed a calm intelligence and real love of wine.

The rain stopped after ten minutes, and Jamie looked up at the sky again and said, "Never mind my staff. It sounds like something *I'd* like to do."

I headed back to pack up with Deborah, not entirely surprised by Jamie's comment, given the details he'd asked about.

I had a number of columns and articles I'd written about the County, and a few days later when I happened to be in Toronto I dropped off an envelope of photocopies at Jamie's restaurant.

It wasn't until the next spring that I found a message on my answering machine: "Hello, Geoff, it's Jamie Kennedy . . . It's been a while, I know. You dropped off a whole bunch of articles at the restaurant for me to read after we met at Feast of Fields last year. I just wanted to tell you that I've really, really enjoyed reading them. And so has my wife – *my* Lorren . . . We've decided that maybe we'd like to make Prince Edward County a destination for a holiday this summer. We were wondering if we could just come and visit you there maybe one day in the not-too-distant future, say hello or whatever, and find out a little bit more about Prince Edward County. . . ."

I mentioned the message to Lauren, and she just smiled like I was mad. She went and played it herself.

"There's no way *we* can afford to buy the Taylor farm," I told her. And her expression changed slightly, indicating a little surprise at my sudden jolt of sanity.

Mary Taylor had died earlier in the year, and her sons had just put the farm on the market. Our right of first refusal would have to be exercised soon, and we'd have no choice but to let it go. As depressing as that was, I was thinking about who our neighbours might be. Sharon Armitage had shown the farm to one or two people already. Would they appreciate the gaggle of rundown buildings that made up the heart of the hamlet? How would it affect our farm, nestled up against the eastern boundary of the Taylors'? More poisonous sprays drifting across our hedge? Would the ridge ever be properly cleared and planted in vines now, and allowed to become one of the best vineyards in the County?

"If we don't tell Kennedy about the place," I suggested to Lauren, "and it sells before they come out in the summer, we'll kick ourselves. I'm going to tell him."

I phoned, and a few days later Lauren and I and the girls were waiting outside our house in Hillier for Jamie and his family. An old black-and-faux-wood station wagon about the size of a whale glided into the village. It pulled up on the gravel near Mary's house, and Jamie unfolded himself from the driver's seat and introduced Lorren and their three boys, Micha, Jackson, and Nile. The adults fell into a fairly easy conversation about the village, and we began to tour the forlorn buildings. The girls kept fairly close, while the boys ebbed and flowed from their parents to intriguing piles of clutter.

It was a pleasant walk, and I explained the history of the place and the little secrets of the farm. We circuited the fields, climbed fences, and walked back along the old railway bed that cut the Taylor farm in half. The kids picked up pieces of metal left behind when the tracks were uprooted and sold to China a few years before and gathered handfuls of the round iron pellets that had spilled and accumulated over years of freight travel from the Marmora mines to waiting ships in Picton. As we got closer to Station Road, the lilac hedges beat back the oxygen with the scent of their flowers, and Lorren, who otherwise appeared to be a strong-minded and sensible person, lost herself to the perfume, the bright sky, and warm May sunshine. She was clearly enchanted with it all.

As I strongly advised, they spent time with Sharon Armitage looking at other properties in the County, but they had recognized the same charm and potential in the Taylor farm that Lauren and I had.

In short, they became our neighbours. Jamie wanted to be a vigneron.

Pinot Noir had taken another hostage.

It seemed natural. The talent, the dedication, and the drive displayed by Jamie and the handful of other chefs performing at his level are precisely those qualities demanded by Pinot Noir. The introduction to his second cookbook, *Jamie Kennedy's Seasons*, practically reads like a covering letter for an application to grow Pinot Noir:

Framing my cooking within the seasons as they relate to people living in Southern Ontario gives me a platform for my creativity. The notion of preserving fruits and vegetables in the summer and fall and using them in winter and spring recipes helps to focus my creative energy and is an honest response to where I live. Good results are more easily attained when we focus on the produce that's available locally and seasonally.

You will find several cross-references . . . between fresh ingredients of one season being preserved for use in another. This is not a new approach to cooking: it's how people fed their families before the advent of "global shopping" in which there is no such thing as seasons. Cooking with seasonal produce has new significance today because it's now about supporting the local economy. It is also a recognition of the artisanal approach to growing produce and processing food, and it flies in the face of agri-business and poor stewardship of the land.

Slowly, Jamie and I planned how to turn that ridge, a jewel under two decades of scrub, into a small vineyard. Although it was now in the hands of another, I couldn't conjure up a better pair to hold it. And in return for my help and guidance, Lauren and I would have use of a third of an acre of that slope – three *ouvrées*, or about two barrels each vintage at full maturity.

It was not hard to wonder just how that slope would change the wine. The vines would still be growing on Hillier Clay Loam, but the slopes, the increased warmth and drainage, and the underlying rock of the bluff were all different and would show themselves in the grapes in a way that would surely set themselves apart from our original plots. Or Ken's and Dan's.

Fretting about the amount of replanting I needed to do, and experiencing a moment of quiet desperation because of it, I opened one of my few remaining bottles of 1999 Pinot Noir. I had only a single bottle of my first vintage, 1998, left in the cellar, and wine writer Tony Aspler had made me promise not to open it, pointing out that as it was the very first Hillier Pinot Noir it should be kept. One day it *will* have to be opened, as wine is meant to be enjoyed and not hoarded or collected as an investment. But that day hasn't come yet. All I can remember of it now is ripe strawberries and a note of rich buttery pear – a taste that caught me completely by surprise – and the gentle teases of cinnamon and clove starting to overtake a shadow of dark cocoa. The colour was deep for Pinot Noir – meaning that it was light compared to Cabernet Sauvignon or Aussie

Shiraz, varieties loaded with pigments – and it grabbed and danced with the light in a playful and elegant way.

With the 1999 I had then made the horrible beginner's mistake of topping up the carboys of wine with a smaller amount kept aside for the task that had not been sealed carefully. It had oxidized gradually and developed volatile acidity. As I poured, even though it was a small amount, I knew on some level I'd regret it. The volatile acidity of the top-up immediately marred the dark fruit and ripe strawberries of the base wine. Yet, with intelligent tasters who could look past the obvious mistake, they could glimpse the fruit quality, the balance of acidity and tannin, and that hint of pure Pinot Noir joy. I saved half of the bottle I had opened, and dropped it over to Jamie, who seemed to be in a similarly haunted mood, brought on, in his case, by contemplating professional changes in Toronto.

He poured a few glasses out, and we both enjoyed that particular dance of transparent deep crimson and light. I warned him of the flaw and let him search over it for the fruit . . . for the future of his own wines. These trial wines had never seen a barrel, and so offered a chance to look at raw Hillier fruit – not "raised," or having undergone *élevage*, the French term for the aging process in cellar.

A few days later I received an e-mail from Jamie describing a lunch he had put on for some special clients. Great wines were poured, and, very kindly, samples were set aside for him to try. He made me smile when he wrote that one, Armand Rousseau's 1990 Chambertin, "was kinda like your Hillier Pinot, Geoff." We both knew that the "kinda" was an important qualifier, but there was something that *did* offer precisely that promise. He could see it now, too, and it had helped raise his enthusiasm.

Certainly, the low crop coming from the high density of vines helps the flavours, concentration, and balance of the early wines. But that can't explain all of it. The vines themselves are decades too young to show signs of our terroir – our unique taste of "somewhereness." In the white wines made by other growers in the County there is a noticeable mineral quality, although they are also too young to be showing terroir. Yet something is there. It may be the vines, though still like very small children, are offering a reassurance that they *will* turn out to be the amusing, productive adults we hope they'll be. While we can't yet shake hands with the limestone under their roots, maybe they're grabbing our finger in their hand – just like a small child – letting us know that the day is not as far off as we imagine. Or fear.

◈

With the farm sold, Hillier was abuzz for the auction of Mary Taylor's furniture and massive accumulation of belongings. Over the course of the day, people came and went, locals looked for odds and ends that would remind them of the Taylor family, tourists stopped in because it was impossible to resist, hard against the Loyalist Parkway, with everything spilling onto countless tables in the farmyard.

Ron Alexander came over to us. "What do you think of that clock?" he asked.

"I really don't know, Ron. It's big," I commented. It was a mantel clock, but that's all I could tell.

"Well I kinda like it. I think I'll see if I can get it."

Only a few things caught my eye that might be within our budget. An original copy of *Belden's Atlas* would be a popular lot. I was shocked when I had the winning bid at only sixty dollars. It should have gone for at least twice that, and even new reprints sold for about ninety dollars. I knew a few people we had chatted with wanted it too; they let me have it out of neighbourliness. I could have managed only another twenty bucks, and had expected to lose it.

I picked up a few other items: an old Hillier duck decoy, a few Quaker doors, and a box full of bundles of red and white labels from the Taylors' chicken cannery in the old cider mill (Chicken Broth, Boneless Chicken Solid Pack, Chicken Spread, and Chicken Giblets in Gravy). Lauren bid on and won a small wooden box of Mary's recipes, thinking there might be something unusual in there. There wasn't, but it did have Jack Taylor's Individual Liquor Permit for 1956-57 from the Liquor Control Board of Ontario. This little green passport – no. 315396 – had to be shown, stamped, and signed every time Jack went in to Trenton to buy alcohol: twenty-three bottles of "spirits" and nine half-bottles for the year.

Phil Wilson, who, with his wife, Marlene, had purchased the old schoolhouse to the east of our house, managed to buy a few boxes of books I had considered. They contained some rare local titles that I already had, so I didn't bid against him.

Phil was maybe in his early sixties, and had surprised me. Tough, with longish white hair and sideburns and a ready quip or tease for everybody, when he first bought the place I was a bit nervous. He had run what can only be called a junkyard at his previous home just west of Wellington, overlooking Lake Ontario and the distant gleam of Sandbanks. But once in Hillier, Phil organized his work yard and metal scraps very tidily, spent a small fortune in landscaping, and turned out to be a gifted jack-of-all-trades. And a philosopher, raconteur, and often perceptive critic. I've come to call him Perfesser, and, from time to time have heard him call me a whole range of things, depending on his mood. "Just kidding. Eh? Eh?" he'll add, smiling and poking me with an elbow.

He has designed and manufactured things that have saved the vines of a number of growers in Hillier, and repaired countless breaks and malfunctions. But he works to his own schedule; the more unusual and challenging a problem or task, the more likely it'll be completed swiftly.

Phil walked away with his books; Ron didn't get the clock; and probably the largest single pack-rat collection ever accumulated in the County was dispersed among new owners, or carted away to the dump.

❧

When they could steal away from Toronto, Jamie and Lorren came up to try to restore order to the farm, working hard, camping outdoors, and cooking on an open fire. They began renovations to the old Taylor houses to make them habitable. I dug up phylloxerated roots when Jamie came by our plots, or showed him just how small Pinot Noir berries and clusters were as the summer and fall progressed. He and Lorren were introduced to other growers around the County.

An early-February Sunday I told Lauren we had to stop by Dan Taylor's to share out some cuttings, and that he'd said the girls were welcome to come too while he and I sorted through the canes. Though she didn't really want to go out, Lauren agreed any break in the routine might distract her for a while, and let her forget she was pregnant again.

Our girls ran off upstairs to play with the Taylors' kids.

Lauren sat on a kitchen stool and chatted with Dan's wife, Carrie. Wine was opened. Then another couple we knew arrived, followed by another, and another.

"Do you know what's going on?" someone asked Lauren, referring to all the spontaneous arrivals. People stopping by with wine at the Taylors' was not terribly unusual.

"Yes," she said.

"You do?" the person replied, stunned by Lauren's matter-of-fact tone. "Ah, I don't think you do, Lauren. It's for you."

She just looked and him, and then at the bottles of wine being uncorked, and the platters of food spreading across the counters.

"It's your baby shower."

If people were hoping for a good reaction, they got it. Lauren's eyes welled up, and she told them she'd thought it was a *little* strange.

Our friends and fellow winegrowers had decided Lauren deserved and needed a party. I was amazed by their generosity. Dan had told me that Carrie had taken to calling Lauren "The Saint" because of the years she'd quietly put in with me out here, and it seemed others thought so too. They organized everything; once Carrie agreed to host it, all I had to do was get Lauren there. It was a great afternoon.

Less than two weeks later, on February 13, Lauren struggled to give the girls dinner promptly, and as soon as they had settled down, she finally impressed upon me why it was more urgent than I appeared to realize. She called the hospital and warned them she was on the way in.

At Bloomfield, Lauren was on the verge of bearing down, just as we raced past Angeline's. I talked her out of it, and got us to the hospital parking lot in Picton.

"I can't, I can't. I'm not going to make it. It's coming out," Lauren sobbed as I tried to get her up and out of the car. I somehow continued to chatter enough encouragement to get her across the snow to the hospital door. I went to the southern door, which I knew was closer to the maternity ward, just a few steps and an elevator ride to the second floor.

We got through the doors, and I hit the elevator button. The doors opened, and I lifted Lauren in and frantically felt for the second-floor button with one hand just as I discovered the baby's head crowning with the other. The elevator door opened right in front of the nurses' station, and everybody's eyes popped and jaws dropped when they saw us – they had all been watching the wrong security camera, expecting we'd come in by the main door at the northern end of the hospital. They jumped into action.

"Can you sit down?"

"I'm not going anywhere!"

Lauren made that clear to everybody; she would deliver right there, on her feet, and all at once nurses were removing items of her clothing while others herded patients out of the halls and back into their rooms. I held Lauren just outside the elevator, leaning against the door jamb for support. Lauren had one leg up on a wheelchair. Her obstetrician got to the floor, rolled on her back, and tried to orient herself for delivery.

"Here, let's see. I think that's right."

"Can I push now?"

"Yes. Here we come. That's it."

And out came the Elevator Baby. In the chaos, I was handed scissors to cut the umbilical cord.

The boy was taken to the nurses' desk, where the newborn-testing equipment had been rolled. He was evaluated, cleaned, warmed up, pronounced healthy and well-sized, and then wheeled off down the hall to follow Lauren, who had been gently guided into the wheelchair and taken the thirty-five yards to the maternity room.

Over the next few days most of the staff came by to peek at the Elevator Baby and his mother. And Lauren said a number of the patients who had to be hustled into their rooms came by too. In the same hospital, and almost a year to the day, we had been in a small room with Betty. I could see that realization wash across Lauren now and again.

I joked with the nurses that the baby had earned the nickname Otis, and how I was glad I chose that elevator instead of the other one, which was made by the Swedish firm Rudolpheson. Sometimes people still ask after little Otis.

Lauren and I named him Micah, after the Hebrew prophet, a man of the green and fertile countryside of Moresheth. The same prophet also provided the motto for my coat of arms – "*Non erit qui deterreat*" (None shall make them afraid) – rendered from part of Micah 4:3,4:

And he shall judge among many people, and rebuke strong nations afar off; and they shall beat their swords into plowshares, and their spears into pruninghooks: nation shall not lift up a sword against nation, neither shall they learn war any more.

But they shall sit every man under his vine and under his fig tree; and none shall make them afraid: for the mouth of the Lord of hosts hath spoken it.

As for our vineyard, well, that now has a name too.

It's a forgivable pun on "Lauren," going back to a visit she once made to France to see her sister, who was working there as an au pair. The children in Debbie's care couldn't comprehend why she called her sister *la reine*, or "the queen," all the time.

Domaine La Reine.

It's the least I could do.

Our first commercial barrel of Pinot Noir is safely housed at a friendly Hillier winery, slumbering inside a one-year old François Frères Allier oak barrel. The 2003 Pinot Noir fruit was bought from Ken Burford and Yvonne Millman, who enjoyed their first small commercial crop that year and saw it ripen nicely in a challenging but about average County season. Planned, planted, and maintained organically, their vineyard has thrived. As their consultant, I've seen to it that they haven't repeated the mistakes I made, and I'm thrilled to see them tend their vines as carefully as I would if they were mine. As one of only two buyers of their brilliant fruit, I'm ecstatic.

One barrel will yield less than thirty cases – barely a drop in the lake of Canadian wine, let alone the vast oceans gushing from ever-multiplying world vineyards. Already the clear ruby liquid makes captured light leap and pirouette in the glass, and an aroma of cherries and strawberries is emerging through the slow months of élevage. There is concentration in the middle, and very surprising length and presence in the mouth, given that the vines are only three years old. The slight awkwardness of fine tannins, acidity, and blue edges to the colour are reminders that this is still only a child, with much growing up to do. Living with the wine, topping it up every week or so, tasting, observing, shows that, like a child, it can be moody and unpredictable, but it will gradually settle down.

It's a promising start on the long two-year process from berry to bottle. Our own new replantings on Station Road in Hillier will produce a little this year, though not enough to ferment separately and start providing answers to the question of differences between Ken's site and our own. If planting goes well this spring, Lauren and I will be back to two acres of Pinot Noir and St. Laurent, replacing all the vines we lost to phylloxera.

The winter of 2002-03 was brutal, and yet Ken Burford and Dan Taylor – part of a very small club of County growers who respect winter and work hard to protect their vines – managed to take first commercial harvests from their rows. This past winter of 2003-04 has been even colder – with temperatures down below -30 Celsius – and it is likely only the same handful of growers will see fruit again this year. Spring is always a time of quiet terror as we wait for the extent of vine damage to show itself; this year the devastation may well break the spirit of some County growers.

In their place will come dozens more. Even with brutal winters these past two years, the dream of owning a vineyard is too alluring. Numerous County farms have sold recently to hopeful vinegrowers and winery owners. I've already lost count of the properties that changed hands between fall and spring.

The dream is nice, and sometimes it should remain a dream. We, however, are as firmly rooted as our vines, and desire no other home or purpose. Our story continues, and if it's not to be recounted in the pages of a book, it can be read in the glass.

ACKNOWLEDGEMENTS

Most of the people I needed to inspire and draw out this book are already mentioned in its pages. At least one – Lauren's sister Joanne – doesn't get anything near the credit there she deserves for the help she provided by taking on without complaint a role somewhere between über-aunt and third parent, all the while making it look easy.

Very few of the other County winegrowers are mentioned, and each has a unique story to tell. One regretted round of edits removed friends James Lahti, Victoria Rose, and Steven Rapkin of Long Dog Vineyards in the very south of the County. James, especially, understands the brutal requirements of editing, and I hope he will forgive me.

A small band of friends who would check on us and occasionally visit also didn't make it into these chapters, but Rob Frater, Katherine Scott, John MacMillan, and Will McDowell helped ease the change and remind us we were not forgotten. Will was also invaluable in keeping me and other *Frank* co-conspirators out of prison, and earns another nod for that.

As well as my amusing fellow *Frank*sters through the first nine years of the magazine (and allies Rick Salutin and Terry Mosher), I also need to acknowledge a handful of magazine and newspaper editors (many underwritten by Conrad Black) who helped keep our family alive, especially Patricia Holtz,

John Geiger, Ellen Vanstone, Tom Cruickshank, and Matthew Church. Before them all was Lynn Cunningham, who taught me to accept and appreciate the work of an intelligent and selfless editor, and probably made their jobs easier.

Some sections of this book have previously appeared in different versions in the pages of *Saturday Night* and within the "Citizen's Weekly" section of the Sunday *Ottawa Citizen*. I've written sporadically on wine, viticulture, and Prince Edward County through four different incarnations of *Saturday Night*, but owe my first chance to Zsuzsi Gartner and Dianna Symonds, and to Ken Whyte, who told me I'd better be taking notes, as it sounded like a book to him. At the *Citizen*, I'm most grateful to Susan Allen for taking me on as a columnist for seventy weeks, to Julius Majerczyk for careful edits, and to Lasha Mutual for her illustrations.

The late Carole Corbeil contacted her agent, Anne McDermid, after kindly reading some of the columns I had written, and Anne believed she could get a decent book out of me, if I left the columns behind and began again. She was right (and patient), and found a home for it at McClelland & Stewart, thanks to the interest of Doug Gibson and my editor, Alex Schultz. If this book reads with any clarity and unity it's because of Alex's ability to deftly remove vast amounts of debris from a manuscript and bring order and polish to what remains. Like Anne, he showed great patience, and knew when to leave me alone, and when to rattle my cage.

GSH
Consecon
April 1, 2004